Othello's Island 1

Selected Proceedings
from Othello's Island: the Annual Conference
on Medieval and Early Modern Studies

Nicosia • Cyprus

Edited by
Dr Jane Chick, University of East Anglia
and Dr Michael Paraskos, Imperial College London

Othello's Island working in collaboration with:

www.cvar.severis.org

and partners from:

    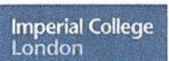

Othello's Island 1 is published by the Orage Press
in association with the Centre for Visual Arts and Research (CVAR), Nicosia, Cyprus

The Orage Press
16A Heaton Road
Mitcham
Surrey CR4 2BU
England

ISBN: 978-1-9993680-0-5

© 2019 The Individual Authors retain full copyright in their own written contributions to this publication. All rights reserved by those authors. No part of this publication may be reproduced or distributed in any form or by any means, or stored in a database or retrieval system, without the prior written permission of the relevant copyright holder(s).

Cover image: Interior of Famagusta Cathedral, Cyprus

Othello's Island 1

In memory of
Benedict Read (1945-2016)
Co-founder of Othello's Island

Contents

Introduction
Jane Chick and Michael Paraskos   8

Wine, Women and Song: Entertainment in Lusignan Cyprus
Nicholas Coureas   13

The Legal Status of Muslims in the Assizes of the Court
of Burgesses in the Lusignan Kingdom of Cyprus
Mabrouka Kamel Deif Youssef   39

The relations between Beirut and Cyprus during the fourteenth
and fifteenth centuries
Pierre Moukarzel   57

The concept of Fortune in the birth of the tarot
James Frost   73

Footfalls on the boundary of another world
Richard Barnes   100

Step-by-Step: The Non-Figural Mosaics of Late Antique Cyprus
Jane Chick   127

Mens sana in sano corpore: The nobility of Grand Duchy
of Lithuania travels to spa from 16th to 18th centuries
Milda Kvizikevičiūtė   155

The Setting of Shakespeare's Othello: Its Symbolic Significance
Jamal Subhi Ismail Nafi' 172

Desdemona's Appetite
Robert Appelbaum 195

*Omkara: Moor of Meerut: Reconfiguring the Sacred
and Profane of Othello*
Natasha Cooper 216

Nine Plates, Two Adventūs and One True Cross
Richard Maguire 239

*Tea-trays and longing: mapping Giorgione's Sleeping Venus
onto Cyprus*
Michael Paraskos 271

*The Old English Translation of the Orosius's History
Against Pagans as a Homiletic Text*
Zoya Metlitskaya 292

*Escaping the Island of Tyrants: Pseudo-Hugo Falcandus, Sicily,
and European Historical Writing in the Twelfth Century*
Philippa Byrne 308

*Cultural negotiations: eastern music in early modern
travel writing*
Claire Bardelmann 328

Introduction
Jane Chick and Michael Paraskos

OTHELLO'S ISLAND IS a conference focusing on the medieval and early modern periods, held annually on the Mediterranean island of Cyprus. It was started in 2013 by Professor James Fitzmaurice of the University of Sheffield and Northern Arizona University, Ben Read of the University of Leeds and Dr Michael Paraskos of Imperial College London, and as is so often the case with events like this, it was the product of our personal friendship as much as a recognition that there is a wealth of history and culture relating to Cyprus and the mediaeval and early modern periods that often goes overlooked. This frequent neglect includes not only the extraordinary wealth of Byzantine art on the island, such as the painted churches of the Troodhos mountains, but also the non-Byzantine medieval and early modern artefacts, including the dramatic gothic cathedrals of Nicosia and Famagusta and the Ottoman *hans* (inns) of Nicosia and Paphos. Then there is the impact of Cyprus on western culture through the island's surprisingly frequent appearances in the works of writers ranging from Geoffrey Chaucer to Cervantes, and William Shakespeare to Mary Wroth. It all suggested, to us at least as we sat enjoying a beer and an ouzini cocktail in a Larnaca bar, that there was room for an annual multi-disciplinary conference for people with open minds and broad-ranging interests.

For the first two years of its existence Othello's Island was hosted by the Cornaro Institute in the city of Larnaca, but in 2015 the conference moved to the Centre for Visual Arts and Research (CVAR) in Nicosia, which has been its home ever since. With that move we developed the conference to include new people on the organisational side, and new strands into the conference itself. This included a number of academics from universities outside Cyprus, including Dr Jane Chick of the University of East Anglia, Professor Lisa Hopkins of Sheffield Hallam University, Dr Sarah James of the University of Kent, Dr Richard Maguire of the University of East Anglia, Dr Laurence Publicover of the University of Bristol and Professor David Rollo of the University of Southern California. This additional expertise has strengthened the conference so that it has become a genuinely diverse gathering, with papers looking at aspects of the medieval and early modern periods with or without a Cyprus connection.

A key example of this is the involvement in Othello's Island of the Department of English Studies at the University of Cyprus, and in particular Dr Stella Achilleos, whose work with James Fitzmaurice has helped turn our event into one of the 'go to' annual international gatherings for academics interested in early modern women writers. Working with Dr Henry Bell of the University of Sheffield, Stella Achilleos and James Fitzmaurice have also encouraged the staging of historical plays at the conference, opening up the event to a wider public. Henry Bell has also worked with Stella Achilleos at taking research into local schools in Cyprus, introducing children from diverse communities on the island to new ways at looking at Shakespeare.

Although there was a desire to publish the proceedings of the conference right from the start, it has been a long-delayed project. A number of papers presented at the earlier conferences have already been published in a special volume of *The Journal of Mediterranean Studies* (vol. 25, no.1, 2016), edited by Lisa Hopkins, but those were papers which fitted in with the parameters of the journal, and several Othello's Island conferences have taken place since then. Plans for a more catholic volume of proceedings were further delayed by the death in 2016 of Benedict Read, who we had hoped would edit the volumes.

Not all papers have been submitted for publication, and so those included here are only an incomplete snapshot of the diversity of themes covered at Othello's Island, and we still have a backlog of further papers for publication in future volumes. However, this is a start, which we hope will be a useful and permanent record of our meetings.

The papers in this volume do not come from a single staging of Othello's Island, but are drawn from across first seven years of the event. This principle will be true also of subsequent published volumes. Our approach to editing the papers has been primarily to edit for consistency in formatting, but with minimal interventions in the papers' texts. For us, this light touch approach seems appropriate due to the diversity of topics reflecting the diversity of nationalities who attend Othello's Island. In presenting these papers as proceedings the aim is to reflect the papers *as presented* rather than imposing explicitly western notions as to what constitutes 'correct' academic style on researchers from other parts of the world. We make no apologies for this approach, although we acknowledge it can result in some papers having non-standard English phrasing, syntax and grammar.

Our special thanks go to Dr Rita Severis, the extraordinary founder and Director of CVAR, whose help in staging Othello's Island is invaluable. We also thank all the speakers who have submitted papers for inclusion in this volume and those that will follow it, and to our original hosts at the Cornaro Institute (then part of the Cyprus College of Art) for giving us the original space in Larnaca in which to start this annual event.

As well as our academic organising committee, thanks are also due to our academic board, which includes our academic organising committee plus Dr Nicholas Coureas (Cyprus Research Centre, Cyprus), Dr Rita Severis (CVAR, Cyprus), Professor Astrid Swenson (Bath Spa University, UK) and, Dr Violetta Trofimova (St Petersburg University, Russia). And last, but not least, thanks to our helpers each year, including Lara Benjamin, Rosamund Fitzmaurice, Alexander Head, Edward Head and Angela Witney.

Dr Jane Chick, University of East Anglia
and Dr Michael Paraskos, Imperial College London

Wine, Women and Song: Entertainment in Lusignan Cyprus

Nicholas Coureas (Cyprus Research Centre, Cyprus)

IN THE LUSIGNAN and Venetian periods of Cypriot history, from the thirteenth to the late sixteenth centuries, the forms of entertainment available broadly resembled those in Western Europe in the same period. In this paper entertainment involving music, dancing, taverns and prostitution will be discussed, but not hunting and martial arts such as fencing and jousting. Cyprus at this time appears to have had a lively tradition of entertainment in the ways mentioned above. These types of entertainment, not surprisingly, did not meet with universal approval, so that both the church and the legislator passed proscriptive or limiting legislation in order to put a stop to or at least minimize what were perceived to be the immoral and harmful effects of such diversions, especially but not exclusively those involving drink and women. Various forms of evidence from Cyprus records the kinds of entertainment practiced. These include chronicles, secular legislation, ecclesiastical legislation and notarial deeds. What is not included are administrative and court records, unfortunately not extant for this period of Cypriot history, that would impart information such as the incomes and outgoings of taverns or from practicing prostitution, the salaries of musicians and entertainers or legal cases involving persons engaged in various types of entertainment.

Song, music and games

Music in Lusignan Cyprus was present not only at celebrations and festivals, as one would expect, but also at funerals, something that excited the disapprobation of the Latin Church, established in Cyprus from 1196 onwards as the official church of the island, shortly after the Latin conquest of 1191. In the rulings of a provincial synod of the Latin Church that took place sometime between the years 1252-1257 under Hugh of Fagiano, the Latin archbishop of Nicosia, the twentieth canon prohibited the presence of women known as 'singing women' from playing the flute and singing during the performance of funeral rites for the deceased. Such women were accused of disrupting the divine service but also of exciting other women present 'to wail, beat and wound themselves'. Any such 'singing women' defying this ecclesiastical prohibition were to be 'captured, beaten, put on the rack, and put into prison …until they abstain from this sort of activity'. Their activity was likened in the relevant ruling to pagan and Judaic ritual and so contrary to Christian teaching, 'because in death the faithful should find consolation and be joyful with our Lord Jesus Christ' (*Synodicum* 2001: 100-101). Nevertheless, the reference to them playing the flute, a musical instrument, indicates that this instrument was played on Cyprus. Over two centuries later, in 1474 when the Venetians effectively took control of Cyprus in the reign of Queen Catherine Corner, the widow of King James II, a flute player named George was arrested on suspicion of involvement in the conspiracy by supporters of the former queen Charlotte to seize the coastal town of Kerynia, although he was released subsequently (Boustronios 2005: §144).

The pre-eminence of the flute as a musical organ on Cyprus, at least by the end of the Venetian period, is recorded by the Dominican friar Stephen de Lusignan, who witnessed the capture of the island by the Ottomans in 1570 and wrote two chronicles of its history while in exile in Europe. In the first of these chronicles, the *Chorograffia* published in 1573 in Bologna, he states apropos of how Cypriots entertained themselves:

> All enjoy themselves by singing and by playing all kinds of musical instruments. But the flute is the more popular than any other musical instrument. Two Cypriots out of three know how to play some musical instrument (Lusignan [1573] 2004a: 85).

The Cypriots' fondness for music is described in greater detail in Stephen de Lusignan's later work, the *Description*, in which he draws certain distinctions based on the gender and the social class of those singing and playing musical instruments.

> They enjoy ... playing the flute and have a strong love of music so that there is practically no nobleman who does not know the art of music and of playing the flute to perfection, with women playing the harp. The people, that is to say the burgesses and those of a lower station go to their gardens following their meals for entertainment, giving themselves over to games and dancing. Besides, they have a natural aptitude for poetry, which they themselves compose without having any art or knowledge. Furthermore, they sing very sweetly and with a fine voice, as one read formerly about the Druids and Sardons who were in France, that they used to call Gaul. On occasions when some noble or famous man dies they have certain dirges and laments, changing their voice according to the occasion (Lusignan [1580] 2004b: 460-461).

A number of Cypriot songs known to this day as *Akritic* ballads originate from the Lusignan and Venetian periods of the island's history. As example is provided by the so-called popular ballad of the queen and Arodaphnousa, which recounts the illicit love King Peter I of Cyprus felt towards Joan d' Aleman, the wife of the Frankish nobleman

Jean de Montolif, who has the name Arodaphnousa in this popular ballad. This ballad is based to some extent on historical fact. The king's illicit love provoked the wrath of Eleanor, the king's Aragonese wife.

Following the king's departure for Rome to gather support for a crusade Eleanor sent her retainers to seize Joan, already eight months' pregnant with a baby conceived by the king, and put her through the most horrendous tortures to force her to abort the baby. After the failure of these methods she had Eleanor sent home to give birth, but gave instructions to the mid-wives to have the new born baby brought to her, as came to pass. The baby's fate is unknown, although one can imagine what became of it, while Elanor was imprisoned in the dungeons of Kerynia on the queen's instructions. On learning of these events the enraged king threatened the queen with dire consequences, and she, perhaps fearing his anger, had Eleanor released from custody on condition that she should enter a nunnery. Joanna chose the Franciscan house for females of St Clare near Nicosia, but the king had her released on his return, and according to the ballad her beauty had remained unblemished despite her tribulations. The ballad, as is often the case, differs from historical reality in attributing two sisters to Arodaphnousa, named Chrystallo and Anthousa, while King Peter on his return discovered that his wife had had Arodaphnousa decapitated, and had thrown her severed head into the fire according to one variant (Makhairas 1932: I, §§234-237; Hill 1940-1952: III, 1108-1109).

Another popular ballad that draws on material originating from the wars of King Peter I of Cyprus is the song of Armouris. This song in the version current in the rest of Greek medieval literature focuses on the diachronic conflict between Byzantium and the Arabs in the borderlands of Asia Minor, its locus being the town of Amorion in Phrygia. In the Cypriot version, however, Amorion becomes Anemourion, a town on the southern littoral of Asia Minor and the Saracen raiders are replaced by Frankish ones. In this manner, the altered ballad constitutes an echo of the raids conducted under King Peter I against the Turks of southern Asia Minor and the Mamluks of

Syria and Egypt throughout the 1360s. Other well-known Cypriot popular ballads, recounting the Ottoman siege of Malta in 1566, the Ottoman capture of Cyprus in 1570 and the Lament of Cyprus, likewise relating its seizure by the Ottomans, originate from the late Venetian and early Ottoman periods of the island's history. It is significant, however, that the tradition draws its earliest historical content from the glorious if turbulent reign of King Peter I (Grivaud 2009: 179-180; Proussis 1943: 24-29).

The fifteenth century J.II.9 manuscript located in the national library of Turin in Italy provides valuable information on the musical compositions played in the royal court of Cyprus during the later Lusignan period, and in particular under King Janus. This manuscript is sub-divided into five fascicules. The first fascicule contains monophonic chants, an office and a mass dedicated to St Hilarion, a mass dedicated to St Anne, three full cycles of the Mass Ordinary and three sets of Kyrie, Sanctus and Agnus. The second fascicule contains polyphonic Mass settings, the third fascicule forty-one Latin and French motets, that is short lyrical compositions for a choir, the fourth 102 French ballads and the fifth twenty-one *virelais*, that is dances to singing and music, mixed with forty-three *rondeaux*, these last being round dances with lyrics (Kügle 1995: 152-153). The compositions indubitably draw on elements from the French musical tradition current among composers in the courts of the kings of France and the dukes of Savoy in the fourteenth and early fifteenth centuries, as also from the court of the dukes of Burgundy and from Cambrai cathedral. The various compositions in the manuscript, mainly liturgical and religious in nature, were composed chiefly to be performed within the royal court of the Lusignan kings (Kügle 1995: 154-157, 160-164 and 170-172). Indeed, two lyrical compositions dedicated to St John the Baptist were possibly prepared for the celebrations following the birth or christening of John, heir to the throne and the son of King Janus, who had been born on 16 May 1416. The liturgical chant in the first fascicule of the manuscript dedicated to St Anne was perhaps written to celebrate the wedding between King Janus's daughter Anne and Louis the son of Duke Amadeus of Savoy, that took place on 7 February 1434. An earlier date for the composition of this chant is also possible, either to celebrate Anne's birthday on 24 September 1419 or even for her first name day which fell on 26 July 1420 (Kügle 1995: 155, 166-167 and 175-176).

The manuscript also affords indications for the identification of certain of the composers who had written compositions found in it. The fifteenth century Cypriot chronicler Leontios Makhairas refers in his chronicle to two persons accompanying King Janus's wife Queen Charlotte of Bourbon on her initial arrival in Cyprus on 25 August 1411 as cantors. These were Jean Hanelle and Gilet Velut (Makhairas 1932: §§638 and 642). Both are recorded in documents from the French town of Lille as 'petits vicaires' or young clerics in Cambrai cathedral between 24 June 1410 and 24 June 1411, shortly before their arrival in Cyprus. In addition, recent research in documents originating from the court of the dukes of Savoy has brought to light references to Jean Hanelle as 'cantor of the king of Cyprus' and present at the ducal court of Savoy on 14 August 1434, a few months after the marriage between Anne de Lusignan and Louis of Savoy. Two years later, on 16 November 1436, Jean Hanelle is referred to again in the court of Savoy as '*Hanelle, mestre de chapelle du Roy de Chippres*'. Jean Hanelle appears to have arrived from France in Cyprus along with Queen Charlotte in 1411, to have worked as a cantor and composer of music in the Lusignan royal court until 1433 and then to have returned to France to take up a position in the ducal court of Savoy. Furthermore, on 4 August 1428 Pope Martin V postulated him for a clerical benefice in the Latin cathedral of the Holy Wisdom of Nicosia. As for Gilet Velut, about whose career less is known, he seems to have returned to Europe earlier (Kügle 1995: 170-173).

Associated with the pleasures of music, dancing and singing were the professions of jesters, mimics and actors and so mention of them is in order. The entertainment they offered was present in Cyprus as in other parts of medieval Europe, but such diversions did not find favour with all sections of society. They could be considered as dangerous distractions from moral rectitude. Hence in the eighth canon of the regulations of the Latin Church of Nicosia, promulgated in around 1252 under Archbishop Hugh of Fagiano, clerics were expressly prohibited from attending the performances of mimics, jokers and actors. The occupation of juggling engaged the attention of the secular legislator as well. According to the relevant articles of the Assizes of the Court of Burgesses, one of the reasons for which parents could disinherit their children was 'if the son or daughter consort with jugglers without the consent of their father or mother, with the son becoming a juggler …'. From the relevant ecclesiastical and secular articles of legislation it comes through clearly that performers, jugglers and actors were seen as engaged in socially disreputable and nefarious activities, and that those engaging in them were perceived as being on the margins of society (*Synodicum* 2001: 92-93; *Assizes* 2002: Codex One, §228, Codex Two, §226). This was not the case with another game popular in Cyprus and throughout the middle east among all social classes but also played in Europe to this day, namely backgammon. The chronicle of George Boustronios, written in the early sixteenth century and recounting the history of Cyprus from the end of King John II's reign to that of Queen Catherine Corner in 1489, recounts how when in the spring of 1458 Hector de Chivides, the viscount of Nicosia, visited James the illegitimate son of King John II and the future contender for the throne, he found him playing backgammon with Sir Anthony Silouan, the vicar of the Latin cathedral of the Holy Wisdom in Nicosia. It is not possible from this passage to know when the game of backgammon was introduced to Cyprus and the extent of its social and geographical diffusion on the island by the mid-fifteenth century, but it manifestly constituted one of various entertainments (Boustronios 1995: §20).

Wine, Taverns and Gambling

In the middle ages as now drinking and gambling were standard pleasures and taverns were a popular venue, in Latin Cyprus as throughout Europe and the northern Mediterranean. Such activity excited disapprobation on Cyprus, especially among the clergy. This is reflected in the relevant ecclesiastical statutes passed in the diocesan and provincial synods of the Latin Church of Cyprus, which denounced clerics engaging in such activities seen as incompatible with the clerical vocation, although to what extent these denunciations altered the culprits' behaviour is an open question. Members of the laity were also denounced in these synods, especially for gambling. Pope Urban IV in several letters dated 3 and 23 January 1263 and addressed to the Latin archbishop of Nicosia and to the *bailli* and nobles of Cyprus refers to the denunciations submitted to him by Archbishop Hugh of Fagiano against some of the lay population of Nicosia. According to the archbishop:

> Several men of the city and diocese of Nicosia, both clerics and laymen, put aside the fear of God ...to contaminate themselves in blasphemies, others in sorcery, others in games of chance in which they frequently swear and take oaths illicitly...' (*Cartulary* 1997: nos. 11, 75-77, 79 and 81).

Various archbishops tried to combat gambling and drunkenness, especially among the clergy, through the promulgation of statutes. According to the thirteenth article of the regulations either Archbishop Hugh de Fagiano or the papal legate Eudes de Châteauroux read out to the populace of Nicosia on Palm Sunday of 1251 or 1252 among those condemned as excommunicates, severed from all forms of contact with the Roman Catholic Church, were 'all those who publicly maintain and sustain gambling in their houses'. At around the same time, according to the eighth ruling of the regulations of the Church of Nicosia promulgated in around 1252 and mentioned above, Archbishop Hugh expressly stated that clerics 'should completely avoid taverns except in cases of necessity while travelling. They should not gamble or play at dice, nor be present at games of this sort'. Greek as well as Latin clergy were instructed to abstain from gambling, for in the Constitutions passed for instructing the Greeks at a provincial synod held under Archbishop Ranulf of Nicosia in around 1283, the seventh article of the fifteenth ruling condemned as excommunicates those who allowed gambling to take place within their houses (*Synodicum* 2001: 92-93, 136-137 and 156-157).

The repetition of prohibitions usually indicates their inefficacy, and the Latin Church's prohibitions against gambling and drinking were repeated from the end of the thirteenth until well into the fourteenth century. In a diocesan synod held in 1298 in the Latin diocese of Limassol under the direction of Archbishop Gérard de Langres of Nicosia, Bishop Nicholas Hungarus of Paphos and Bishop Berard of Limassol the eighth section of the fourth article of the statutes condemned once again 'all those who publicly maintain dice games in their houses'. The fact that this and previous statutes prohibiting games of chance refer repeatedly to gambling activities as taking place within private houses as opposed to more public venues such as taverns strongly suggests that this like acting, mimes and dancing was regarded as a socially disreputable activity, even if no laws prohibiting it are found in the secular statues of the Lusignan kingdom of Cyprus. By way of facilitating the return to the bosom of the Church of those condemned as excommunicates on account of gambling, the fifth article of the same statutes instructs confessors to encourage gamblers to return their ill-gotten gains to those whom they had acquired them from, or else to their heirs, or to make them over to the church itself if neither the original owners nor their heirs could be found. If those who had acquired gains from gambling could not return the proceeds at once on account of poverty, they could wait and return them once their financial situation had improved (*Synodicum* 2001:

192-195). Clearly the Latin Church, aware of the difficulty in persuading such people to return their winnings, no longer relied on simple condemnation of transgressors as excommunicates. By the close of the thirteenth century it had facilitated the process of recovery of the ill-gotten gains and the return of the culprits to the flock from which they had strayed by allowing them to return their winnings once they could do so without suffering financial hardship. Despite this the problem continued into the fourteenth century. In a provincial synod held in Nicosia in 1313 by the papal legate Peter of Pleine-Chassaigne the bishop of Rodez, at a time when the archbishopric of Nicosia was vacant, it was decreed in the fourteenth article that:

> No cleric shall ... play games publicly or secretly, nor pay attention to, associate with, or welcome the players, or give them or any evildoers advice, assistance or favour (*Synodicum* 2001: 214-215).

From the phrasing of this articles two things stand out; one that games of chance on Cyprus could be played publicly as well as secretly and secondly that clerics could be led astray in joining such games by sinful members of the laity, whose company they were to avoid. Seven years later, in 1320, the sixteenth article of the regulations of John del Conti, the incumbent archbishop of Nicosia, for implementation by the cathedral chapter and clerics of the diocese of Nicosia urged clerics 'of whatever condition or status to flee from taverns, indecent places and games of chance' (*Synodicum* 2001: 232-233). Those ignoring or defying this prohibition were to be punished. As will be seen below, this and previous prohibitions on clerics frequenting taverns were honoured more in the breach than in the observance.

In 1428 an especially interesting incident regarding a cleric visiting a tavern together with friends took place. This cleric, named Anthony Mansour the son of Abraham from Pera, happened to be in the tavern with his friends in October 1428 to eat and drink. A resident of Famagusta named Bisarra was in the same tavern with his own party and at some stage the two parties came together and started carousing. The cleric Anthony, who happened to be holding a knife in order to cut the bread and pasta which all of them were eating, to his misfortune, struck Bisarra by accident, neither premeditatedly nor in jest, wounding him so badly in the chest so as to cause his death. Consequently, the captain of Famagusta or his officers arrested Antonio, initially gaoling him and then handing him over to the Latin bishop of Famagusta, once they had realised that he was a cleric. The bishop likewise had him placed in custody, but Anthony managed to escape and make his way to Rome where he sought absolution for his offence, given that it had not been premeditated. Racello de Auro de Bononia, a Hospitaller and the papal representative, granted him the absolution requested so as to enable him to return to Famagusta in his former official capacity and to recover his former honours and privileges, without having to undergo trial there before a secular court. His advocate conveyed his request to the doge and senate of Genoa, who accepted it and decreed him absolved from all accusations levelled against him (Bliznyuk 2005: no. 8). This incident does explain, at least to some degree, the prohibitions on clerics frequenting taverns to be found in the councils and the decrees emanating from them promulgated by the Latin Church of Cyprus in the course of the thirteenth and fourteenth centuries.

The allusion to bread and pasta being served at the tavern is interesting. It constitutes one of the all too scarce references to types of food served at these establishments in Famagusta. Given that both these victuals are made from wheat it highlights, albeit indirectly, the importance of the grain supply for this Genoese enclave within the Lusignan kingdom of Cyprus. The registers of the two Genoese treasurers, the *massari*, of the city, although incomplete for the period of Genoese occupation of Famagusta afford important information in this regard. Kept according to the double-entry accounting system practised in Genoa since the 1340s, the entries on the left consisted of the *exitus* or outgoings while those on the right were the *introitus* or revenues. The purchase of grain, for instance, was registered as an outgoing, but the grain itself was registered on the right as something coming in, in the revenues section. The Genoese imported grain into Cyprus from Sicily, and one of the towers on the ramparts of the walls circling Genoese Famagusta was called the grain tower in the treasurers' accounting records, the *massaria*. Besides, by the end of the fourteenth century, by which time urban expansion had become a thing of the past, mills had been constructed within Famagusta, and more specifically within the neighbourhoods or *contrade* of the hairdressers, St Cosmas, St Mary of Mount Carmel and Limassol (Balard 2008: 237-241; Blijnyuk 2005: nos. 2-4, 6-7 and 17-18).

The notarial deeds drawn up in Famagusta between the years 1296-1310 by the Genoese notaries Lamberto di Sambuceto and Giovani de Rocha impart valuable information on tavern keepers and their activities, but they also have their limitations. The tavern keepers referred in such deeds are practically all Genoese, Venetians, Anconitans, Milanese or originating from other parts of Italy. Given the presence of Greek inhabitants and the numerical preponderance of Syrians, usually refugees from the Latin states of Syria and Palestine conquered by the Muslims from 1260 to 1291, one can reasonably deduce that Syrian and Greek tavern keepers were also present but there are no extant records for them (Coureas 2012: 65-68). One interesting aspect regarding tavern keepers in Famagusta, however, is the presence of women in this occupation. The first mention of a female tavern keeper, Marinaria, appears in January 1310, when she acknowledged the loan of a sum of 200 white bezants from the Genoese Pagano di Porta Sancti Andree, advanced to her the previous year. As she herself admitted, she had borrowed this sum 'for the purchase and sale of wine in the tavern', promising to repay him the whole sum including interest 'in good faith and without deception' (*Notai Genovesi* 43 (de Rocha) 1984: no. 38).

A second recorded instance of a female tavern keeper is encountered in the year 1448, the person concerned being a certain

Marossa Pansana. Appearing before the judges in the course of the judicial inquest being held over the charges brought against Pietro di Marco, the former Genoese captain of Famagusta, she submitted two specific accusations against him. According to the first of these, during his term of office a Catalan named John de Letta had stolen from her a gold vessel worth 30 ducats. When she denounced him before the captain the latter had the accused taken to the torture chamber. Marossa, who was present there, demanded that he be tortured so that in his terror he would return the gold vessel, but the captain showed himself to be highly unwilling to take such a step. According to the second accusation Marossa levelled against the captain, a certain Antonio de Alba owed her 15 white bezants together with a quantity of silver worth 25 white bezants. The said Anthony was placed in custody on his return to Famagusta and the relevant receipt was impounded by Giustiniano Fatinanti. Following this, however, Captain Pietro di Marco instructed Giustiniano to relinquish this receipt despite Marossa's objections, and as a result Antonio departed without paying her what he owed her (*Genova e Cipro* 1984: no. 17).

The former captain Pietro di Marco declared in his defence apropos of the first accusation that he had indeed subjected the accused to torture but that on ascertaining that no incriminating evidence resulted he was unwilling to continue. Regarding the second accusation, he stated that he had indeed given Giustiniano orders to relinquish the receipt in his possession. The final outcome of this case is not known, even though Marossa brought forward two witnesses who upheld the veracity of her accusations in their testimonies (*Genova e Cipro* 1984: nos. 18-25). In February 1455, however, Marossa Panssana is mentioned again, this time as the purchaser of a house with a tavern attached to it from a certain Barnabas Ternatio. This establishment was located on a street extending from the area of the marketplace to the customs house of Famagusta. The document recording her purchase is invaluable not only for stating the general vicinity in which the tavern was located, clearly a central artery of Famagusta, but also for recording how a house was attached to the tavern, proof that as elsewhere in Europe and the Mediterranean houses had commercial premises attached to them, serving in architectural terms the dual purpose of residence and workplace. Furthermore, in June 1455 Marossa is referred to once more as the employer of a certain man named Losa from Nicosia, who owed her the sum of four ducats, the price 'for his supper and for a bed'. In addition, Marossa is recorded in the register of debts submitted during the term of office of the Genoese captain Bartholomew de Levanto during the years 1455–57, twice as a creditor and once as a debtor (*Un enquête* 2000: 242).

Another tavern keeper recorded in Genoese state archives of the mid fifteenth century was Serini Cachotripitri, who ran a tavern in a house owed by a Genoese. Her name was perhaps a corruption of Eirini Kakotripiti, in which case this tavern keeper was not only female but also ethnically Greek (Balletto 1996: 42 and n. 27). The active participation of women from Cyprus in running taverns or hostels, where wine could also be obtained, extended beyond the confines of the island to Alexandria in Egypt. A notarial act of Niccolo Venier drawn up in August 1421 refers to Maria of Cyprus, an innkeeper in Alexandria who had lent four ducats to a certain George Deliono, who possibly originated from the town of Nuoro in Sardinia and was now resident in Famagusta. It is possible that Maria is identical to the 'Mariona de Zipro' mentioned in a notarial act of December 1421 regarding the purchase of 81 butts of wine by three Venetians resident in Candia, Crete. The Venetians acknowledged owing 1106.5 ducats for this purchase to Lord Angelo Michael, a Venetian living in Venice, and the wine sent from Crete to Alexandria was sold to three persons explicitly mentioned as tavern-keepers, one Greek, one Anconitan and one Coptic, as well as to Mariona, who although not mentioned as a tavern-keeper must have either been one or have been engaged in a similar occupation, for why else would she have purchased this wine? Several Cypriot women maintained hostels in the city. Sometime before 1422 Peter Zexomeno, a Greek from Cyprus, became Cypriot consul there. A deed of March 1422 alludes to an agreement concluded in Alexandria by his wife Euphemia and his sons Nicholas and James with Sir Blaxinus Ordo, the consul of the Greeks of Crete, over certain mutually agreed undertakings, unfortunately not specified, which were still pending. In a subsequent deed of July 1422 Peter's son James married Maria, an Abyssinian slave manumitted by her master Bartholomew Lomellini on the same day and given a dowry of 60 ducats by him, clearly so as to marry James (Verlinden 1981: 66, 69-70 and 81; Ashtor 1983: 410).

Nicosia the capital of Cyprus also boasted taverns, although the sources for their existence are from the sixteenth century onwards, by which time Cyprus was under Venetian rule. These taverns are called *canutes* in the language of the time, the word, possibly of Armenian origin, signifying a tavern or a small shop. The chronicle of George Boustronios, refers to a certain James of Malta marrying the daughter of a tavern keeper named Nicholas of Palermo, who prior to his emancipation had been a serf belonging to the count of Tripoli but afterwards opened a tavern and made a great deal of money (Boustronios 2005: § 93). Clearly taverns in Cyprus could be lucrative if not for people of high social station. Until 1474 there were five *canutes* in the suburbs around Nicosia, and because they were outside the city their owners were considered exempt from the payment of the municipal tax on consumables entering the city, the so-called *gabelle*. During the Venetian period the local authorities granted permission for the opening of seven additional *canutes* from 1531 onwards, but following their establishment a fierce competition ensued resulting in the decline of certain *canutes* within the city. Such establishments acquired a reputation as centres of extravagance and moral laxity on account of the drink they sold to their clients, and were regarded as discouraging Christians from the observance of the divine offices (Coureas, Grivaud and Schabel 2012: 150-151). Yet despite their nefarious reputation they continued to function throughout the

Lusignan and Venetian periods of Cypriot history, both in Nicosia, the capital of Cyprus, and Famagusta, the island's principal port.

Women as Prostitutes and Mistresses

Cyprus, famed throughout history as the island of Venus, maintained this reputation to the hilt during the Lusignan and Venetian periods of its history. The records of the Latin and Greek Churches on the island attest to the propensity of the clergy of both denominations to seek the company of prostitutes and mistresses, despite the declared prohibitions and condemnations. Cypriot secular legislation also addresses the issue of paid sex with females, on both a one-off and a diachronic basis, while the later sixteenth chronicler Stephen de Lusignan, writing shortly after the fall of the island to the Ottoman Turks, saw Cypriots of both sexes as potentially more libidinous than either their ancestors or the people of other nations.

Latin clerics on Cyprus faced condemnation from the outset in cases where they lived sexually dissolute lives. As early as 1204, only eight years after the foundation of the Latin Church on Cyprus, the papal legate Peter Capuano in a letter directed to Alan the incumbent Latin archbishop of Nicosia made the following remarks concerning them:

> We have heard that some [clerics] in your parts are such slaves to filthiness of the flesh that they shamelessly have concubines in their own houses, while others, even if not in their own houses, still openly maintain them in other houses and supply them with their needs …we strictly command that from now on anyone who is in holy orders who openly has a concubine shall be stripped of the proceeds of his prebend for two years by the diocesan bishop. And if he openly maintains her in some other house likewise he shall still be stripped of the proceeds for one year. And if this shaking up does not make him understand, but

he chooses to rot in his own excrement like a mule [cf. Joel 1.17] so that he becomes completely filthy, rather than to devote the due servitude to the Lord in the vocation to which he has been called, from then on what is canonical shall be inflicted. The genitals, especially those of ministers of the altar, must be kept contained even more than burning lamps in one's hands [cf. Luke 12.35], so that they should understand what was said to them [Isaiah 52. 11]: 'Be ye clean, you that carry the vessels of the Lord' (Synodicum 2001: 285, no. 5 [6]).

Latin prelates also condemned paid sex among the Greek clergy. According to the sixteenth article of the constitutions instructing the Greeks promulgated in around 1283 under Ranulf, the Latin archbishop of Nicosia at that time, Greek monks were expressly prohibited from keeping women in their houses. Yet in 1313, over one century after Peter Capuano's prohibitions, the fortieth article of the regulations passed under the papal legate Peter de Pleine-Chassaigne for instructing the clergy threatened all clerics keeping concubines with public excommunication and the loss of benefices, as well as the right to minister in the orders they had taken. In 1320, the regulations of Archbishop John del Conti aimed at instructing the cathedral chapter of Nicosia and the clergy of the same diocese likewise ordered clerics on pain of punishment to flee from 'indecent places' by which brothels were meant (*Synodicum* 2001: 138-139, 224-225 and 232-233). The repeated prohibitions, in the matter of paid sex as with regards to the issues of gambling and drinking, betoken their ineffectiveness.

The problem of clerics, Latin and Greek, consorting with concubines persisted into the mid-fourteenth and early fifteenth centuries. The Latin archbishop of Nicosia Philip de Chamberlhac wrote a letter some time before 7 October 1348 to the papal penitentiary Stephen, cardinal priest of SS John and Paul, requesting the grant of absolution after the customary manner of the church for up to 50 clerics and lay persons who had incurred sentences of excommunication under provincial or synodal statutes for maintaining concubines. Cardinal Stephen granted Archbishop Philip the power to commute the sentences to suspensions, with the culprits being warned not to keep concubines at their own houses or in those of other persons. The culprits are not named, and given the distance between Cyprus and the papal curia in Avignon it was natural that the archbishop of Nicosia should request the power to grant absolutions on the spot in order to save penitent transgressors the time and expense, as well as the dangers attendant on a sea voyage across the Mediterranean, of journeying from Cyprus to Avignon in Provence. Nonetheless, the very submission of the request shows that the phenomenon of maintaining concubines among clergy and laity on Cyprus persisted (*Cartulary* 1997: no. 126).

Greek as well as Latin clergy were accused of maintaining concubines. The Constantinopolitan monk Joseph Bryennios visited Cyprus at the start of the fifteenth century in order to examine the application of the Greek clergy of Cyprus to enter communion in secret with the Ecumenical patriarchate of Constantinople while openly remaining subject to the jurisdiction of the popes and the Latin archbishops of Nicosia. He eventually rejected the application as being hypocritical and forming a bad precedent for other Greek churches in lands under Latin rule, and while in Cyprus he convened a synod in a mountainous region of Cyprus on 28 July 1406. In the course of the synod he castigated the Greek clergy of Cyprus for their shortcomings, stating the following regarding concubinage:

> For among the clergy that happen to be among you there is no-one who does not maintain concubines openly, while his lawful wife is living and even more so on her death, and even prior to marrying her. Furthermore, all the bishops and the monks all at once, served by women brought in and clearly begetting children by them, officiate without hindrance and, performing all immoral acts with them freely, celebrate the divine service

> together, and have made custom into law, and I keep quiet about the other things (Katsaros 2000: 40; Hill 1940-1952: III, 1085-1088).

Turning to the laity, one observes that their own enjoyment of paid sex with women occupied the attention of the legislator. Several articles of the Assizes of the Court of Burgesses, which in Cyprus dealt not only with issues concerning the burgess population but also functioned as a criminal court, deal with the issues of prostitution and concubinage. One of these laws specifies where prostitutes were to reside:

> Truly if I have rented out my house to a woman who happens to be a procurer, or an evil woman, or is a bad person from a bad social background, or of ill repute, I should indeed have her leave my house before the end of the fixed term, and have her pay rent for as long as she has been in the house, for it is not right for such people to live among good people, but only in the communal area which has been ordained as the dwelling place of such people (*Assizes* 2002: Codex One, §90, Codex Two, 90).

The intent of the above law was not to eradicate prostitution but to control it spatially, by ensuring that prostitutes were concentrated in one neighbourhood and not throughout the urban space. Yet the practice of prostitution was also discouraged, for one of the articles of the Assizes stated that parents could legally disinherit their daughters if the latter chose to become prostitutes and refused to be married as their parents wished (*Assizes* 2002: Codex One, §228, Codex Two, §226).

Concubinage was also dealt with in an article of the Assizes, the intent being not to eradicate or limit this phenomenon, but to provide compensation for claimants who had fallen out with their concubines after being in a long-term relationship with them. The procedure decreed for obtaining this compensation, however, must have deterred all but the most determined claimants:

If he kept the company of a sinful woman on a regular basis, or even once, and he spent all he had on wining and dining her, on clothing her and buying her shoes, and did this for himself and for her, should he then quarrel with the sinful woman and ask her to give back whatever he spent on her, the law judges and decrees that he should never get back any of what he spent upon her, except by a contemptible form of justice and baseness. Should he wish to get back whatever he gave the sinful woman, it should be arranged for a Muslim to come to a house and sleep with him there with a wooden rod, of the same thickness as a man's penis, or of that of the man who wants back what was his, and it should be thrust up his anal passage for as many times as the woman declares upon her faith that the man slept with her. Once this has been done to him, the woman is obliged to give the man back everything which is discovered as having been made over to her by him. And if all the things that has been expended or consumed are not found the woman does not have to return them anew but shall remain absolved for the other services she rendered for him, this moreover being what is right and lawful according to the assizes (*Assizes* 2002: Codex One, §211, Codex Two, §209).

The reasoning behind the above article was that the since claimant had paid the woman to penetrate her sexually, he could only recover what he had spent by being penetrated himself, and that with the assistance of a Muslim, a sworn enemy of Christendom.

Prostitution on Cyprus is also referred to in sources from the Venetian period. The chronicler George Boustronios recounts in his narrative how shortly before the arrival of Queen Catherine Corner in Nicosia, on 21 October 1473, Nicholas de Morabit the viscount of Nicosia ordered all prostitutes to depart from the city and to betake themselves to the camel yard and to the place where coaches congregated, so as not to soil the city with their presence during the queen's visit.

Famagusta, the kingdom's premier port, also had prostitutes, and these are referred to in the chronicle of Florio Bustron, a relative of Boustronios who wrote his chronicle in Italian towards the end of the Venetian period. His account of the incident in Famagusta involving the city's prostitutes, fuller than that of the same incident given by George Boustronios, states how a disturbance took place as the result of the visit some Italians had paid to the local prostitutes on 19 May 1474. The irate Italians, dissatisfied with the services they had received, refused to pay the prostitutes and hurled abuse at them. In response, the prostitutes summoned the Franks of the city, who were clearly their procurers and who came armed to confront the Italians, accompanied by certain Greek inhabitants of the city. A fight ensued and the Venetian *provveditore* of Famagusta had to separate the warring parties and gaol those causing the disturbance. Subsequently, however, he had released all those involved except the Greeks. The Venetian garrison commander Gonsalvo informed the popular leader John the Saracen of this discrimination at the Greeks' expense. Nonetheless, when the latter accompanied by relatives of those remaining in gaol protested before the Venetian *provveditore* the latter had them placed in custody, as a result of which further disturbances broke out. The Venetians dealt with the matter by reinforcing the city's garrison, and on 26 May 1474 their fleet arrived and disembarked 200 men at arms (Boustronios 2005: §§146 and 276-277; Bustron 1886: 452-453).

Shortly after the Ottoman conquest of Cyprus in 1570 the Dominican friar Stephen of Lusignan, writing in exile in Bologna, Italy, said the following as concerned the Cypriots in his work titled *Chorograffia*:

> Besides, all of them in common are hot-blooded by nature, which is why you will encounter poets and other authors calling Cyprus an island given over to sensuality. Therefore, they are hot-blooded, sensual and extremely romantic, nevertheless they always respect honesty and honour, so that were it not for these two characteristics they would truly be extremely dissolute. Furthermore, there are more brothels here than in any part of the

world. The nature, the air and the character of the place inclines them towards this, and not only the indigenous inhabitants but the foreign residents as well are inclined towards these things (Lusignan [1573] 2004a: 84a).

One decade after the Ottoman capture of Cyprus Stephen de Lusignan, by now in Paris, penned the following description of the women of Cyprus in his second major work about the island, the *Description*:

> And yet I would not be remiss in narrating this matter, and particularly that the women of Cyprus would still be regarded and would have the popular perception of being more devoted to the voluptuousness of Venus than those of any other nation; if it were the case that they were so greatly enslaved to pleasure as not to prefer their honour to their own lives, something that restrains them with such force that appetite being constrained by reason they have disciplined with the aid of virtue the shameless desire that seeks in every way to breach that which every damsel or woman should guard most thoroughly (Lusignan [1580] 2004b: fol. 219r).

Subsequently in the same work Stephen de Lusignan has the following to say about the desires of Cypriots in general, women and men:

> For I assure you then that if the Cypriots gave free rein to their desires, and placed their affection in worldly issues they would be worse, more dissolute and villainous than their ancestors, regarded as divine by the ancients, had ever been, and more unbridled and lascivious than deceitful Venus had ever been (Lusignan [1580] 2004b: fol. 220r).

The common thread running through all the three passages of Stephen de Lusignan mentioned above is that the Cypriots are extremely libidinous but nonetheless respect honesty and honour and are able to discipline their carnal impulses. Given that Cyprus since classical times has been regarded as the island of Venus, the carnality of the Cypriots and even of long term foreign residents of Cyprus is a literary topos. Yet on the other hand he seems anxious to stress that despite their carnality the Cypriots can and do discipline themselves and so are not totally promiscuous. This contradiction is resolvable. Stephen de Lusignan wrote both the works mentioned above after the Ottoman capture of Cyprus, and his chief motivation for writing them was to galvanize Western Christendom into recovering the island from the Ottomans through war. Maintaining that the island's inhabitants were complete moral degenerates would hardly provide Western Christendom with a suitable incentive for its recovery. Therefore, the author here stresses the Cypriots' capacity to overcome their desires, thereby depicting them as deserving of Western assistance against their Ottoman conquerors.

Conclusion

Lusignan Cyprus was a multicultural and multi-denominational kingdom, although with a Christian majority population. Most of the information on entertainment on the island derives from Latin or Greek sources and so any forms of entertainment specific to smaller Christian denominations such as the Copts or the Armenians, or even to non-Christian groups like Muslims or Jews is not recorded. In general, however, the forms of entertainment to be found in Cyprus were closer to those of Western Europe that to those of the Middle East, to which Cyprus is far closer geographically. This is attributable to the mainly Christian composition of the population and to the influences of the Latin aristocracy that governed the island in the period under discussion.

Reference Sources

- Ashtor, E. 1983. *Levant Trade in the Later Middle Ages*, Princeton: Princeton University Press
- *The Assizes of the Lusignan Kingdom of Cyprus*. 2002. Translated by Coureas, N., Nicosia: Cyprus Research Centre
- Balard, M. 2008. 'La *massaria* génoise de Famagouste'. In *Diplomatics in the Eastern Mediterranean 1000–1500: Aspects of Cross-Cultural Communication*, edited by Beihammer, A., Parani, M. G. and Schabel, C. D., 235-249. Leiden: Brill
- Balletto, L. 1996. 'Ethnic groups, cross social and cross cultural contacts on fifteenth century Cyprus'. In *Intercultural Contacts in the Medieval Mediterranean*, edited by. Arbel, B., 35-48. London: Frank Cass & Co. Ltd
- Blijnyuk, S. 2005. *Die Genuesen auf Zypern ende 14. und im.15. Jahrhundert*, Studien und Texte zur Byzantinistik 6. Edited by Schreiner, , Frankfurt: Peter Lang GmbH
- Boustronios, G. 2005. *A Narrative of the Chronicle of Cyprus 1456-1489*. Translated by N. Coureas, Nicosia: Cyprus Research Centre
- Bustron, F. 1886. 'Chronique de l'île de Chypre'. Edited by Mas Latrie, R. de, in *Collection des documents inédits sur l'histoire de France: Mélanges historiques*, V Paris: Imprimerie Nationale
- *The Cartulary of the Cathedral of the Holy Wisdom of Nicosia*. 1997. (ed.) Coureas, N., and Schabel, C., Nicosia: Cyprus Research Centre
- Coureas, N. 2012. 'Taverns in Medieval Famagusta', in *Medieval and Renaissance Famagusta: Studies in Architecture, Art and History*, edited by Walsh, M.J.K., Edbury, W. and Coureas, N., 65-72. Farnham: Ashgate Publishing
- Coureas, N, Grivaud, G. and Schabel, C. 2012. 'Frankish and Venetian Nicosia 1191-1570'. In *Historic Nicosia*, edited by Michaelides, D., 115-229. Nicosia: Rimal Publications
- De Lusignan, S. [1573] 2004a. *Chorograffia et breve historia universale dell' isola de Cipro principiando al tempo di Noe per in fino al 1572*. Nicosia: Bank of Cyprus Cultural Foundation
- De Lusignan, S. [1580] 2004b. *Description de toute l' isle de Chypre*. Nicosia: Bank of Cyprus Cultural Foundation
- *Genova e Cipro: L'inchiesta su Pietro di Marco capitano di Genova in Famagosta (1448–1449)*. 1984. Edited by Fossati Raiteri, S.. Genoa: Collana Storica di Fonti e Studi 41
- Grivaud, G. 2009. *Entrelacs Chiprois: Essai sur les lettres et la vie intellectuelle dans le royaume de Chypre 1191-1570* Nicosia: Moufflon Publications

- Hill, G, 1940-1952. *A History of Cyprus*, 4 vols. Cambridge: Cambridge University Press, III (1948)
- Katsaros, B. 2000. 'Ioseph Bryenniou, ta praktika tes synodou tes Kyprou (1406)'. *Byzantina* 21: 21-53
- Kügle, K. 1995. 'The Repertory of the Manuscript Torino, Biblioteca Nazionale J.II.9, and the French Tradition of the 14th and Early 15th Centuries'. In *The Cypriot-French Repertory of the Manuscript Torino J.II.9*, edited by Günther, U. and Finscher, L. 151-181. Neuhausen-Stuttgart: Hänssler-Verlag
- Makhairas, L. 1932. *Recital concerning the Sweet Land of Cyprus entitled 'Chronicle'*. (ed. and trans.) Dawkins, R. M., 2 vols. Oxford: The Clarendon Press
- *Notai Genovesi in Oltremare: Atti rogati a Cipro da Lamberto di Sambuceto (31 Marzo 1304 – 19 Luglio 1305, 4 Gennaio – 12 Luglio 1307) e Giovanni de Rocha (3 Agosto 1308 – 4 Marzo 1310)*. 1984. Edited by Balard, M. Genoa: Collana Storica di Fonti e Studi 43
- Proussis, K. 1943. 'Ta istorika kypriaka tragoudia', *Kypriakai Spoudai* 7: 21-46
- *The Synodicum Nicosiense and other Documents of the Latin Church of Cyprus 1196-1373*. 2001. Translated by Schabel, C. Nicosia: Cyprus Research Centre
- Verlinden, C. 1981. 'Marchands chrétiens et juifs dans l'État mamelouk au début du XVe siècle d'après un notaire vénitien'. *Bulletin de l'Institut historique belge de Rome* II: 19-86
- *Un enquête à Chypre au XVe siècle: Le sindicamentum de Napoleone Lomellini, capitaine Génois de Famaguste (1459)*. 2000. Edited by Otten-Froux, C.. Nicosia: Cyprus Research Centre

The Legal Status of Muslims in the Assizes of the Court of Burgesses in the Lusignan Kingdom of Cyprus

Mabrouka Kamel Deif Youssef (Damanhur University, Egypt)

MUSLIMS WERE AMONG the minorities in Cypriot society under the rule of the Lusignan dynasty. The Latin Kingdom of Cyprus comprised several minorities beside the Greek majority population, such as Syrians, Samaritans, Nestorians, Jacobites and Jews. The legal system was able to accommodate all these minorities. This research discusses and analyses the legal articles concerning Muslims in the Assizes. Although the Assizes regulated what should be practiced instead of what does exist, they still reflect the law compilers' perspective on Muslims at the time. They also provide us with an indication of the status of Muslims' in Cypriot society compared to other minorities.

The articles include provisions on social, economic and criminal aspects of life which made it possible to have a perception of Muslims' lives in Cyprus during the 13th and 14th centuries. Major issues of their lives, most importantly conversion and manumission along with their legal consequences will be discussed. In addition, some of the important queries in this research are the legal penalties imposed on Muslims in various criminal cases. Moreover, the points of difference and similarity between Muslims and other minorities in different judiciary matters such as court summons, offering testimonies and giving oaths are to be investigated. Furthermore, the nature of trials between Muslims and Latins in case of dispute and the penalties forced on Muslims by law are also to be discussed. This research highlights the commercial aspects of the legal articles as one of the major aspects of the relationship between Muslims and Latins. The papal prohibition on trade with Muslims in force from 1291 until 1344 contradicted the laws permitting such trade, and it was subject to violation. Moreover, some of the decrees concerning prohibition of sexual relations between Muslims and Christians, trade and consulting Muslim doctors issued by Archbishops of Nicosia will be reviewed.

Before discussing these articles it is necessary to be acquainted with the historical information about Muslims on the island during the 13th and 14th centuries through the information imparted by Islamic and Latin sources. Islamic sources provide us with information not mentioned in Latin sources. Muslims in Cyprus were mainly captives of the mutual raids between the Lusignan Kings of Cyprus and the Mamluks Sultans. The unsuccessful Ibn-Hasson raid targeting Cyprus in Shawwal 669 A.H/ 1270 A.D was one of these raids. The chronicler Al-Qādī Mohy al-deen Ibn Abd al-Zahir indicated that the Latins captured all Muslims on board the eleven galleys[1] that were destroyed by the winds near Limassol or *Nimasson* as it is named in Arabic sources (Ibn 'Abd al-Zāhir, 1976, 387).

The captives' numbers could be estimated at around 1,650, some of whom were freed by a ransom while others remained slaves in the Lusignan Kingdom of Cyprus. Those Muslim captives were mentioned in the letter from Sheikh Al-Islam Ibn Taymiyya known as *Al-risala al-qubrussiya* or The Cypriot Letter, and thought to have been

---

[1] The word for galleys in Arabic is *Al-sheeny*. It is a large military ship, that was one of the most important ships in fleet of Muslim countries. *Al-sheeny* is the name that all ships' names are derived from in Arabic according to historical sources. The name indicates the ship's role such as *Al-tareeda* (The Speedy) and *Al-Ghorab* (The crow). Al-Nuwaryi Al-Iskandarani specified the number of soldiers of each ship to be 150. Al-Nakheely, 1979, 84-83.

addressed to John II the exiled lord of Jubail[2] in 1304. This letter's content was clearly based on what had occurred with Abo Abbas El Maghraby who was one of the captives of Ibn-Hasson raid. Abo Abbas El Maghraby along with *Rai'es* of Alexandria and *Rai'es* of Damietta was mentioned by Al-Nuwaryi as one of the important figures held in captivity up until 673A.H, when Sultan Baybars sent Fakher al-Deen al-Maqry to negotiate and pay their ransom (Al-Nuwaryi, 2004, 115). Ibn Taymiyya asked the letter's recipient to treat the Muslim captives humanely in his kingdom and to abstain any attempts of conversion of Muslims. Affirming that the Messiah had commanded to help the poor and the weak and to obtain mercy, he expressed his astonishment that Christians should capture people of any nation perfidiously or deservedly whom they were not at war with. He even cited that the Messiah said 'But I tell you not to resist an evil person, but whoever slaps you on your right cheek turn the other to him also and if anyone wants to sue you and take away your tunic let him have your cloak also' (Matthew 5:39-40). Muslim captives in Cyprus had been seized wrongfully because while Muslims were right to wage war against the Christians who had corrupted God's religion, Christians could never be justified in waging war on Muslims because neither God, nor the Messiah or apostles had ever sanctioned attacks or killed those following the religion of Abraham. Ibn Taymiyya asserted that most of the Muslim captives in Cyprus were poor and weak with no one to pay for their ransom. He also mentioned that Sheikh Abo al-Abbas's ransom was paid with difficulty (Ibn Taymiyya 1974, 30,31,34,35; Coureas 2016, 404).

The Alexandria raid in Muḥarram 767 A.H /October 1365 was one of the most important Cypriot raids in the 14th century.

---

[2] This letter caused disagreement between scholars about the person receiving this letter. It was not clear if it was John II the lord of Jubail a member of Embriaci family who lived in his exile in Cyprus or William de Villaret, the Hospitaller Grand Master. Ibn Taymiyya 1995, 87-91 and 125-202; Cucarella 2010, 187-212.

Muhammad bin Qasim al-Nuwiry al-Iskandarani could estimate the number of Muslim captives in this raid as he had witnessed these events himself. He believed that the Latins held 5,000 men and women in captivity from among the Muslims, Jews and Christians, in addition to children. Those captives were taken from Egypt and distributed in cities all around Cyprus (Al-Nuwaryi, 1968-1976, 2/166-167, 177, 179, 207). These estimates of the numbers of captives were also confirmed by Maqrizi (Al-Maqrizi 1997, 284). The Cypriot fleet under the command of King Peter I returned to Cyprus carrying spoils (Mas Latrie, 1877, 109). Afterwards, negotiations for peace were initiated and messengers were sent to Cyprus to request the redemption of the Muslim captives as a condition of maintaining peace between both sides. King Peter I agreed to these conditions and all Muslim captives returned back to Cairo (Makhairas 1932, 1 and 163-165).

Many of the Latin sources provide important information about Muslims in the Kingdom of Cyprus. One of the most important notarial collections is that of Lamberto di Sambuceto,[3] that contains valuable information concerning major issues such as the price of Muslim slaves, examples of their being traded, marriages among these slaves, the conversion of Muslim slaves and the changing of their

---

[3] Lamberto di Sambuceto who had been working in the Black Sea port of Caffa before he moved to Famagusta, where he lived from 1294-1307. He held an official position of 'Notary and scribe' for the Genoese community. See, Ahmet Usta, 'Evidence of the Nature, Impact and Diversity of Slavery in 14th Century Famagusta as Seen Through the Genoese Notarial Acts of Lamberto di Sambuceto and Giovanni da Rocha and the Venetian Notarial Acts of Nicola de Boateriis,' PhD dissertation, (Eastern Mediterranean University, 2011),7.

names.[4] The writings of pilgrims who had passed through Cyprus in their journeys to the Holy Land likewise contain significant information on Muslims in Cyprus. For instance, the German pilgrim Ludolf of Suchen who visited the island between 1336 and 1341 pointed out that the Templars employed more than 100 Muslim slaves in the vineyard of Engaddi in the district of Paphos. Their only mission was to clean and guard the vineyards. Obviously, this occurred before the dissolution of the Templars in 1312.[5] It is also worth mentioning that naval piracy played a major role in the maintaining the supply of Muslim slaves to Cyprus. Following the disaster of the Genoese invasion in 1373, pirates would seize Muslims' ships and capture thousands of Muslims to be sold as slaves in the markets of Cyprus and Rhodes. Most of the time the Muslim slaves sold in Cyprus would work in the labour intensive sugar plantations in the district of Limassol, belonging to the Hospitallers, the Venetian Cornaro family and the Crown (Mas Latrie 1891-93, 498; Grivaud 1990, 61-62; Ashtor 1983, 225; Coureas 2016, 394). These Cypriot and Rhodian pirates continued raiding the Egyptian and Syrian coastlines, especially on account of the Cypriot nobles' desire to enrich themselves through piracy and obtain workforces for their estates. This policy was not practiced only by

---

[4] Cornelio Desimoni, ed. 'Actes passes a Famagousta, de 1299 a 1301, par devant le notaire génois Lamberto di Samuceto,' ,Archives de l'Orient Latin,II,(Paris:Ernest Leroux,1884), Documents,no. 86,95,110; Notai genovesi in oltremare: Atti rogati a Cipro da Lamberto di Sambuceto, Universita di Genova, Istituto di Paleografia e Storia Medieval, Collana storica di fonti e studi diretta da Geo Pistarino, 5 vols. (Genoa, 1982), No 31, (3 Luglio 1300-3 Agosto 1301), ed. Valeria Polonio, Documents no. 256.; No 32, (6 Luglio-27 Ottobre 1301), ed. Romeo Pavoni, (Genoa, 1982), Documents no.55,58,117,156.

[5] Excerpta Cypria: Materials for a History Of Cyprus, trans. Claude D.Cobham (Cambridge: Cambridge University Press,1908),16.see also, Coureas,'Latin Cyprus and its Relations',409;Peter Edbury, 'The Templars in Cyprus,' In The Military Orders: Fighting for the Faith and Caring for the Sick, ed. Malcolm Barber,189-195.(Cambridge: Variorum,1994), 191,193.

nobles. The Lusignan Kings were also forced to conduct raids on the Mamluk lands due to declining royal revenues and the need for a workforce in their sugar plantations.6

It is important to mention that Muslims in Cyprus were not only Arab Muslims but also Turkish Muslims who had been captured in the Cypriot raids on the coasts of Asia Minor or had reached the kingdom through slave trade. Turkish slaves were brought to Cyprus by Latin raiders, Catalans, Hospitallers.7

Therefore, it is clear that most Muslims in the Kingdom of Cyprus were captives who had lost their freedom and lived in Cypriot society as slaves who were usually exploited in agricultural work. It also seems likely that Muslim women taken as slaves were sexually exploited. Archbishop Gerard issued a warning in 1298 prohibiting any sexual involvement with Muslim or Jewish women considering this act as a major crime that made its perpetrator subject to his jurisdiction.8

Although there is no statistical count of the Muslims in the Lusignan kingdom of Cyprus or on the evolution of their existence in different time periods, just like other minorities they were included in

---

6   King Janus of Cyprus conducted a raid on the Egyptian coasts in AD 1415 to suffice the deficiency in workforce in his sugar plantations. He captured 1500 Muslims and refused to release them. He replied to Mamluk Sultan al-Mu'ayad that they were needed in the plantations, although Emmanuel Pilotihas mentioned that around 535 slaves were ransomed that year. Mas Latrie 1891-93, 499-500; Ashtor 1983, 225; Ouerfelli 2004, 333-4; Coureas 2016, 394.

7   It is worthwhile to note that Turkish raiders also captured Greeks from the Aegean area which was 'The Turkish ghazi principalities of Western Anatolia, or the towns of Satalia and Candelore in Southern Anatolia, all of which were active in this trade'. Makhairas 1932, 143; Arbel 2000, 154; Usta 2011, 15 and 40.

8   For slave categories and peasants refer to peasant, Usta 2011, 42-43.

legislation of the Assizes of Lusignan Cyprus.[9] The number of legal articles relating to Muslims is more than 20, concerned with different aspects of their lives.

Issues of slaves and slavery represented a great portion of the articles of law in the Assizes. The Assizes approached topics such as conversion of Muslim slaves and its legal consequences. Freeing those slaves was one of the consequences of conversion, Nevertheless, the former slave cannot summon his master in court. The law considered a former slave, who summons his master in court a criminal who had to redeem his actions through the corporal punishment of cutting out his tongue and paying a fine (Coureas 2002, 16, 192 and 193). The manumission of slaves after their conversion to.[10] However, the law preserved some rights to the owners of former slaves. It stated that in case a former slave passes away without a will or children, all his possessions are transferred to his former master and his offspring (Coureas 2002, 193). However, in cases where the slave did have illegitimate children, he was to bequeath one third of all his properties to his master who had freed him and to his children. When this law was not followed, the master had the right to receive a third of the properties bequeathed to the slave's family within a year and a day (Coureas 2002, 192).

---

[9] The earliest editions of the assizes were translated in Venice in 1535. The first modern edition of the burgess court Assizes was published in 1839 by Èdouard Kausler from the manuscript of Munich. In 1839 Victor Foucher published Italian and Old French version of the manuscript of 1535. Beugnot also published an edition in 1843 in volume II of the Lois in the RHC.There is also an English translation by Nicholas Coureas of the two Greek manuscripts written in Cyprus. They were translated from the French or Italian originals I depended on these English translated versions, Kausler 1839; Le Comte Beugnot 1843; Coureas 2002.

[10] One of the forms of manumission stated in notarial acts was manumission of the slave by paying an agreed sum to his master. Manumission could also be granted as some sort of gratitude from his master. There was also manumission as a remission of sins for the master's soul. Usta 2011, 85.

Manumission was one of the ways used to encourage Muslim slaves to convert to the Latin faith (Kedar 1984, 76-7). It was the only way for Muslim slaves to escape from the harsh life, conditions, violence and ill-treatment of their condition. The slaves' subjection to torture and brutality at the time were widely mentioned in notarial deeds. Slaves were thrown off building roofs and murdered by their owners. Torturing slaves was not just physical, but both men and women slaves were also sexually exploited. Through the notarial acts drawn up in Cyprus during the fourteenth century it comes through clearly that the ownership rights of a master included the right to sell, rent, donate, set her /him free and use for pleasure. However, there were also other masters who insisted on preserving their slaves' safety after selling their slaves to another master (Lamberto di Sambuceto 1982b, 239; Lambardo 1973, 76; Makhairas 1932, 465; Usta 2011, 41 note, 114 and 83).

In the Lusignan Kingdom of Cyprus, manumission was not facilitated since the masters of Muslim slaves did not allow these slaves to convert to Christianity. They were also constantly in demand for cultivating fields and vineyards, labour intensive industries like sugar and viticulture in Kolossi and Episkopi in the district of Limassol, as well as in Engadi, Lemba and Emba in the district of Paphos (Coureas 2005, 106-107; Usta 2011, 41; Mas Latrie 1852, 212). Slave masters also doubted the sincerity of Muslim conversions to Christianity. Although the law theoretically and clearly stated that the slave's manumission should fully safeguard his or her freedom, in practice slaves were only granted a conditional manumission. Slaves were obliged to stay under the control of their masters performing the same service for a certain period of time; they were not granted full freedom instantly. In the 12th century, an originally Muslim girl was recorded in a notarial deed to have continued to be a slave to her master for 10 years after her supposed manumission. Another example of a female slave was a woman called Elen. She was kept under a status of conditional manumission according to the relevant notarial deed dated 9th of April

1300 for five years. She was to serve her master during these five years both inside and outside his house (Lamberto di Sambuceto 1982b, 97; Phillips 1985, 102; Usta 2011, 85 n. 285).

It was apparent that conditional manumission was being granted under the influence of the Papacy. One of the letters dispatched by Pope Gregory IX to the Patriarch of Jerusalem in 1237, expressed concern that many slaves who desired conversion to the Catholic faith were being denied manumission. The Pope gave his advice that manumission was only for slaves who were willing to pledge to serve their Latin masters' after the manumission (Tautu 1950, n. 228, 307-308; Nader 2006, 166-7). Some of the Muslim slaves after baptism were called by Christian names, usually names of Saints. A Turkish Muslim slave was documented as sold through an act in 1301 to Rex of Voltri after his baptism and his name had been changed to Michali by his former Genoese owner Guillelmus de Aste (Lamberto di Sambuceto 1982a, 256; Usta 2011, 81). Therefore, it was clear that even though the Muslim slave had converted to his owner's religion, he was traded away and not granted his freedom. The law stated that when a slave fled his master – whether Muslim, Christian, Jew, Syrian or Samaritan – to an Muslim country and aimed at returning to a Christian one to convert to Christianity, he was to be granted his full rights for converting into what they believed to be the true faith. His previous master would have no rights over him. On the other hand, in cases where the slave fled from his master to a Christian state — even if he became a Christian there — his master's rights were fully preserved. In such cases and the law stated he had the right to sell him to a new master who had to be a Christian (Coureas 2002, 238).

It also seems like the presence of Muslims in Cyprus was not limited to slaves but also included a social middle class resident in Cyprus. This is proved by a warning to the Christians in 1252 and 1280 from the Latin archbishop of Nicosia not to seek Muslim doctors. Nevertheless it is not confirmed that Muslim doctors did live in the 13th century in Cyprus. However, it is well known that Muslims headed to the royal courts of King Hugh IV of Cyprus in the midst of the 14th century for philosophical and theological debates (Schabel 2005, 162). The law had set criteria for overseas doctors coming from Muslim countries or others concerning the practice of medicine. Primarily, the Muslim or overseas doctor had to prove his competence before the best doctors in Cyprus. Afterwards, the doctor had to obtain the bishop's permission to practice medicine in the city of his choice (Coureas 2002 Codex 1, 227 and Codex 2, 225).

The legal articles concerning litigation were broadly similar in dealing with Muslims and other non-Latins as opposed to Latins. A case in point is offering testimony as the law primarily stated that non- Latins were not allowed to testify against Latins in the Burgess court. On the other hand, Muslims, Syrians, Greeks, Jacobites, and Nestorians were allowed to act as witnesses for or against members of their own faith (Coureas 2002 Codex 1, 132 and Codex 2, 129; Bishop 2011, 67).

In addition, Muslims, Greeks, and Syrians did not enjoy the right to challenge any Latin in a judicial duel in the court (Coureas 2002 Codex 1, 26 and Codex 2, 258). As for court summons regarding changeable debts or some owed livelihood, the law stated that in cases where Muslims and Syrians denied the debt along with the lack of witnesses on the side of the Latin defendant, Muslims or Syrians would be obliged to testify under oath that they did not owe the Latin anything. On the other hand, the law did not compel Latins to testify under oath in case of debt denial along with the lack of witnesses (Coureas 2002 Codex 1, 57 and Codex 2, 58). Nevertheless, when giving an oath in the covered market court the law obliged the Muslim to swear by the Qur'an and the Jew by the Torah. It also compelled the Syrians, Samaritans, Greeks and Nestorians to swear by the Bible of their own language (Coureas 2002 Codex 1, 291 and Codex 2, 291).

The trials between Muslims and minorities were regulated by the litigation laws in different disputes. Being summoned in court for owing debt between a Muslim and a Samaritan with the Samaritan in denial of the debt would force the latter to call Muslim witnesses since

Samaritans were not allowed to testify against Muslims. That is also the case in all disputes between Muslims, Jews, Samaritans, Jacobites and Syrians. In general, the law desired 'every race being accused with witnesses of the same race, and no other witnesses' (Coureas 2002 Codex 1, 61 and Codex 2, 63).

The law treated the non-Latins equally. Moving to a Muslim country and changing one's religion to become a Jew or a Samaritan was one of the causes children could invoke to deprive their parents of their inheritance (Coureas 2002 Codex 1, 228 and Codex 2, 227). That was the point of similarity between Muslims, Jews and Samaritans. All minorities were equally treated in handling their cases such as debt, lost commodities or regarding any behaviour exhibited by Muslims, Jews, Nestorians, Greeks, Samaritans, or Jacobites before the marketplace court. They were not allowed to bring charges against anyone over any action which anyone had committed against them before any court other than the court of their marketplace, with the exception of charges of murder, conspiracy, or the drawing of blood since these charges needed to be submitted before the court of Burgesses. The number of assessors defined by law was six trust-worthy assessors in the marketplace. Four of them were Syrians and two Christian Latins. Their role was to pass judgement over all cases brought before the *bailli* (Coureas 2002 Codex 1, 228 and Codex 2, 287).

The law did not discriminate between Muslims, Syrians, Jews, and Samaritans in defining the conditions required for appointing the *bailli* in the marketplace. Earning people's trust, a good reputation, and being honourable were among the requirements for this position (Coureas 2002 Codex 1, 288 and Codex 2, 286). Moreover, there were similarities in the treatment of Muslims and Latins within the laws concerning Muslim or Latin clerks in the employ of the ruler in the covered market or the court chain, such as in case either of them was involved in state embezzlement or bribery. If a clerk receives a bribe from a merchant to allow the entry of his goods without paying his dues to the ruler or if the clerk retained half the amounts due to himself conspiratorially, the law stated that this clerk shall be blindfolded and paraded around the town, then, hanged to death (Coureas 2002 Codex 1, 274 and Codex 2, 272). Hiring a Muslim clerk was one of the forms of domestic slavery, and these domestic slaves' jobs were described as unproductive labour, because the slaves are not producing foodstuffs, or urban products like pottery, jewellery or furniture (Phillips 1985, 8; Usta 2011, 31-32).

One of the important distinctions in law between Muslims and minorities in the penalties prescribed was stating that in cases where a Muslim slave assaults a Latin man or woman, the Muslim should have his hand cut off, be paraded through out the town, and exiled (Coureas 2002 Codex 1, 294 and Codex 2, 294). On the other hand, when a Syrian assaulted a Latin man or woman, the Syrian was simply obliged to pay a fine of 50 Bezants (Coureas 2002 Codex 1, 279 and Codex 2, 277). This distinction is not simply religious, it is also social, the Muslim is a slave but the Syrian is a free man. Slaves in general were hanged or burnt if the assaulted free men who died as a result, but only if they died (Coureas 2002 Codex 1, 203 and Codex 2, 201). The Muslim could be hanged even if the victim did not die, so the law on Muslim assailants was stricter.

The Assizes dealt with Muslim involvement in criminal theft. If a Muslim fled after robbing orchards, vineyards or residences the ruler would be forced to confiscate all the Muslim's belongings and assets to compensate the victim's loss. The remainder of the Muslim's possessions would then be transferred to the ruler of the country (Coureas 2002 Codex 1, 234 and Codex 2, 232).[11]

Regarding commodities stolen or transferred to Muslim territories and their return later on to Christian ones; the law stated that the owner of the commodity had to have two witnesses to prove his

---

[11] This law applied in Cyprus but was more relevant to the Latin states founded in Syria by the Crusaders. A Muslim fleeing Cyprus after robbing orchards would have to find a ship and cross the sea, whereas in Syria he could simply cross a land frontier.

ownership and deny that it has been stolen. Moreover, the subject who had lost this commodity beforehand had to pay the same expenditure that the buyer had paid to make the purchase. The new buyer had the right to verify the amount of expenditure to be paid to him through witnesses or oaths. However, the initial owner, before fully redeeming his commodity, needed two witnesses taking an oath on the Gospels, had to affirm his previous ownership. In addition, the redeemed owner had to take an oath on the Gospels stating that he had not sold, granted or given the commodity as security. On the other hand, if it was proven that the current owner was a thief, who had stolen this commodity from its original owner with the lack of any witnesses who had seen him purchase it, the commodity was to be redeemed immediately to the original owner without further charges. The thief had to be hanged and all his possessions had to be confiscated by the ruler of the country where he had committed his crime (Coureas 2002 Codex 1, 221 and Codex 2, 219).

The law strictly prohibited interreligious Muslim-Christian marriage. It also stated that Christians belonging to different confessions could not marry on certain festival days of the Christian calendar, or the children of their own god sons or god daughters who had been born after the christening (baptism) of their god sons or god daughters (Coureas 2002 Codex 1, 171 and Codex 2, 169). This law prohibiting marriages between Muslims and Christians was not always observed in Cypriot society. Interreligious marriage was mentioned in an act between Salveto Botario and Vivaldus de Asta on the 25th of September 1301. This act records Vivaldus' sale of a 20 years old Muslim slave named Ballabam and his Christian mother Mariam, who was 60 years old. It appears as though Ballabam's father was a Muslim; therefore, he could follow the ethnic group of his father and be recorded as a Muslim (Lamberto di Sambuceto 1982b, 156; Usta 2011, 75).

The Assizes included articles to regulate trade between Muslims and Christians. It specified legal penalties on false Christians who exported prohibited goods such as weapons, helmets, spears, chain mail, bows, metal skewers and bits for horses to Muslim lands. The merchant was to be sentenced to death by hanging and all his possessions were to be confiscated by the ruler, if his prohibited trade was proven by witnesses (Coureas 2002 Codex 1, 45 and Codex 2, 46). Similarly, popes issued a series of bulls forbidding trade with Muslims and archbishops enforced equivalent decrees. The Latin archbishop Hugh of Fagiano's decree in 1251 condemned as excommunicated those false Christians who exported timber, weapons and iron to the Mamluk lands. His successor Archbishop Ranulf renewed this prohibition in 1280. Pope Nicholas IV announced in August 1291 the prohibition of Christian trade with Mamluk Sultanate for 10 years on pain of excommunication (Coureas 2016, 404-405). An article also stated the prohibition to trade Christian slaves to Muslims. He who committed this crime knowingly or unwittingly was to be hanged (Coureas 2002 Codex 1, 200 and Codex 2, 198). The Assizes also contained customs duties payable for all commodities transported by land or sea, including goods exported to Muslim countries (Coureas 2002 Codex 1, 295 and Codex 2, 297). It also specified duties paid for goods imported from Muslim countries (Coureas 2002 Codex 1, 296 and Codex 2, 298).

    In conclusion, Muslims reached The Latin Kingdom of Cyprus due to mutual raids between the Kingdom and the Mamluk Sultanate and pirate raids in the Mediterranean Sea. There is no accurate evidence on their exact number in Cyprus although according to notarial acts there was a large number of Muslim slaves on the island. Most Muslims were of Arabic and also Turkish extraction who reached the Kingdom through piracy raids on the coasts of Asia Minor, Syria and Egypt or through the active slave trade at that time, especially on account of the increasing needs of the workforce. Most Muslims lived in adversity in the Cypriot society; they lived as slaves in vineyards and sugar plantations. The fact, however, that, warnings were issued against seeking Muslim doctors was an indication of their existence in the Lusignan Kingdom of Cyprus. It also showed that even middle class

Muslims living in the kingdom suffered discrimination and did not have full rights and privileges due to their religion.

Latins, the dominant ethnic and religious group, enjoyed all privileges and their full rights under the umbrella of the law and while conversely all non-Latin minorities were bound by strict laws. The Assizes show clear similarities between Muslims and other minorities in the matters of testimonies and courts summons, where the law treated them on equal terms. Nevertheless, it displayed major differences, especially in cases where Muslims were ill-treated. In cases where a Christian Latin was assaulted by a Muslim, his hand was cut off while a Syrian committing the same offence would only pay a fine. The prohibitions against interreligious marriage, seeking Muslim doctors, exporting strategic goods to Muslims and breaking trade restrictions in disregard of the successive papal bulls and decrees issued by archbishops are examples of the legal articles aimed against Muslims.

Reference Sources

- *Al*-Maqrizi. 1997. *Kitab al-Suluk fi Maarifat Duwal al-Mulauk*, ed. Mohammed Abd Al qader Atta. Beirut, Lebanon: Dar Al Kitab Al E'lmeya.
- Al-Nakheely, D.1979. *Al-Sofon Al Islameya ala Horoof Al-Mog'am*. Alexandria: Dar al- Ma'aref.
- Al-Nuwaryi, Ahmad Abdel wahab. 2004. *Nehait al-arab fe fonoon al-adab (The final purpose of Literature Arts)*, ed. Moustafa Nageeb fawaz and hekmat Keshky fawaz. Beirut: Dar al –Ketab Al E'lmeya.
- Al-Nuwaryi al-Iskandarani, Muhammad bin Qasim. 1968-1976, *Kitab al-Ilmam bl-Alam fi-ma-gart-bu-al-ahkam-wa-al-omor- al-Maqdia-fi-wakat-al-askandria* 767 A.H, (the book of knowing public figures in what happened in the raid of Alexandria), three versions preserved in the Library of Faculty of Arts, Alexandria University under the number:1-738M (version preserved in Bankipur library in India under 2335 Arabic), B-667M (Berlin version number 9815 in the Ahlodart list, number 359-60 in Feterschtein list,) G737 M.(version in the Dar al Kotob Al masreya in Cairo under the number: 28558, ed. Aziz Surial Atiya,with the contribution of Ethan Comb for the first part) in seven vols. India: Dar Al -Ma'aref Al -Othmaneya.

- al-Zāhir, Ibn 'Abd, 1976. *Al-Rwad al-Zāhir fi Sīrat al-Malik al-Zāhir*, ed. Abd al-Aziz Khuwaytir: Riyadh.
- Lambardo A, ed.1973. *Nicola de Boateriis, notaio a Famagosta e Venezia (1355-1365)*, Venice.
- Arbel, B. 2000. 'Slave Trade and Slave Labour in Frankish Cyprus(1191-1571)'. In *Cyprus, Franks and Venice, 13th -16th Centuries*, IX , 151-190. Aldershot: Ashgate
- Ashtor, E. 1983. *Levant Trade in the Middle Ages*. New Jersey: Princeton University Press.
- Bishop, A.M. 2011. 'Criminal Law and the Development of the Assizes of the Crusader Kingdom of Jerusalem in the Twelfth Century." PhD dissertation, University of Toronto.
- Cobham, C.D. trans. 1908 *Excerpta Cypria: Materials for a History of Cyprus*. Cambridge: Cambridge University Press.
- Coureas, N. 2002. *The Assizes of the Kingdom of Cyprus*. Nicosia: Cyprus Research Centre.
- ---. 2005. 'Economy'. In *Cyprus: Society and Culture 1191-1374*, ed. Nicolaou-Konnari, A., and Schabel, C., Leiden: Brill.103-152.
- ---. 2016. 'Latin Cyprus and its Relations with the Mamluk Sultanate 1250-1517'. In *The Crusade World*, ed. A. Boas, New York: Routledge. 391-418.
- Cucarella, S. 2010. 'Corresponding across Religious Borders: The Letter of Ibn Taymiyya to a Crusader in Cyprus'. *Islamochristiana* 36:187-212.
- Desimoni, C. ed. 1884. 'Actes passes a Famagousta, de 1299 a 1301, par devant le notaire génois Lamberto di Samuceto'. In *Archives de l'Orient Latin*, II. Paris: Ernest Leroux.
- Edbury, 1994. 'The Templars in Cyprus', In *The Military Orders: Fighting for the Faith and Caring for the Sick*, ed. Malcolm Barber, 189-195.
- Cambridge: Variorum.Grivaud, G. ed. 1990. *Excerpta Cypria Nova*, vol, 1. Nicosia: Cyprus Research Centre.
- Ibn Taymiyya, 1974. *Al-risala al-qubrussiya* .Cairo: Dar Al Ketab.
- Ibn Taymiyya, 1995. *Lettre à roi croisé (al-Risāla al-Qubrusiyya)* Traduction de l'arab, introduction, notes et lexique par J.R. Michot, Louvain-la-Neuve: Tawhid, Lyon.
- Kausler, E.H. ed. 1839. *Livre des assises de Jérusalem*. Stuttgart.
- Kedar, B.Z. 1984. *Crusade and Mission: European Approaches Toward the Muslims*. Princeton: Princeton University Press.
- Lamberto di Sambuceto. 1982a. *Notai genovesi in oltremare,Atti rogati a Cipro da Lamberto di Sambuceto, Universita di Genova, Istituto di Paleografia e Storia Medievale,*

Collana storica di fonti e studi diretta da Geo Pistarino, 5 vols: No. 31, (3 Luglio 1300-3 Agosto 1301), ed. Polonio, V., Genoa.
- ---. 1982b. *Notai genovesi in oltremare,Atti rogati a Cipro da Lamberto di Sambuceto,Universita di Genova, Istituto di Paleografia e Storia Medievale, Collana storica di fonti e studi diretta da Geo Pistarino*, 5 vols: No. 32, (6 Luglio-27 Ottobre 1301), ed. Pavoni, R., Genoa.
- Le Comte B. M. ed. 1843. 'Livre des assises de la cour des Bourgeois', In *RHC Lois*, II. Paris: Académie Royal des inscriptions et Belles-Lettres.
- Makhairas, L. 1932. *Recital concerning the Sweet Land of Cyprus*, entitled "Chronicle", ed. Dawkins, R.M., 2 vols. Oxford: Oxford University Press.
- Mas Latrie, L. 1852. *Histoire de l'île de Chypre sous le règne des princes de la maison de Lusignan,II*. Paris: A l'imprimerie Nationale.
- --- Guillaume de Machaut, 1877. *La Prise d'Alexandrie ou chronique du Roi Pierre Ier de Lusignan*, Généve: Imprimerie Jules-Guillaume Fick.
- Mas Latrie, R. ed. 1891-93. 'Chronique d' Amadi'. In *Chroniques d' et de Strambaldi*, 2 vols.Paris: A l'Imprimerie Nationale.
- Nader, M. 2006. *Burgesses and Burgess Law in the Latin Kingdoms of Jerusalem and Cyprus 1099-1325*. Aldershot: Ashgate.
- Phillips, W.D. 1985. *Slavery from Roman Times to the Early Transatlantic Trade*. Minneapolis: University of Minnesota Press.
- Ouerfelli, M. 2004. 'Les relations entre le royaume de Chypre et le sultanat mamelouke au XV siècle'. In *Le moyen Age*, CX, 2:327-344.
- Schabel, C. 2005. 'Religion'. In *Cyprus: Society and Culture 1191-1374*, ed. Nicolaou-Konnari, A. and Schabel, C., Leiden: Brill. 157-218.
- Tautu, A.L. ed. 1950 Gregory IX *Acta (12271241)*. Rome: Vatican City.
- Usta, A. 2011. 'Evidence of the Nature, Impact and Diversity of Slavery in 14th Century Famagusta as Seen Through the Genoese Notarial Acts of Lamberto di Sambuceto and Giovanni da Rocha and the Venetian Notarial Acts of Nicola de Boateriis.' PhD dissertation.Eastern Mediterranean University.

The relations between Beirut and Cyprus during the fourteenth and fifteenth centuries

Pierre Moukarzel (Lebanese University Beirut, Lebanon)

THIS PAPER AIMS to show the importance of relations between Cyprus, especially Famagusta, and Beirut during the Mamluks era and sheds light on the Cypriot merchants settled in Beirut during the first half of the fourteenth century.

During the fourteenth and fifteenth centuries various military, economic and political factors favoured the development of relations between Beirut and Cyprus, in particular Famagusta its main port, allowing them to play an essential role in the Mediterranean trade within the framework of the trade exchanges between East and Europe, and being able to attract the deployment of the European trade in the oriental Mediterranean Sea.

After the fall of Acre in 1291, Cyprus played a great role in the trade with the Mamluk sultanate. In addition, it became a very important base of the European merchants, and served as a reloading point for many shipments of European products. The products of Cyprus, such as sugar, cotton, wheat and salt had a great market in many European countries. Its main port, Famagusta, formed the base from which the European merchants shipped to the West the spices, the cotton of Syria, and many other commodities coming from the dominions of the Mamluk sultan (Ashtor 1983, 39). Since the end of the thirteenth century, Venice organised a line of regular convoys of galleys connecting it to Cyprus, functioning under the control and the supervision of the Venetian Senate. The galleys were sometimes authorized to continue their voyage to Syria (Stöckly 1995, 119).

Cyprus became a great centre for the distribution of oriental products and its commercial exchanges with the Syrian ports were intense (Ashtor 1983, 40). The acts of Lamberto di Sambuceto, notary of Famagusta, from the years 1299 to 1301, contained five commendas given on October 7, 1300, by Syrian Christians, consisting of spun cotton and amounting 2920 dinars. The merchandise was to be sold either in Apulia or in Venice. The merchants who gave them were from Latakia and Beirut. The same merchants also exported cotton to Ancona, giving commendas to Anconitan merchants (Desimoni 1893, 103, 106, 123, 126, 349, 353, 362, 366). So Christian merchants from Beirut and other Syrian coastal cities came over Cyprus and exported the cotton of their country from there. On the other hand, Cypriots, especially the Syrian immigrants, travelled to Syria to buy the merchandises they needed. The Nestorian family Lakhan provided an important part of the traffic between Famagusta and the Syrian coasts (Richard 1981, 91).

The notary's acts concluded in Famagusta during this period revealed the Genoese commercial activities with the Syrian coast: in 1302, a Genoese bequeathed 100 besants (Byzantine gold coin) to the Church of Rome to travel to Tripoli, and in 1307, a company was formed to make the travel to Beirut and Damascus with a storehouse in Beirut (Richard 1976, 222). The Italian ships conducted the transport of goods between Cyprus and the Syrian coast. Sometimes, in years of scarcity, the Italian merchants exported grains to Syria and despite the papal prohibition of trade with the Mamluk sultanate many contracts were signed for trade with the dominions of the sultan or indicated 'Syria' as the destination of the voyage (Ashtor 1983, 41; Richard 1984, 120-134; Heyd 1959, 23-25). At any rate, the numerous commercial contracts drawn up in Famagusta at the beginning of the fourteenth century leave no doubt as to the intensity of trade between Cyprus and Syria.

Cypriots were also engaged in the commerce of arms and slaves with the inhabitants of Keserwân Mountains to the northeast of Beirut. According to the Islamic scholar and theologian Ibn Taymiyya (died in 1328), Ismailis, Nusayris, Druze and other inhabitants of Keserwân sent to Cyprus a great number of Muslim prisoners, arms and horses following the defeat of the Mamluk army facing the Mongols in 1299-1300. In addition, they installed a market at the coast for twenty days to sell prisoners, arms and horses to the Cypriots (Ibn Taymiyya 2004, 400).

Beirut was the main economic and commercial basis of Syria. The chronicler Sâlih bin Yahyâ (died after 1436) an emir of the family Banû Buhtur who lived in Beirut quoted that after the fall of the city in the hands of the Mamluks in 1291, the European ships returned gradually to visit the port of Beirut for trade and the king of Cyprus sent regularly to Beirut aboard two galleys the goods of the Venetians landed in Famagusta. The Cypriots had churches in Beirut and a group of merchants permanently settled in the city. They also had their own taverns. Sālih bin Yahyā added that later all that was abolished (Bin Yahyâ 1969, 35). In the port of Beirut, the role of Cypriots seemed to be important. They transported merchandise on their ships to Cyprus. Furthermore the king of Cyprus played a major role in stimulating the commercial activities of Beirut with the Europeans.

The development of trade between Cyprus and Beirut during the fourteenth century

Undoubtedly the development of trade between Cyprus and Beirut knew an important expansion because of favourable conditions and privileges granted by the Mamluk sultans. The sources did not mention that the king of Cyprus had signed a treaty with the Mamluk sultan to obtain the most favourable conditions of trade for Cypriot merchants but it seemed that there was a secret agreement between both sovereigns to maintain commercial exchanges between Cyprus and

Beirut and other Syrian coastal cities. Probably the agreement was not declared in order not to put Cyprus in a difficult position with the main European powers because the disrespect of the papal prohibition of trade with the dominions of the sultan.

The privileges granted by the sultan to the Cypriots in Beirut were the result of an agreement between two States, offering concession made by the sultan for a group of foreign traders living on his territories. This concession protected them as far as it recognised them legally, not only granted the protection of their persons and goods, but especially gave a legal and social existence to the merchants. Cypriots settled in Beirut, as European merchant communities living in the ports and cities of the Mamluk sultanate, were not subjected to the status of dhimma that was a protection to the non-Muslims for a levy, but they enjoyed a promise of protection ('ahd al-amân), which meant that a non-Muslim being a member of 'the land of the war' (dâr al-harb) was protected by the law following an agreement which fixed frames of a particular status of the current law in the countries subjected to the sultan (Al-Qalqashandî 1988, 322). The amân (safe-conduct) offered an easier basis for the establishment of commercial relations with European States than the law of armed truce. It was valid when there was a declaration of war between Muslims and the community to which the non-Muslim in question belonged or when the war had been temporarily suspended by a treaty or truce. With the development of the trade between the Christian powers and the Muslim world since the end of the twelfth century, the institution of the amân was in practice replaced by treaties concluded between the sultan and the main European merchant cities, particularly the Italians, which offered to the foreigners, the traders or the pilgrims, more security and more rights. The amân given by the sultan did not have its origin in the Muslim notion of amân. It was not about a protection for a limited period of time once it was expired the protected would be in danger. According to the religious of the various law Muslim schools the duration of the amân might not exceed one year; it looked like more as a kind of treaty between the sultan and the European merchant cities (Wansbrough 1971, 20-35). There were two types of amân given to the Non-Muslims: general ('âmm) and particular (khâss). The first was granted to an unlimited number of persons, such as the inhabitants of the same region, and it was only given by the sultan or his deputy (al-nâ'ib), as in the case of truce, while the second was given to one person or a limited number of persons by any taxpayer Muslim even those who did not have the ability to fight as slave, woman, old man, stupid and insolvent (Al-Qalqashandî 1988, 322). With the development of the trade between the Christian powers and the Muslim world since the end of the twelfth century, the institution of the amân was in practice replaced by treaties concluded between the sultan and the main European merchant cities, particularly the Italians, which offered to the foreigners, the traders or the pilgrims, more security and more rights. Because the development of trade during the thirteenth century, treaties had not been limited to ten years claimed by Islamic jurists (Al-Mâwardî 1989, 69). Of course sultans were not weak and fearful in their treaty with Cypriots or Europeans in general. But it was a policy adopted by the sultans and supported by the jurists forming a situation that had a religious origin but had been modified according to the circumstances, the interests of the sultans and Muslim community (Qalqashandî 1988, 8).

According to the text of Sâlih bin Yahyâ, Cypriots living in Beirut were only merchants settled for trade. They didn't have their wives with them. The lack of such privilege did not favor the long duration of their stay and opposed the formation of a new local population. In general, European traders living in the Muslim Levant towns were not authorised to be accompanied or joined by women of their religion. Sources quoted that in Alexandria the household of merchants was assured by servants coming from many European countries. In addition to these servants, the merchants also had slaves, more often slave-girls from the Oriental countries (Ashtor 1983, 407-408; Vallet 1999, 203-204; Bauden 2005, 273-274). We don't know if the same situation existed in Beirut concerning the Cypriot merchants because we have to take into consideration that Beirut was a very small city compared to Alexandria and European merchants of different nationalities in Alexandria were numerous. Furthermore, the slave trade in Egypt was very active (Christ 2012, 126-129). The confining of the Cypriots in the space of their lodging houses in Beirut restricted their demographic and social settlement and contributed to the growth of their residential and social segregation, forming a barrier against their moving closer towards the local population and the integration in the eastern society (Valérian 2004, 676-698). Thus, the nature of the presence of Cypriot traders in Beirut was illustrated by two phenomena: they retained their own individual names, and they formed a social group distinguished from its oriental surroundings. They became part of Levantine society without fully integrating into it. The traders were identified by the city where they were from, they were mentioned in the text of Sâlih bin Yahyâ by Cypriots (al-Qabârisa), but no time described or presented them as locals.

The Cypriots in Beirut obtained the privilege to have their own churches to celebrate the mass. Probably the churches were located inside the houses of the merchants and not outside in some places in the city. The Western pilgrims who visited Beirut since 1335 mentioned only two churches: Saint Saviour inside Beirut served by the Franciscans and Saint Georges outside the city (Moukarzel 2010, 93-97). The local authorities in Beirut were aware of the importance of maintaining the separation between the Cypriots and the Muslim inhabitants of the city in order to avoid problems and disputes with Muslim jurists. The Cypriots were considered as foreigners in the land of Islam who had a different religion and culture. For that reason, a strict and rigorous control on these foreigners by gathering them in definite places could help the local authorities to master the situation and to impose their power (Moukarzel 2013, 339-354). In addition, the houses must be near the port and close to each other because the main goal for the Mamluk authorities in Beirut was to regulate the trade and so gathering the

Cypriots in definite places presented to the local governors an instrument to facilitate fiscal and control operations on the traders and their activities providing the conduct of the commercial revenues to the State treasury.

The Cypriots had also their own taverns in Beirut to drink and sell wine. It was strictly forbidden to the traders to exercise commercial transactions concerning wine with the Muslim inhabitants: According to the Islamic law, the commerce of wine was allowed among dhimmîs but it was forbidden among Muslims or between Muslims and dhimmîs (Fattal 1995, 151). It seemed that the number of Cypriots living in Beirut was important so they had stores, houses, churches and taverns. All these buildings didn't belong to the Cypriots but were exclusively at their disposal. Sâlih bin Yahyâ talked only about the Cypriots in Beirut and their possessions so we can wonder if the other European merchants travelling from Cyprus to Beirut during the first half of the fourteenth century claimed to be citizens of the kingdom of Cyprus to enjoy the privileged status of the Cypriots in Beirut. We have to take into consideration that Catalan, Genoese and French ships frequented the port of Beirut during the first half of the fourteenth century: in 1334, a Catalan ship was present at the port of Beirut (Bin Yahyâ 1969, 97), and in the acts of a Genoese notary drawn up in 1344 in Damascus and Beirut appeared the names of Genoese and French merchants. Some of the Genoese merchants were living in Beirut and there was a French consul in the city (Ashtor 1983, 49-50). Although the Cypriots enjoyed commercial facilities, for sure they never got the privileges that gave them complete freedom of trade. For strategic and economic reasons, they remained, like all Europeans, under the control of local authorities in Beirut during their residency in their houses and also when they frequented markets or moved inside the city: it seemed that public places were open to traders but they were prohibited from entering mosques (Semeonis 1997, 974). Furthermore, according to the text of Sâlih bin Yahyâ, it seemed that Cypriots and other European merchants settled in Beirut were not influenced by the attacks launched against the city by Europeans: in 1299, many Frankish vessels tried to operate a landing at Beirut, but they failed because of the winds which dispersed them; and in 1334, the Genoese attacked Beirut. The battle lasted two days and the attackers succeeded to enter inside the port (Bin Yahyâ 1969, 97).

The sultan had the desire to attract Cypriots and other European traders to the markets in Beirut, Tripoli, Alexandria and other coastal cities and ports to develop and expand the commerce. He granted privileges to the traders, but at the same time local authorities in the cities and ports did not lose any opportunity to collect from them money (administrative procedures, customs dues and taxes). The most important was the perception of money because all relationships with the kingdom of Cyprus or other European countries were essentially based on material interests. The main objective of the sultan was to accept foreigners and take advantage of their wealth to provide supplies for the Treasury. During the same period, sources did not quote that traders from Beirut settled in Cyprus. But an English pilgrim who visited Famagusta in 1344-1345 evoked the presence of Muslim traders settled in the city coming from the sultan countries (Hoade 1970, 61). We can not exclude the idea that among the Muslim traders living in Cyprus there were merchants from Beirut.

During the first half of the fourteenth century, Cyprus was defying the papal prohibition of trade with the dominions of the sultan by maintaining its commercial activities with Beirut. It was until August 3, 1350, that Pope Clement VI granted to the king of Cyprus Hugh IV (1320-1361) the permission to send, during a period of five years, two galleys in Alexandria and other territories submitted to the sultan (Deprez and Mollat 1961, 317). This decision was the result of changes in papacy position concerning the trade with the Mamluk sultanate after the absence of security in the Black Sea in 1343 following the Tatars attack of the Italian merchant communities in Tana which was the major trading city on the Sea of Azov. In fact, the prohibition of trade was not lifted, but sometimes the pope granted licenses by special grace to exceptional cases (Coureas 2005, 395-408).

In 1365, the king of Cyprus Peter I (1358-1369) attacked Alexandria and sacked it (Al-Nuwayrî 2008; Al-Maqrîzî 1970, 104-108; Van Steenbergen 2003, 123-137). That year was a turning point in the relations between Cyprus and the Mamluk sultanate. The intermediary commerce between Cyprus and Syria was interrupted. The Venetians did not rely any more on the Cypriots ships to transport their merchandises to Beirut; they sent their own ships directly to Beirut. On September 8, 1366, three Venetian galleys arrived to Beirut (Thomas 1966, 111, 113-114). The expedition against Alexandria had nothing to do with Christian motives for recovery of the Holy Land. On the contrary, its motives seemed to have been purely commercial. The changing trade routes from the Black sea towards Egypt and Syria after 1343 and the economic effects of the Black Death (1346-1353) threatened Cyprus' commercial position, while the economic element at the same time favoured the Mamluk sultanate and in particular its main port Alexandria. The main goal of Peter I was to occupy Alexandria in order to derive profit from its commerce or to destroy the city so its commercial revenues would revert to Famagusta (Balard 1995, 104; Edbury 1977, 97).

The Mamluk authorities in Egypt and Syria took measures of precaution against other raids and wrought vengeance on the Christian subjects and on the European traders. Venetian merchants in Beirut and Alexandria were arrested and according to the chronicler Ibn Kathîr (died in 1373) the European merchants in Damascus were imprisoned and their goods were confiscated after the attack of Alexandria (Ibn Kathîr 1932-1939, 314, 322). The sources did not mention if the Cypriots in Beirut were arrested or had fled when they knew about the attack of Alexandria. Whatever the case could be they were not present anymore in Beirut and the port of the city became the target of attacks launched by the king of Cyprus having an objective to exercise pressure on the Mamluks governors. In 1369, four galleys sent by the king of Cyprus attacked Beirut. The city was well defended, the tower at the entrance of the port was equipped by soldiers and inside the city there was an army composed of four hundred soldiers, infantrymen and horsemen. The galleys did not succeed to reach the shore because the port's entrance was too narrow, so they abandoned the idea of attacking the city and continued their way towards Byblos (De Mas Latrie 1891, 116). In general, these military operations did not have any utility because they were punctual and limited, and they did not come within a frame of a general and organized Crusade.

In 1370, peace was concluded between the sultan and the main European powers: the Venetians, the Genoese, the Cypriots and the Catalans. This peaceful agreement had a duration of twenty years and contained a series of conditions among which returning all the plundered goods from Alexandria was mandatory (Ibn Qâdî Shuhba 1994, 380). The regular commercial exchanges with the Mamluk dominions started again and European vessels visited the ports in Egypt and Syria. Cypriots did not return to Beirut; they definitively left the city.

The trade between Cyprus and Beirut after the peace agreement in 1370

After 1370, a series of events influenced the circulation of trade in the Mediterranean Sea and opened a new period of commercial activity between Venice, Beirut and Cyprus. In 1374, Genoa ruled Famagusta and supplanted all the other merchant cities in Cyprus (Richard 1976, 221-229; Hill 1940, 414-415). In the face of such situation, Venice chose Beirut to establish a new economic base in the Mediterranean Sea in order not to interrupt its trade with the Levant, and organised a line of regular convoys of galleys connecting Venice to Beirut, replacing the maritime line of Cyprus, functioning under the control and the supervision of the Venetian Senate which decided to send every year two galleys from Crete to Beirut passing by Cyprus loading merchandise and returning to Venice. The functioning of this shipping line formed a very important economic turning point for both cities: on the one hand for Venice which fixed a centre for commercial support in Syria, and on the other hand for Beirut which gained prosperity and economic development which will mark it throughout the fourteenth and fifteenth centuries. To organise this new shipping line, the Venetian Senate specified the route to be followed and the duration of the stay in Beirut. These two galleys had to make the annual three journeys from Crete to Beirut, the last one before the end of October, and they were authorised to stay 22 days in Beirut during the first journey, 15 days during the other two ones (Senato Misti 34, 82, 85, 87). In 1375, Venice concluded a treaty with the Mamluk sultan providing privileges for the Venetian merchants in Syria (Thomas 1966, 162, 168-171; Predelli 1880-1889, 104). From then on, the Venetian Senate mentioned in its deliberations the galleys of Beirut and the muda of Beirut. In addition, Venice established at the end of the fourteenth century a line with Beirut for the transport of pilgrims to the Holy Land which was complementary to those of the commercial transport. Besides the Venetian official maritime networks, there was a real fleet of private ships not controlled by the Venetian authorities, sailed towards the various ports of the Mediterranean Sea, among which were Famagusta and Beirut (Luzzatto 1954, 53-57), (Hocquet 1991, 397-434). Famagusta was the main port of call of these maritime networks before reaching Beirut. The great part of the commercial exchanges between Famagusta and Beirut was henceforth maintained by the Venetian merchants.

But the projects of crusades which the kingdom of Cyprus joined resulted in bloody confrontations ended by the Mamluk conquest of Cyprus in 1427 (Ziada 1933-1934, 90-113, 37-57; Darrag 1961, 239-267; Edbury 1999, 223-242). The peace was restored and the Mediterranean trade reached its highest levels. The new relationship established between Cyprus and the Mamluk sultanate since 1427 opened the space of the Eastern Mediterranean for free trade; European merchants, particularly the Venetians, benefited greatly from this situation to establish good relations with the sultans of Egypt and to increase their hold over the Mamluk commerce. Venetian merchants living in Cyprus went to Syria and Egypt to sell the island products such as salt, sugar, wheat and molasses. In 1445, the Venetians renewed the function of the line of regular convoys of galleys travelling between Venice and Cyprus (Stöckly 1995, 126-127). The maritime convoys assisted by the private navigation allowed Venice to pursue a firm policy to seize the trade of spices and cotton in Syria and to exercise a commercial supremacy in the oriental Mediterranean Sea dominating the trade of Cyprus with Beirut.

Conclusion

During the fourteenth and fifteenth centuries, commercial relations between Beirut and Cyprus, especially Famagusta, did not stop progressing. Beirut and Famagusta became the termini of the merchant galleys carrying on board goods and merchants who frequented Syria for the trade. They were the meeting place of traders, European pilgrims and travellers who wished to visit Syria. Various military, economic and political factors favoured the development of Beirut and Famagusta allowing them to play a major role in the Mediterranean trade. The commercial relations between Cyprus and Beirut were still present and had gone through all the phases of confrontation and war between Cyprus and the Mamluk sultanate during the fourteenth and fifteenth centuries. They increased when Beirut and Famagusta became an important pole of the Venetian network of navigation towards which converged various other networks: those of the private and public navigation of Venice. These networks connecting Cyprus with Beirut complemented each other and competed mutually.

Reference Sources

- Archivio di Stato di Venezia, Senato, Misti, reg.34, f.82, f.85, f.87.
- Ashtor, E. 1983. *Levant trade in the later Middle Ages,* Princeton: Princeton University Press.
- Balard, M. 1995. 'Chypre, les républiques maritimes italiennes et les plans de croisades (1274-1370).' In *Cyprus and the crusaders, Papers given at the International Conference,* Nicosia, 6-9 september 1994, eds N. Coureas and J. Riley Smith, 97-106. Nicosia.
- Bauden, F. 2005. 'L'achat d'esclaves et la rédemption des captifs à Alexandrie d'après deux documents arabes d'époque mamelouke conservés aux Archives de l'État de Venise (ASV)', *Mélanges de l'Université Saint-Joseph* 58 : 269-325.
- Bin Yahyâ, S. 1969. Târîkh Bayrût wa huwa akhbâr al-salaf min dhuriyyat Buhtur bin ʿAlî amîr al-Gharb bi-Bayrût, eds Hours, F. and Salibi, K. Beirut: Dâr al-Machreq.
- Christ, G. 2012. *Trading conflicts: Venetian merchants and Mamluk officials in late medieval Alexandria,* Leiden: Brill.
- Coureas, N. 2005. 'Controlled contacts: the papacy, the Latin church of Cyprus and Mamluk Egypt, 1250-1350.' In *Egypt and Syria in the Fatimid, Ayyubid and Mamluk eras. IV, Proceedings of the 9th and 10th International Colloquium* organized at the Katholieke Universiteit Leuven in May 2000 and May 2001, eds Vermeulen, U. and Van Steenbergen, J., 395-408. Leuven: Peeters Publishers.
- Darrag, A. 1961. *L'Égypte sous le règne de Barsbay* 825-841/1422-1438, Damas: Institut français de Damas.
- De Mas Latrie, R. ed. 1891. *Chroniques d'Amadi et de Strambaldi,* Paris: Imprimerie Nationale.
- Deprez, E. and Mgr Mollat, G. eds 1961. *Lettres closes, patentes et curiales intéressant les pays autres que la France publiées ou analysées d'après les registres du Vatican,* Paris: de Boccard.
- Desimoni, C. 1893. 'Actes passés à Famagouste, de 1299 à 1301, par devant le notaire Lamberto de Sambuceto', *Revue de l'Orient Latin* 1 :58-139, 275-312, 321-353.
- Edbury, W. 1977. 'The Crusading Policy of King Peter I of Cyprus, 1359-1369.' In *The Eastern Mediterranean lands in the period of the Crusades,* ed. Holt, M., 90-105. Warminster: Aris and Phillips.

- --- 1999. 'The Lusignan Kingdom of Cyprus and its Muslim neighbours.' In *Kingdom of the Crusaders. From Jerusalem to Cyprus.* ed. Edbury, W., 223-242. Aldershot: Brookfield.
- Fattal, A. 1995. *Le statut légal des non-musulmans en pays d'islam.* 2nd ed. Beirut: Dâr El-Machreq.
- Heyd, W. 1958. *Histoire du commerce du Levant au Moyen Âge,* Trans. Raynaud, F., 2 volumes, Amsterdam: A.M. Hakkert.
- Hill, G.F. 1940. *A History of Cyprus, 2, The Frankish Period 1192-1432,* Cambridge: Cambridge University Press.
- Hoade, E. ed. 1970. *Western pilgrims: The itineraries of Fr.Simon Fitzsimons (1322-23) a certain Englishman (1344-45), Thomas Buggs (1392), and notes on other authors and pilgrims,* Jerusalem: Franciscan Printing Press.
- Hocquet, J-C. 1991. 'L'armamento private.' In *Storia di Venezia. Temi. Il Mare,* eds Tenenti, A. and Tucci, U., 397-434. Roma: Istituto della Enciclopedia Italiana fondata da Giovanni Treccani.
- Ibn Kathîr, 'Imâd al-dîn. 1932-1939. Al- bidâya wal-nihâya fî al-târîkh, 13-14, Vol. 7, Cairo.
- Ibn Qâdî Shuhba, Abû bakr bin Ahmad. 1994. Târîkh Ibn Qâdî Shuhba, ed. Darwish, A., Vol.2, Damascus: Institut Français de Damas.
- Ibn Taymiyya, Taqî al-dîn Ahmad. 2004, Majmû' fatâwa shaykh al-islam Ahmad bin Taymiyya, Vol.28, ed. Abd al-Rahmân bin Muhammad bin Qâsim, Al-Madîna al-Munawwara (Saudi Arabia): Mujamma' al-Malik Fahd li-tibâ'at al-mushaf al-sharîf.
- Luzzatto, G. 1954. 'Navigazione di linea e navigazione libera nelle grande città marinere del Medioevo.' In *Studi di storia economica veneziana,* ed. Luzzatto, G., 53-57. Padova: CEDAM. (Al)-Maqrîzî, Taqî al-dîn. 1970-1973. Kitâb al-sulûk fî ma'rifat duwal al-mulûk, Vol.1, ed. Abdel Fattah Ashour, S., Cairo: Dâr al-kutub.
- (Al)-Mâwardî, Abu-l-Hasan 'Alî. 1989. Al-ahkâm al-sultâniyya wal-wilâyât al-dîniyya, ed. Mubârak Al-Baghdâdî, A., Kuwait: University of Kuwait.
- Moukarzel, 2010. *La ville de Beyrouth sous la domination mamelouke* (1291-1516) et son commerce avec l'Europe, Baabda (Lebanon : Éditions de l'Université Antonine.
- --- 2013. 'The Latin traders in Egypt and Syria during the XIVth and the XVth centuries: Privileged communities under a strict control.' In *Mediterráneos. An Interdisciplinary Approach to the Cultures of the Mediterranean Sea,* eds Carro M. Arturo, S. et al., 339-354. Newcastle upon Tyne: Cambridge Scholars Publishing.

- (Al)-Nuwayrî, Shihâb al-dîn. 2008. Waqʻat al-Iskandariyya min kitâb al-ilmâm lil-Nuwayrî al-iskandarî, ed. Suhayl Zakkar, Damascus: Dâr al-Takwîn.
- Predelli, R. 1880-1889. *I libri commemriali della Republica di Venezia*. Regesti, Venezia: Deputazione Veneta di Storia Patria.
- (Al)-Qalqashandî, A. 1988. Subh al-ʻasha fi sinâʻat al-inshâ, ed. Muhammad Husayn Shams al-Dîn, Vol.13-14, Beirut: Dâr al-kutub al-ʻilmiyya.
- Richard, J. 1976. 'La situation juridique de Famagouste dans le royaume des Lusignans.' In *Orient et Occident au Moyen Âge : Contacts et relations (XIIe-XVe s)*, 221-229. London: Variorum Reprints.
- --- 1981. 'Une famille de 'Vénitiens blancs' dans le royaume de Chypre au milieu du XVe siècle: Les Audeth et la seigneurie de Marethasse', *Rivista di Studi bizantini e slavi* 1 : 89-129.
- --- 1984. 'Le royaume de Chypre et l'embargo sur le commerce avec l'Égypte (fin XIIIe-début XIVe siècle)', *Comptes Rendus des Séances de l'Académie des Inscriptions et Belles-Lettres*, 128 (1) :120-134.
- Semeonis, S. 1997. 'Le voyage de Symon Semeonis d'Irlande en Terre Sainte.' In *Croisades et Pèlerinages. Récits, chroniques et voyages en Terre Sainte XIIe-XVIe siècle*, ed. Régnier-Bohler, D., 959-996. Paris: Robert Laffont.
- Stöckly, D. 1995. *Le système de l'Incanto des galées du marché à Venise (fin XIIIe-milieu XIVe siècle)*, Leiden-New York-Köln: Brill.
- Thomas, G.M. 1966. *Diplomatarium Veneto-Levantinum sive acta et diplomata res veneta greacas utque Levantis illustrantia (1300-1350) (1351-1454)*, Vol.1-2, New York : Burt F. Valérian, D. 2004. 'Le fondouk, instrument du contrôle sultanien sur les marchands étrangers dans les ports musulmans (XIIe-XVe siècles) ?' In *La mobilité des personnes en Méditerranée de l'Antiquité à l'époque moderne: procédures de contrôle et documents d'identifications*, ed. Moati, C., 676-698. Rome: École française de Rome.
- Vallet, É. 1999. *Marchands vénitiens en Syrie à la fin du XVe siècle : Pour l'honneur et le profit*, Paris: Adhe.
- Van Steenbergen, J. 2003. 'The Alexandrian Crusade (1365) and the Mamluk sources. Reassessment of the kitāb al-ilmām of an-Nuwayrī al-Iskandarānī (D. A.D.1372).' In *East and West in the crusader states: context, contacts, confrontations*, eds. Ciggaar K. and Teule, H.G.B., 123-137. Leuven: Peeters Publishers.
- Wansbrough, J. 1971. 'The Safe-Conduct in Muslim Chancery practice', *Bulletin of the School of Oriental and African Studies* 34: 20-35.
- Ziada, M. M. 1933-1934. 'The Mamluk conquest of Cyprus in the fifteenth century', *Bulletin of the Faculty of Arts* 1-2: 90-113, 37-57.

The concept of Fortune in the birth of the tarot

James Frost (Canterbury Christchurch University)

THE PACK OF cards now known as the tarot or *tarocchi* emerged in Northern Italy around the mid-fifteenth century. The tarot consists of twenty-one trump cards appended to a fifty-six card version of an ordinary Latin-suited pack, along with the wildcard known in Italian as matto or 'madman'. Fifteenth century sources refer to the game as trionfi or 'triumphs', rather than 'tarot' (Dummett 1980, 80-84). The trump cards are important for the 'trick taking' gambling games that were played with the pack. The additional trump suit serves to triumph over or 'trump' the suit cards in order to win the trick. Michael Dummett identified three main variations of trump sequence associated with the regions of Ferrara, Milan and Bologna (Dummett 1980, 387-417; 1986, 6-8). Although very few early packs are numbered it is essential to know the correct sequence of trumps in gameplay.

The trump cards include many allegorical personifications such as Love, Death, and the cardinal virtues. Some make astrological references such as the Star, Moon and Sun cards. In this paper I will focus on one particular card and, through comparative analysis, locate it in medieval cultural history and thought.

The card of Fortune tends to appear somewhere in the centre of the sequence. In packs common to Ferrara, Milan and later standard French packs its position is represented by the Latin 'X', which could be associated with the spokes on Fortuna's wheel. The image stands out as it represents a principle that presides over both uses of the cards; as a game of fortune, and later, in the telling of fortunes.

There is little scholarship on the early iconographical development or origins of the tarot images: most academic studies take a cursory glance over individual cards rather than engaging in sustained and focussed hermeneutic explication. Michael Dummett stated that the early designers made a random and insignificant selection of the memorable images of the time, a practice common in later card design (Dummett 1980, 387-388). An iconographical study of the images was not his concern or his field: as an Oxford Professor of Logic his concern was predominately in the rules and logic of gameplay. His small book The Visconti-Sforza Tarot Cards (1986) gives a few interpretative suggestions but is lacking in sustained analysis. Before his publications the librarian, Gertrude Moakley, attempted an iconographical analysis of the Visconti-Sforza cards (Moakley 1956, 62-68; 1966, 61-115). Many of her suggestions are worth pursuing further, and are referenced by Dummett. However, she was so keen to discover a coherent story in the cards that she tended to force interpretation into an exclusively Petrarchian scheme rather than consider a broader network of influences. As Helen Farley pointed out in A Cultural History of the Tarot (2009), the details of Petrarch's poem I Trionfi do not fit as precisely with the trumps as Moakley suggests, although they are an important influence. Farley refers to these as 'superficial correspondences' but the themes are pertinent and provide a reference point in mediæval popular culture. In Farley's view, this and other suggestions concerning the origin of the tarot collectively 'infer that the imagery displayed upon the tarot trumps was common in Mediæval and Early Modern literature, theatre and art' (Farley 2009, 45-49). Farley provides a convincing explanation of the earliest Italian hand-painted cards in relation to the history of its patrons, the fifteenth-century dukes of Milan. However, she does not aim to provide a comprehensive iconographical study and each trump card receives a small amount of attention, which is understandable given the ambitious scope of her study.

The Fortune Card

The earliest known representations of the Fortune card; also known as 'The Wheel of Fortune', or 'The Wheel', appear in two closely related packs: the Brambilla tarot in the Pinacoteca di Brera in Milan and the Visconti-Sforza pack which is split between the Piermont Morgan Library in New York, the Accademia Carrara and the private collection of the Colleoni family in Bergamo. It is generally accepted that these cards were made in the Cremonese family workshop of the Late-Gothic artist Bonifacio Bembo, around 1440-1460s (Moakley 1966, 19-34; Dummett 1980, 68-69; 2007, 16-22; Bandera Bistoletti 1991, 13-16, 27-34; Bandera and Tanzi 2013, 36-37). The line work and facial characterisation distinctive of this workshop can be seen in the highly inventive Arthurian Tavola Ritonda manuscript in the National Library, Florence (Luyster 2012). Also in Cremona itself, the frescoes of San Agostino and the biblical panels for the Meli family in the Museo Civico are clearly of the same hands. These works, among others, have been variously attributed to Bonifacio and his brother Ambrosio, who were probably close collaborators on the cards (Tanzi 2011, 46-47; Bandera and Tanzi 2013, 28-34, 58-60, 64-69). The same doll-like faces which look out from the gilded tarot cards, look out from these works also. The six late additions to the Visconti-Sforza pack still tend to be assigned to Antonio Cicognara around the 1480s (Bandera and Tanzi 2013, 50) However, Dummett attributes them to the Ferrarese-influenced classicised style of another of the Bembo brothers, Benedetto (Dummett 2007, 22). The stylistic similarities between the putti of these cards and Benedetto's surviving frescoes in Castello di Torrechiara are striking. If this is indeed the case, we can assign the entire group of cards to the Bembo family workshop.

Both the Brambilla and Visconti-Sforza cards depict a blindfolded and winged goddess Fortuna at the centre of a wheel, around which are arrayed four figures. In both cards the ragged figure at the bottom bears the wheel on his back. Ascending on the left is a figure in green with ass's ears. At the top sits an enthroned figure, also with ass's ears. A figure on the right descends on the wheel. Of the two, the Brambilla pack looks to be the earlier. Primarily, there are heraldic indications elsewhere in the packs. The suit of coins in the Brambilla pack shows an actual coin impression from the rule of Filippo Visconti whereas the Visconti-Sforza pack has motifs adopted by Francesco Sforza when he came to power in 1450 (Bandera Bistoletti 1991, 9-12; Bandera and Tanzi 2013, 50). In visual terms the Visconti-Sforza card seems a more developed and mature design. The figures are larger: they inhabit the pictorial space in a more confident manner. The image of Fortuna has a more defined costume with carefully rendered folds around her waist and sleeves, whereas the Brambilla Fortuna is naïve and schematic. In the Visconti-Sforza card the figures clinging to the left and right of the wheel tuck their left feet around the back of it in an effort not to fall off. The figure descending on the right has an animal tail, barely distinguishable in the burnished gilding and not present in the Brambilla card. Important additions to the Visconti-Sforza card are inscriptions issuing from the mouth of each figure. The ascending figure utters Regnabo, 'I will reign'; enthroned at the summit, Regno, 'I reign'; descending, Regnavi, 'I have reigned'; and at the bottom Sum Sine Regno, 'I reign not'.

    The earliest known text to refer unmistakably to the tarot, is an anti-gaming sermon by an anonymous Franciscan friar, dated somewhere between 1450 and 1480 (Steele 1901, 319). It is directed against three types of game: dice, playing cards, and the ludus triumphorum, the game of triumphs. All are derided as inventions of the devil Azarus or 'Hazard' (Steele 1900, 187). This friar responds to the cards in the most hostile fashion, but also with remarkable familiarity and precision as if, perhaps, he had been a well-seasoned player himself. The trump cards are referred to as the twenty-one steps down to Hell and are listed individually (Steele 1900, 185-187). Each one is recognisable, including Fortune. The author annotates his mention of 'La Rotta', the Wheel, with 'id est regno, regnavi, sum sine regno'. He may have been familiar with cards bearing this inscription, or may have been contextualising the image within a well-known tradition of representation.

Bien-advise Mal-advise

The four figures on the wheel were familiar in medieval popular culture. Mechanical wheels of fortune were constructed for morality plays from as early as 1100 (Nelson 1980, 227-228). The play Bien-advise Mal-advise by Antoine Vérard, performed at Rennes in Brittany in 1439, included the four characters as well as personifications of 'Good Advice' and 'Bad Advice'. When the wheel turned and they assumed the position of Regno each would give a speech adapted from the series of poems, Alcune Poesie Inedite del Saviozzo et di Altri Avtori. Once the wheel had turned full circle they all disembarked for confession. The characters of Bad Advice, Regno and Regnabo (depicted in the tarot with the asses' ears of a fool) were cast into hell. Whereas those of Good Advice, Regnavi (of the tail) and Sum Sine Regno were given salvation (Nelson 1980, 229-230).

As found in other literary sources, mankind is an active agent; invited to ascend and voluntarily submitting to the rules of Fortune (Patch 1927, 147-159). In his speech, Sum Sine Regno clearly has a choice about whether to mount the wheel or not:

> I am, as you see, without reign, down low in wretchedness. Fortune has disclaimed me. If I should mount on this wheel, every man would be friendly to me. Let each take warning who considers me [...] (Nelson 1980, 165-166).

In the Visconti-Sforza image this aged figure has white ragged clothes a little like the 'Fool' or 'Madman' in the same pack and he bears the wheel like a burden. The position of Sum Sine Regno might remind us of the traditional images of vice crushed by virtue, although the implication here is different. Fortuna is certainly not a virtue, nor can we assume Sum Sine Regno to be a vice, it is more likely that the image represents a subversion of this convention with vice over virtue.

The struggle with virtue is present elsewhere in the early tarot cards. Faith, Hope and Charity trampling the vices are seen in the incomplete pack, held at Yale University and known as the Visconti di Modrone (likely earlier than the Brambilla pack). Whereas only three out of the four cardinal virtues, Justice, Fortitude (in this instance as a Herculean Sforza) and Temperance, are present in the Visconti-Sforza and all other traditional tarot packs to the present day.

The usual remedy for Fortune given in medieval texts is to seek God and virtue, but to take care not to covert the gifts of virtue too much (Patch 1927, 68-70). This is the downfall of Regnabo, in this passage from Bien-advise Mal-advise:

> I shall reign if Fortune pleases and the wheel turns to the fourth place. I shall be above and rule all the world. How great is my pleasure then! Virtue moves me to speak such words, because I plan to do justice and punish those who have maliciously robbed the men of good estate. What joy shall I have to be able to punish them. (Nelson 1980, 165-166).

Regnabo's parting line sounds a lot less than virtuous, and the righteous and punishing aspect of justice is represented in the Visconti-Sforza tarot by the mounted knight in the top section of the Justice card.

Ancient Fortuna

So where did this powerful image originate? Fortuna was a Latin Goddess who was not supplanted during the Christian middle ages. There was no theological equivalent or replacement for 'chance', a force that still appeared to be active and present in the Christian world.

Allusions suggestive of Fortune's Wheel are found in ancient Greece. Sophocles uses the metaphor in a surviving fragment from an unknown play:

> Menelaus: But my fate is always revolving on the fast-moving wheel of the goddess and changing its nature, just as the appearance of the moon cannot remain for two nights in the same shape, but first emerges from obscurity as new, making its face more beautiful and coming to fullness, and when at its loveliest, it dissolves once more and comes to nothing. (Lloyd-Jones 1996, 381).

The goddess here is identified by Hugh Lloyd-Jones as Tyche. This Greek goddess of fortune often represented one's lot from birth. Here we see her representing sudden change, but it was usually more favourably. She has few personified descriptions and no attached myth, and doesn't seem as developed as the Roman or medieval Fortuna (Hornblower and Spawforth 1996, 1566).

The motif of the wheel described by Sophocles also appears visually in a mosaic in an excavated villa at Olynthus in northern Greece. In the antechamber before entering the main gaming parlour is an inscription wishing good fortune, above is represented an abstracted four-spoke 'wheel of good fortune' (Robinson 1946, 208-209).

Roman representations often showed Fortuna balanced on the insecure footing of a sphere rather than turning a wheel, a motif revived in renaissance art (Wittkower 1938, 318). The Latin term orbe often applied to Fortuna may be translated as either a sphere or a wheel (Robinson 1946, 212). Like the wheel, the sphere is another symbol of uncertainty or treachery. However, Seneca's phrase 'As Fortune rotates the headlong fates of kings' (Robinson 1946, 212) sounds like a direct inspiration for the medieval representation of Regno and the other characters on a wheel. Her introduction to Rome was traditionally attributed to King Servius Tullius in the sixth century BC. She took on many guises for different kinds of propitious fortune: Fortuna Muliebris (of procreation), Fortuna Redux (of triumphant return from battle), Fortuna Publica Populi Romani (of the Roman people) (Hornblower and Spawforth 1996, 606). I mentioned earlier that the Fortuna of the tarot was blindfolded: in her cult at the forum Boarium in Rome she was draped in two togas making her effigy virtually indiscernible (Hornblower and Spawforth 1996, 606). This may speak of the mystery of her will and workings or of her blindness to class and status. By the time of the empire, Rome had at least eighteen temples or shrines to Fortuna. Hers was a widespread cult venerated by emperors, soldiers and in households (Canter 1922, 66-67). Pliny was highly sceptical of her cults and commented about how she threatened to overshadow real faith (Robinson 1946, 212-213). Also widely read in the middle ages, Pliny echoes Sophocles in defining the character of the goddess as inconstant, a trait that became central to her medieval conception and continued into the renaissance.

Carmina Burana

The iconography of the Fortune tarot card design draws upon the familiar representation of the goddess Fortuna found in the manuscript tradition. In a verse illustration in the thirteenth century Carmina Burana we see the image similar to tarot including the inscriptions, though the figures lack bestial characteristics. Unlike the tarot images, Fortuna is neither blindfolded nor winged, although those were her traditional attributes. This suggests that both Carmina Burana illustration and tarot image were from a common tradition, rather than one being a direct copy of the other. Below the illustration are verses that decry the cruelty of the goddess:

> O Fortune, variable in phase like the moon,
> always you wax or wane;
> detestable is your life's way!

> now she palsies, then in sport she spurs
> the acuity of the mind;
> penury, power,
> she dissolves like ice (Marshall 2013, 18).

Though compiled by wandering Goliard monks two centuries before the appearance of the first documented tarot cards, the verse anticipates the main motifs in the cards: fortune, the moon, poverty and wealth, game play and the struggle between virtue and vice. It is also very close to the simile drawn by Sophocles. Elsewhere in the manuscript are songs of love, drinking songs, celebrations of tavern life, and satirical works such as the gambler's mass. This late medieval culture seems to be the world from which the tarot is born; it is a world where the high culture of scholastic learning is mingled with the crudeness of the tavern.

Traditionally, Fortune is blind because she makes no distinction of merit or status, effort or worth. She is winged because her gifts are fleeting and opportunities are quickly lost (Patch 1927, 44-45). These attributes are also found on another card in the Visconti-Sforza pack. Love is represented by a winged and blindfolded Cupid for the same reasons. The same pack has an unusual image of Death holding a bow and arrow but with a blindfold worn like a bandana, above his sightless sockets. It is fitting that Love, Fortune and Death should be connected through their iconography. All three allegorical personifications strike without warning, in a seemingly arbitrary manner. In the Carmina Burana verses the goddess Fortuna is not indifferently blind, but actually malevolent, monstrous and treacherous. Perhaps this is why she has no blindfold. She plays a game with mankind and like a ruthless gambler she will strip the shirt from her victim's back:

> Luck, fearsome and vain,
> you are a spinning wheel,
> an injurious state, a treacherous salvation,

> always ready to dissolve;
> shadowed and veiled,
> you strive after me, too;
> by the sport of your evil
> my back is now nude (Marshall 2013, 18).

Fortuna gives great gifts; the dignities of honour, fame, and riches, but then takes them back again. Her cruelty is in proportion to her former kindness; the higher exalted, the further there is to fall (Patch 1927, 49-55). It is both Fortune and Death who remove these worldly achievements.

Another verse in the Carmina Burana collection indicates the infernal fate of those who live by Fortune:

> Fortune's wheel now turns:
> diminished, I descend,
> whilst another to the top is raised;
> elevated too high,
> the king is seated at the peak –
> but he should beware of the fall!
> for we read that even Queen Hecuba
> came beneath the wheel (Marshall 2013, 18).

The imagery here refers to Regno and the other characters. This moral message is directed at courtly ambitions, rather than tavern gamblers who presumably do not have so far to fall.

Fortune's gifts are temporal, particularly the gifts of power and royal favours of kingship and empire (represented by the Emperor and Empress trumps). Thus her particular concern is with the fickle world of the court (Patch 1927, 57-64). Such connotations would have had a strong resonance with the dukes of Milan who commissioned these packs. Filippo Maria Visconti, whose insignia dominate the Brambilla pack, came to power after his brother Giovanni Maria had been assassinated (Muir 1924). Francesco Sforza was a condotierre, a soldier of fortune, who fought for and against Visconti and who married Filippo's daughter Bianca Maria. His political and military manoeuvres were mixed with a good deal of luck in wrestling the dukedom from the Ambrosian Republic after the Filippo's death (Ady 1907). Sforza's devices are included in the Visconti-Sforza pack and may have been commissioned by him or by Bianca Maria. Like the figures on the circumference of the wheel, dukes and dynasties fall and soldiers rise from nothing to become powerful despots.

Boethius and Petrarch

Similar illustrations of Fortune's wheel appear accompanying manuscript texts of Boethius' Consolation of Philosophy. In some, such as that displayed in the Wallace Collection, London, the wheel is rendered as a three-dimensional object. The technical details such as notches, pins, supports and spoke holes are so specific that a wheel could be constructed from this model. Thus, such images possibly represented the actual construction of the theatrical wheels. The changeable nature of the goddess is here represented by a second Janus-like face formed from her hair.

The text features the personification of Fortune as a central character with which the character of Boethius struggles. In life, Boethius had experienced the exaltation and then scorn of Fortuna. A former Roman senator of the sixth century, he was imprisoned and then executed by King Theodoric the Great for suspected treason. It was in confinement in Pavia, awaiting execution, that Boethius wrote this meditation on fortune, reason and faith (Watts 1969, 10-19). Presumably there was little else to think about other than how he had arrived at this predicament, ruined by fortune.

In the narrative Fortuna reveals to Boethius her true nature in a speech which may have influenced both the medieval morality plays and the Carmina Burana verses:

> Inconstancy is my very essence; it is the game I never cease to play as I turn my wheel in its ever changing circle, filled with joy as I bring the top to the bottom and the bottom to the top. Yes, rise up on my wheel if you like, but don't count it an injury when by the same token you begin to fall, as the rules of the game will require (Watts 1969, 57).

Given that fortune is at work in game play, it is fitting that Fortuna herself plays a game with mankind, if we choose to follow her rules. It is the personification of Philosophy, however, who informs Boethius that even Fortuna is still subject to divine reason (Watts 1969, 50). The seemingly blind mechanics of Fortuna only hide the intentions of divine Providence. The 'changing faces of the random goddess' are in fact a kind of constancy. Furthermore, Philosophy tells Boethius that Fortuna has her own justice and usefulness whether pleasant or adverse (Watts 1969, 142-144). Ultimately Fortuna rewards or disciplines the good, and punishes or corrects the bad.

It is highly likely that a copy of the Consolation of Philosophy was held in the vast Visconti library at Pavia and known to those commissioning the courtly tarot packs. Furthermore, Boethius was entombed there, where he had been imprisoned.

Another important writer on Fortuna connected with Pavia was Francesco Petrarca, or Petrarch in English. The notion that virtue was a remedy, triumphant over fortune, was transmitted to the renaissance through his vast and influential treatise De remediis utriusque fortunae. In the preface he also employed the metaphor of the wheel as a constant dynamic force which plagues mankind with ills:

> We know of many strung up on the rack of Fortune, many showered with riches, and many being whirled around her wheel with great force (Rawski 1991, 9).

Petrarch was in the service of the archbishop Giovanni Visconti, ruler of Milan, and his son Galeazzo II, frequently visited Pavia in the latter part of the 1360s (Campbell 1879, xc-cxviii; Muir 1924, 222-226). There is evidence that Petrarch used the extensive library at Pavia as his annotated and autographed copy of Virgil was recovered when the library was plundered in 1499 (Campbell 1879, lxix-lxx). Filippo Maria Visconti was certainly aware of Petrarch's work in the 1440s when commissioning packs, as he adopted one of his phrases 'a bon droyt' as a motto, emblazoning both frescoes and tarot cards with it (Bandera and Tanzi 2013, 38). As Moakley (1956) suggested, the notion of trumps in game play were probably influenced by Petrarch's popular poem I trionfi where one principle triumphs over another i.e. Death triumphs over Love and Chastity, Fame triumphs over Death (Campbell 1879, 322-405).

The key influences in the creation of the tarot revolve around the intellectual culture of Pavia in particular. It was an important residence for the dukes of Milan, a centre of learning due to its university and renowned library. It is also where Bonifacio Bembo of Cremona, whose workshop created tarot for the Visconti and Sforza, was employed to restore the Visconti frescoes (Moakley 1966, 22-24; Bandera Bistoletti 1991, 39-40).

As well as being connected to this intellectual culture, the Fortune card reflects popular visual culture connected to theatre, pageantry and the tavern-fuelled literature of the wandering Goliards, as we have seen. The most celebrated of twelfth-century Goliardic writers collected in the Carmina Burana folio, known as the Archpoet, mentions the licentious distractions of the youths in Pavia in his acerbic Confession (Marshall 2013, 231). Thus, Partlett conjectures it may have been written there (Partless 1986, 233). This is an environment ripe for gambling games such as the tarot.

Although the gilded and hand-painted tarot of the Milanese court are considered the earliest in existence we cannot say for certain whether the tarot originated as a courtly pastime or as a popular tavern game with printed packs. The iconography could support either hypothesis and card gaming was known in both contexts.

Popular printed packs

There are a small number of uncut sheets of printed cards surviving from the fifteenth century. There are no finished packs from the period: presumably they suffered such heavy wear and tear through play that they have perished.

The sheet held in the Metropolitan Museum, New York, shows the four familiar characters with their traditional Latin inscriptions. Regno and Regnabo, the two characters damned to hell in the medieval play, are fully transformed into animals here. Sum Sine Regno does not bear the wheel on his back but reclines in a relaxed manner on the ground. Also, Fortuna herself is absent. Such divergences from medieval tradition suggest that humankind is entirely responsible for its fate. We choose to ascend the wheel and then exist as nothing but animals and fools; inevitably we descend again.

Something of the image can be discerned in a damaged sheet in the Rosenwald Collection, Washington. It is not clear whether Fortuna is present but it is difficult to see how she could be incorporated given the limited space remaining. A crowned figure at the top must be Regno, and there are indications of Regnavi and Regnabo. At the bottom is a dog-like animal depicted upside down as if the card can be reversed to transform the king into a beast.

The small surviving fragment on a fifteenth-century Milanese sheet in the Cary Collection of Playing Cards at Yale University shows human figures, but the wheel has a handle instead of the goddess and no inscriptions. Sum Sine Regno can be seen clinging to the bottom of the wheel. It is this pack that in specific details of the Moon, Star and other card fragments, appears to be the origin of the traditional pattern standardised in eighteenth-century France (now known as the Tarot de Marseille). Seventeenth-century variations on this pack saw a progressive bestialisation of the characters. In the pack by the printer Jean Noblet of around 1659 the goddess Fortuna has vanished along with Sum Sine Regno, leaving only three figures. The Wheel has a handle controlled by an invisible force. The figure ascending has become entirely animal and looks a little like an ass, while the Regnavi figure descending looks somewhat ape-like. In Jean Dodal's pack from the turn of the eighteenth century Regno at the top of the wheel is quite poorly rendered and could easily be interpreted as another beast. In the widespread standardised decks, following Pierre Madenie's edition made in Dijon in 1709, even crowned Regno has been fully transformed into beast with a long tail.

Conclusion

In terms of iconographical development there is a transformation of the Fortune's wheel of the middle ages; from figures with animal attributes into fully-fledged beasts, from a wheel controlled by a blind goddess to a mechanised wheel controlled by an unseen force. Some of the changes are probably accidental, the result of inaccurate copying and recopying from one card maker to another. Some changes may be practical: five different figures makes for quite a complex design in simple woodcut, three is much easier to accommodate on a small scale. But they also seem to reflect broader patterns of thought since the renaissance. The rule of fortune makes mankind into nothing but an instinctive animal, disconnected from reason. The law of chance has not disappeared, but the controlling factor is no longer a goddess but an abstract principle.

The mechanical inevitability of Fortune's wheel expresses an understanding of probability – what is up will come down, given time. The understanding that a run of seeming good luck is bound to turn bad, and bad luck is bound to turn good, was expressed through this motif in the ancient world and continued throughout the middle ages and into the renaissance. In fact, as card makers seemed to grasp intuitively, in the dawning 'age of reason' the goddess is not needed at all; the wheel turns itself in a predictable manner. The idea that fortune overshadows faith is just as relevant in today's casinos as it was in the taverns and courts of fifteenth century Italy.

Whether the genesis of the tarot was in court or tavern, Pavia was the right climate for its inception. For centuries Pavia was a cultural and intellectual hub, not only for the Milanese court which fostered it, but for the mobile scholars of Europe who also found less elevated ways of passing the time there. The philosophy of fortune was embedded in this melting pot.

Reference Sources

- Ady, C.M. 1907. *A History of Milan under the Sforza.* London: Methuen.
- Bandera Bistoletti, S. 1991.*Tarocchi Viscontei della Pinacoteca di Brera.* Milan: Martello Libreria.
- Bandera, S. and Marco T. 2013. *Quelle carte de triumphi che se fanno a Cremona: I tarocchi dei Bembo.* Milan: Skira.
- Campbell, T. ed. 1879. *The Sonnets, Triumphs, and Other Poems of Petrarch.* London: George Bell and Sons. http://www.gutenberg.org/ebooks/17650#download.
- Canter, H.V. 1922. "Fortuna' in Latin Poetry' *Studies in Philology,* 19 (1): 64-82.
- Dummett, M. 1980. *The Game of Tarot: from Ferrara to Salt Lake City.* London: Duckworth.
- Dummett, M. 1986. *The Visconti-Sforza Tarot Cards.* New York: George Braziller Inc.
- Dummett, M. 2007. 'Six XV-Century Tarot Cards: Who Painted Them?' *Artibus et Historiae* 28 (56): 15-26.
- Farley, H. 2009. *A Cultural History of Tarot: From Entertainment to Esotericism.* London: I.B. Tauris.
- Hornblower, S. and A. Spawforth, eds. 1996. *Oxford Classical Dictionary* (3rd edition). Oxford: Oxford University Press.
- Lloyd-Jones, H. trans. 1996. *Sophocles: Fragments.* Cambridge, MA: Harvard University Press.

- Luyster, A. 2012. 'Playing with Animals: the visual context of an Arthurian manuscript (Florence Palatino 556) and the uses of ambiguity.' *Word & Image: A Journal of Verbal/Visual Enquiry*, 20 (1): 1-21.
- Marshall, T. trans. 2013. *The Carmina Burana: Songs from the Benediktbeuern* (2nd edition). Los Angeles: Marshall Memorial Press.
- Moakley, G. 1956. 'The Tarot Trumps and Petrarch's Trionfi; Some Suggestions on Their Relationship.' *Bulletin of The New York Public Library* 60 (2): 55-69.
- Moakley, G. 1966. *The Tarot Cards Painted by Bonifacio Bembo for the Visconti-Sforza Family; An Iconographic and Historical Study.* New York: The New York Public Library.
- Muir, D. 1924. *A History of Milan under the Visconti.* London: Methuen.
- Nelson, A.H. 1980. 'Mechanical Wheels of Fortune, 1100-1547.' *Journal of the Warburg and Courtauld Institutes* 43: 227-233.
- Partlett, D. ed. 1986. *Selections from the Carmina Burana.* London: Penguin Books.
- Partlett, D. 1991. *Oxford History of Card Games.* Oxford: Oxford University Press.
- Patch, H.R. 1927. *The Goddess Fortuna in Mediaeval Literature.* Cambridge, MASS.: Harvard University Press.
- Rawski, C.H. trans. 1991. *Petrarch's Remedies for Fortune Fair and Foul: Book I.* Bloomington and Indianapolis: Indiana University Press.
- Robinson, D.M. 1946. 'The Wheel of Fortune.' *Classical Philology* 41 (4): 207-216.
- Steele, R. 1900. 'A Notice of the Ludus Triumphorum and some Early Italian Card Games; with some Remarks on the Origin of the Game of Cards.' *Archaeologia: or Miscellaneous Tracts Relating to Antiquity* 57: 185-200.
- Steele, R. 1901. 'Early Playing Cards, their Design and Decoration.' *Journal of the Society of Arts* 49: 317-323.
- Tanzi, M. 2011. *Arcigoticissimo Bembo.* Milan: Officina Libraria.
- Watts, V.E. trans. 1969. Boethius: *The Consolation of Philosophy.* London: Penguin.
- Wittkower, R. 1938. 'Chance, Time and Virtue' *Journal of the Warburg and Courtauld Institutes* 1: 313-321.

Illustrations

Fig. 1: 'Fortune' Brambilla tarot, before 1447
(Source: © Pinacoteca di Brera, Milan)

Fig. 2: 'Fortune' Visconti-Sforza tarot, after 1450
(Source: M.630.9 © The Morgan Library and Museum, New York)

Fig. 3: Carmina Burana manuscript, c.1230
(Source: Clm 4660, fol. 1. © Bayerische Staatsbibliothek München)

Fig. 4: Manuscript Cutting, frontispiece to Boethius *De Consolatione Philosophiae* Book II, attributed to Maître de Coëtivy c.1460 -1470, France
(Source: M320 © The Wallace Collection, London)

Fig. 5: Tarocchi Cards woodcut sheet from Venice or Ferrara, late 15th century
(Source: 31.54.159 © Bequest of James Clark McGuire, 1930, The Metropolitan Museum of Art, New York)

Fig. 6: Woodcut sheet from Florence, late 15th century
(Source: 1951.16.7 © Rosenwald Collection, National Gallery of Art, Washington)

Fig. 7: Woodcut sheet from Milan, late 15th century
(Source: ITA Sheet 3S © Cary Collection of Playing Cards,
Beinecke Rare Book and Manuscript Library, Yale University)

Fig. 8: La Roue de Fortune, Jean Noblet tarot, Paris c.1659
(Source: FRBNF43634904 © Bibliothéque Nationale de France, Paris)

Fig. 9: La Roue de Fortune, Jean Dodal tarot, Lyon 1701-1715
(Source: FRBNF40918567 © Bibliothéque Nationale de France, Paris)

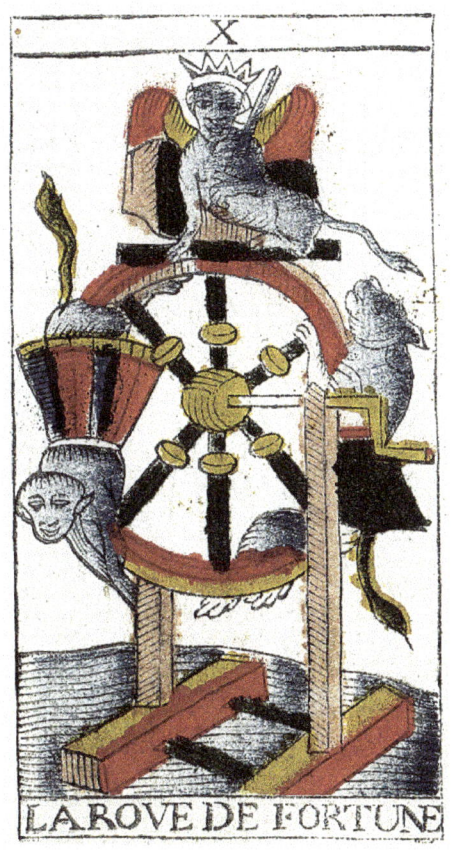

Fig. 10: La Roue de Fortune, Pierre Madenié tarot, Dijon c.1709
(Source: © Musée National Suisse, Zurich)

Footfalls on the boundary of another world

Richard Barnes (City and Guilds of London Art School, UK)

CAST

Death
Arthur Edward Waite
Pamela Colman Smith
and the author as himself

* * *

Part I: The Fool

Midway upon the journey of our life
I found myself within a forest dark,
For the straightforward pathway had been lost.

(Dante, Inferno, Canto I, 1)

LIKE BLACKENED STUMPS of long-rotten teeth the lignum vitae carcass of piers interminably lost to ebb and flow emerge from the glasslike veneer of the water. The slow list of the boat ramp yaws invitingly away through an uncomfortable acquiescence between land and water.

From heavy antediluvian mists pressing down upon the velveteen surface the spluttered throb of a time worn diesel engine is borne upon the ear. There is an inner comfort to be found in the approach of a ferry, breaking the stillness of sound and sight, day to night, of glass to water.

Time and weather worn, a hulk of former majesty speaks to the senses but not to the eyes. The creative licence darkness affords reflected in the lapping of the water.

A deserted profusion of seats along the promenade deck - anodyne two-tone plastic, part scoop, part bucket, an injection-moulded fusion of slippery discomfort.

'Tickets please.'

Overlaying tones of a heavy accent of undetermined origin. Words parroted in a foreign tongue, oft used yet never perfected. My eyes raise to the sound. Topped with grubby faded baseball cap, apathy battles acne to be the conquering feature on the indecipherable visage. Shrink-wrapped in ill-fitting high-vis waterproof, a distant torpid gaze melds with the heavy mastication of a cud-like gum, excreting a bovine aura over awkward late-pubescent growth.

'Tickets please.' An overly loud teenage sigh.
Eyes lowered amid fumbles within darkest pocket recess. Failure to unearth the cardboard stub.

'Tickets please.'

A fresh barrage, yet dissonant from those before. Words spoken with an alluringly deep honeyed eloquence. My eyes raise to the sound. Topped with bright brocaded conductors cap, attentive eyes balance faultless smile. Imperfect symmetry of suit perfectly worn, vertical lode of gleaming brass buttons tumble to gold fob, catenary fall to watch pocket. Silver ticket punch drawn deftly from leather pouch. The picture of efficient elegance.

Ticket unearthed, hand raises. Click of punch. An icy gust blows my hair obscuring vision. The clunk of electric ticket machine preempts the moment before the ticket is thrust back in my hand, and as sight returns I witness boredom in fluorescence slump off down the deck. (MacNeice, 34)

Sudden change of mind.

'Um excuse me, I know it's last minute, but do you have any cabins left?'

Amid another sigh the juvenile motions with his head towards a door halfway down the deck, where a small plastic sign reads 'Pursers Office'.

* * *

A soft knock on the door.

A thump on the door.

Latch undone, metal and plastic cabin door swung open, youth thrusts crumpled paper receipt into my hand, then turning on booted-heel walks away before thanks given.

'I could really do with a drin…'

'Drink sir?..' Says well coiffed beard behind elegant salver.

'Your Sebastian of passage is in the envelope, the drink our compliments. I trust all is to your liking. Good night.'

The louvered mahogany cabin door closes effortlessly on brass hinges. A Victorian revolving chair cradles me between its swept arms and elegant spindle back as I sit resting the tray on the rosewood davenport. Glass to lips, strychnine shock concedes to liquored glow of first deep draft.

From Gladstone bag paper and pen, then a deck of cards. Desk front opened to lush green baize. Cards shuffled and spread. Familiar glide of card across material. Bright colours, signs and symbols arrayed before the eyes.

Nib to page.

* * *

Sip, warmth

In the foreground seated atop a white charger a skeletal figure in black armour carries a black banner emblazoned with the emblem of a white rose. In the midground in front of the horse stands a bishop, hands clasped together in prayer, crosier cast aside. Beside him a woman and child kneel. Between the horses legs a king lies dead, his crown upturned on the ground. In the background a boat in full sail floats on a river running past the bottom of vertical cliffs. Atop these a sun rises between two towers. At the top of the card the number thirteen in Roman numerals, at the bottom the word 'Death'.

Pause.
Ink swells around the nib as it sits on the page.

'That's it?..'
　　Thought-word-form, or something more?
　　Casters enable a panoramic sweep of room. In a sea of pitch the desk floats in a pool of caramel illumination from simple wall sconce.
　　'Is that all you can see?'
　　A voice without beginning or end. On sounding it has always been, on ceasing it never was.
　　'You have been staring at me for quite some time now, is there nothing more to write?'
　　If Received Pronunciation had a source this was the very ancient wellspring.
　　Turning to face the darkness, I watch as blackness steps from itself and ebbs into form. Standing half lit at the edge of the illumined pool is the armoured skeletal figure of death from the tarot card.
　　'Um.. I can see more but I just can't seem to find the words.'
　　'Let's have a little colloquy over it then!'
Warmer tones.
　　'I'm sorry?..'
　　'A chat old man.. a talk, chinwag, tittle-tattle, lets bloviate on the subject a while.'
Joviality itself.

'And while we're at it perhaps a drop to loose the jaw..hmm?'

'I'm sorry I have nothing to offe..'

Death points to the davenport, upon which sits a decanter and another glass.

'And don't stiff me on the measure.. stiff me..!'

A hollow dusty chuckle raises from somewhere within the bowels of the breastplate. Turning to hand him the drink he is already sitting half-swallowed in a deep-buttoned leather wing chair, outstretched legs crossed on matching ottoman.

'Oh you are a dear.' he says.

'Shouldn't we be playing chess or something? Isn't that how it works?'

'Ha! What a chap you are. This isn't Bergman darling! There will be no Totentanz into the final credits. I'm just here for a chat. Is there anything you want to ask me about my card?' (Bergman, 1957).

'Oh ok..tarot cards are Egyptian in origin aren't they?'

Half-choking on his drink, the shock of my statement expressed by an atomized mist of alcoholic spittle hanging heavy in the air between us, he sighs and gives me a withering stare.

'Have you done no research whatsoever?...'

'Of course, why do you ask?..'

He whistles, and a moment later the white charger from the card is at his side. In one fluid motion he is out of chair and into saddle. A smooth tug on the reins and he trots slowly away into the surrounding darkness. Without turning Death calls to me.

'Well keep up boy- I don't have all day!'

Strangely embarrassed as if letting him down, I run to catch up as he disappears into the gloom, a sheepish Sancho Panza to his Don Quixote.

PART TWO: THE MAGICIAN

Stygian murk relents to tremulous gleam. Pressing on we are presently surrounded by milling bodies dispersed between fragments of giant granite sculptures.

'Wait a second, this bears a striking resemblance to..'

'Room 4 the British Museum.. Indeed my eruditely challenged friend!'

Few countenances among the throng are lit with the acquisition of knowledge, most display a descent of active consciousness to museum ennui. In the centre of the room a single figure stands stock still save the tell-tale fidget of pre-teen child. Oily snail tracks of sticky fingers fan from pudgy pre-pubescent digits splayed over the thick glass of an imposing translucent cube. Contained within the glass case a trapezoidal shaped stone.

'The Rosetta Stone?'

Death nods.

'So where did you get this Egyptian origin story from then?'

'I'm not sure, I think it's just part of the accepted cultural history of tarot.'

'Funny things cultural histories, same with urban myths, they are believed because they construct and reinforce the worldview of the group within which they are told, providing us with 'coherent and convincing explanations of complex events'. You are of course familiar with Court de Gebelin's Monde Primitif...Volume 3. from 1781?' (Mosier, 2005, VI, 4)

'Think I missed Volume 3.' I say with a smile.

'Really dear fellow, What do you spend your time doing?!' he replies sardonically.

'In an essay in this tome he gives the account of his intuitive insight into the origins of tarot cards. Dummett describes this one essay as having being the 'fountain-head of the entire occult Tarot mystique!' (1996, 57) 'I scrutinise them and suddenly I recognise the allegory [...] this is in no way the product of our imagination, but the effect of the deliberate and perceptible connections of this pack with everything that is known of Egyptian ideas.' (Court de Gebelin, 1781, 367) He claims that an antique book of wisdom had been disguised by Egyptian sages as a pack of playing cards and thus it managed to survive down through the ages in the guise of a game.'

'Go on.'

'In the same volume the Comte de Mellet names this as the 'Book of Thoth'. Declaring the cards were 'read or interpreted like statements of Destiny'. (1781, 406) He becomes the first to assert the tarot were used for divinatory purposes. He also nominally links the 22 cards to the 22 letters of the Hebrew alphabet.'

'So why the Rosetta Stone?'

'Quite simple *Liebchen*, in 1824 Champollion decrypted the Rosetta Stone.'

'That's forty-three years after Gebelin's 1781 essay.'

'So...?'

'So... He would not have been able to read this mysterious book of wisdom!'

'*Precisement chou-fleur!* Also tarot scholar O'Neill suggests that Egyptian symbolism differed from that illustrated on tarot cards of the time. 'Natural figures appear as elements of the hieroglyphics but are completely absent from the tarot. None of the most important images of themes of Egyptian knowledge are found in the tarot." (1986, 57)

'So where did Tarot originate?'

'Tarot was originally just a trick-taking card game, the result of 22 extra trump cards being added to the ordinary 52 card deck which had been in use in Europe since about the 1370's. These trump cards beat any normal cards in a trick. The tarot deck was probably invented in Italy around 1440; certainly the earliest extant decks we have are from this period and were made for the Visconti-Sforza family by Bembo Bonifacio. (Shephard 1985, pp. 19-20) Here I am.'

He hands me two cards.

'Unlike a regular pack these tarot trumps or Major Arcana have individual images on them that can be said to associate or symbolise particular concepts.'

'What do they stand for?'

'Sheppard suggests the trumps take us into the world of symbolism, and it is in the nature of symbolism that it can be interpreted in many ways and at many levels of meaning. Because symbols are reflective of the worldview in which they are created, he proposes that we think of the deck as 'a systematic allegory of the cosmic hierarchy of the universe in the fifteenth century." (1985, 9)

'Umm?'

Death sighs..

'The four suits of the regular deck are families or nations, ten simple grades from commoner to royalty.'

'The Minor Arcanum in tarot speak?'

'Indeed. Let me illustrate with my deck.'

'So examples from the Major Arcanum such as the Empress and Emperor?'

He deals the cards into my hands.

'Are more important figures yet still inhabiting the human world.'

'Justice, Fortune and Death?'

'Are from the world of the soul. Allegorical in nature.'

'And finally The Devil, and the Last Judgement?'

'Represent the world of life beyond death. All are steps up the ladder of being. So the cards represent a kind of miniature cosmos. Around the same time c.1465, we have a set of 50 playing cards known as the Tarrochi di Mantegna. Engraved picture cards lacking the regular lower suit cards, they are allegorical, depicting a humanist world-view or cosmology of the day. Their hierarchy parallels the tarot depicting the condition of man from beggar to pope, then muses, arts, virtues, planets and stars.'

'So what are the sources of the renaissance tarot imagery?'

'It's up for discussion. Farley postulates that none of the suggested sources such as triumphal processions, Petrarch's poem I trionfi, or medieval theatre, can convincingly explain the source, but collectively they infer the imagery was 'common in Medieval and Early Modern literature, theatre and art." (2009, 49)

Death hands me two more cards.

'So in these early cards it looks like they used the ancient motif of you as Grim Reaper to symbolize death, correct?'

'Not quite no.. O'Neill tells us 'The image of the corpse/skeleton and scythe is not an ancient symbol for Death. Lessing (1879) demonstrates that the Greek and Roman cultures used the image of a young man, often winged, inverting and extinguishing a torch.' (2012) Follow me.'

He leads me past row upon row of large wooden panels covered in black material upon which black and white photos are attached.

'63 in all. About a thousand photographs.'

'Crime scene photo montage?'

'Similar, Warburg's Mnemosyne Atlas. He described it as a 'ghost story for adults'. (1929, III.102.3–4) Using these photos of sculpture, paintings and the applied arts he wanted to show how the motifs of antiquity survived into the renaissance and beyond. Read this..'

He points to a plaque on a panel.

'Ever since the passing of antiquity, the ancient gods had lived on in Christian Europe as cosmic spirits, religious forces with a strong influence in practical affairs: indeed, the cosmology of the ancient world- notably in the form of astrology – undeniably survived as a parallel system tacitly tolerated by the Christian church.' (Warburg, 1920, 598)

'So what you are saying is that old gods and divinities were combined and changed to create new forms?'

'Absolutely. I am a good example of that. The Grim Reaper is a mixture of the Greek gods Saturn- god of agriculture reaping with his scythe, and Thanatos - god of death. Plus the Roman god Cronos- the god of time with his hourglass. Ah here we are!.. Panels 50-51.'

We stop at a panel covered with images of old cards.

'Here Warburg is exploring how ideas of the cosmos as a harmonic system have been expressed visually through the motifs expressed on playing and tarot cards. (1929) Cards are the perfect vehicles of transmission of images through the ages as they are easily transportable and often printed in multiple copies. The motifs and symbols would be adapted to match the differing games and visual language of each region or country. What do you see?'

'Cards displaying the celestial spheres, muses, virtues.. and.. the planets or gods.'

He points to one of the cards.

'This is Saturn from the Mantegna deck we were discussing. Note the scythe, and on one arm he holds the dragon serpent of time, in remembrance of his identity as Cronos.'

'So it's an example of the survival that Warburg is describing.'

'Yes. On the same panel we have images of the Marseille deck from about 1700. Saturn has split, morphing into the wise old man of the Hermit card and also the Death card. The reaping of heads in the field displaying the passage of time.'

'But why the skeletal form?'

'O'Neill suggests it is the merging of imagery from the Danse-Macabre and Book of Revelation. (2012) The way images survive and are recreated by artists in different forms over the centuries is described by the phrase 'The afterlife of antiquity'. Attributed to, yet never confirmed to be said by Warburg.' (Bovino, n.d.)

'So what can you tell me of your current incarnation?'

'Refill my glass and I'll tell you ...' he trills.

PART THREE: THE HIEROPHANT

Dominating a small mahogany side table the polished brass trumpet of a gramophone glistens in the light.

'Arthur' Death expounds.

'Why?' I say quizzically.

'Let's just say that Aleister Crowley once described his writing as 'if his mouth were full of hot potatoes. The length and obscurity of his archaisms renders him almost unintelligible to me, an affectation which I find intolerable.' (1911, 135) 'His Master's Voice' seemed therefore apt! He devoted his life to studying esoteric matters and the occult, but especially to Christian mystic traditions. In doing so he became a member of multiple secret societies. What was it that you wrote in your diary in March 1903 Arthur?'

The gramophone whirs into life, trumpeting loudly in flat scholarly tones.

'If my receptions go on at this rate, I look shortly to be the most initiated man in Europe' (Cited in Gilbert, 1987, 117)

'In 1902 alone he joined at least nine different secret societies. (Higgins, 2013) He began as merely a scholar of the mystics, but later he became one. This set of beliefs later expressed themselves visually in the form I take today. Arthur, your Damascene moment of 1905, if you please?'

'It was late Autumn […] I missed my way on some stairs without banisters and fell heavily. The result was concussion of the brain […] but I was made conscious slowly of a substantial change within, as if some new door had opened in the mind.'(1938, 168)

'What do you know of Christian mysticism?' Death asks me.

'My basic understanding is that western mystical traditions are based upon the belief that there is an absolute or God. From this perfection is created the universe and humanity.

'And the path of the Christian mystic?'

'Because humans were originally part of this perfection, we want to be reunited with it. So the path of the mystic is that of the reconnection with the divine.'

'Yes, that's it.'

'I'm not sure how this relates to the tarot?'

'In 1891 Arthur joined the Hermetic Order of the Golden Dawn. His biographer Gilbert describes it as a society created 'in order to further the systematic study of the occult sciences. It offered its members a sequence of initiatory rituals of a very eclectic nature that combined Egyptian, kabbalistic, and Rosicrucian symbolism." (1987, 107)

'The Golden Dawn ritual scripts are a mass of confused symbolism, but they have one point of importance. The notion of a candidate ascending the tree of life. It is utterly mismanaged throughout, but there it happens to be.' (Waite, 1936, 230)

'The concept of the Tree of Life originates in Jewish tradition. The *Sepher Yetzirah* discusses the 32 paths of wisdom derived from the number of times God's name is mentioned in the first chapter of Genesis. These become associated with the 22 letters of the Hebrew alphabet and the ten basic numerals. In turn they are seen as 'ten emanations, or illuminations of God's Infinite Light as it manifests in Creation'. (Bar-Lev, 1994, 73) They are also seen as ten spheres, which are arranged in a symmetrical hierarchy, connected by 22 pathways. The highest is connected most closely with God and the lowest with the material world. This becomes pictorially expressed as the Tree of Life. Examples of Christians who adapted this scheme are John Dee and Robert Fludd. Dummet tells us 'both developed cosmic schemes involving choirs of angels, planets and alphabetical correspondences.' (2002, 22) The best Renaissance example of this is in Dante's Divine Comedy, in which the protagonist is guided through the nine concentric circles of hell to paradise.'

'So we have the expressions of those cosmic hierarchies springing up again?'

'Indeed. Also the connection of the 22 pathways with the 22 trump cards in the tarot deck.'

'So how did Arthur view the tarot?'

'The tarot embodies symbolical presentations of universal ideas, behind which lie all the implicits of the human mind, and it is in this sense that they contain secret doctrine.[...] The theory is that this doctrine always existed [...] perpetuated in secrecy [...] and recorded in secret literatures like those of alchemy and kabbalism.' (1910, 24)

'And what is the secret doctrine?'

'The secret tradition contains, firstly, the memorials of a loss which has befallen humanity; and secondly the records of a restitution in respect of that which was lost.' (Waite, 1911, ix)

'So these traditions and doctrines contain wisdom and knowledge. A spiritual guidebook if you like that tells you how to return to the divine?'

'Supposedly yes. Although they relate to a felt experience, an inner pathway and journey, so it can't really be expressed in words. More than merely a journey of the body and mind, ultimately it is one of the soul. The spiritual journey of the Christian mystic.
Arthur saw the tarot as a tool to aid the mystic's journey and as such re-imagined the tarot imagery to express these concepts. To accompany it he wrote a Pictorial Key to the Tarot. Arthur tell us what my card represents.'

'The veil or mask of life is perpetuated in change, transformation and passage from lower to higher, and...' (1910, 41)

'Whoa!...Arthur with brevity! I'll explain the imagery and you just...'

Death sighs and shakes his head.

'He thinks I am..'

'Better represented by one of the apocalyptic visions than by the crude notion of the reaping skeleton' (1910, 41)

'The Book of Revelation?'

'Chapter six, verse eight - my favourite!.. 'And I looked, and behold a pale horse: and his name that sat on him was death."' (Revelation, 6:8. King James Version)

He looks proud.

'Look at this.'

On the desk lays a very large tattered folio folder. On the front *'C'est Fin!'* is handwritten in neat cursive script above a hand-painted version of Ensor's 'Death and the Masks'

'Nice likeness!'

'Oh you do flatter me..got a confession to make old boy..bit of a scrap-booker!'

Grinning sheepishly he opens the folio to flick through countless pages adorned with different images of himself.

'Ah..Durer's Four Horsemen from the Apocalypse.'

'Possibly the most known apocalyptic image of you, however you do still have a little meat on your bones and as for the beard!'

'To quote the great Ray Davies 'One week he's in polka-dots, the next week he is in stripes. 'Cause he's a dedicated follower of fashion.' (1966).. In my case, artistic fashion!'

'More especially a card of the death of Kings.' (1910, 41)

Arthur butts in. 'The King of Kings, being Christ? A reference to the Ascension?'

Death nods.

'Could he also be referring to King Arthur? The armour does suggest knight after all!'

'Certainly! The quest for the grail is a strong allegory for the mystic. In his Hidden Church of the Holy Graal Arthur draws parallels between the four suits of the tarot (cup, wand, sword, pentacle) and the grail hallows – four sacred objects of the grail legend (cup, lance, sword and dish.)' (1909, 600-615)

'And the ship on the river could be seen as the barge that carries the wounded body of Arthur to Avalon, or the journey that we take through life. Both physically and spiritually. So the banner displays the quest of the knight, and it's emblazoned with..'

'The mystic rose, which symbolises life..'(1910, 41)

'Springing from death, which is portrayed through the black background. Presumably he is talking about the rose of heaven?'

'In the Paradiso Dante writes:

In fashion as a snow-white Rose lay then
Before my view the saintly multitude,
Whom Christ in his own blood had made his bride.
(*Canto XXXI, 274)*

'Dante ascends beyond physical existence to the Empyrean tenth level of heaven, the level of God. He sees an enormous white rose that symbolises divine love, and eternal life. Any thoughts Arthur?'

'There is a deeper state, which the Paradiso does not reach, beyond the sense of the multitude..and in this state Dante would have become the rose.'(1936, 248)

'Of course! It is just a vision for Dante.'

'So long then that we are in the external appreciation of living things, seeing and understanding by the logical mind, we are in a state of vision.. Beyond these there is a mystical state, in which there is a way into deeper knowledge, direct and not reflective, by inward seeking through the Soul's own being rather than through ways without.' (1936, 249)

'I always enjoyed the Doré engraving of this' He passes me a copy.

'So all we have left is the two…'

'Between two pillars on the verge of the horizon there shines the sun of immortality' (1910, 41)

Death glowers stingingly at the gramophone.

'And the sun of immortality is the state of the divine?'

'Yes the ultimate goal of the mystic – the reunion with the divine.'

'Do the figures falling in front of death illustrate that death comes to all no matter of their station in life?'

'Right, remember the image on one of the Visconti cards? It was a common medieval motif. Death reaping life.

'Arthur, do you have anything else to add?' I say.

Death puts his head in his hands and groans.

'In the exotic sense it has been said to signify the ascent of the spirit in divine spheres, creation and destruction, perpetual movement, and so forth.' (1910, 41)

'So your card is not just about death, it is about change and transformation. All important mystical themes. Arthur, tell us about Pamela.'

***

PART IV: THE HIGH PRIESTESS

'A most imaginative and abnormally psychic artist [...] who, under proper guidance, could produce a Tarot with an appeal in the world of art and a suggestion of significance behind the symbols which would put on them another construction than had ever been dreamed.' (1936, 184)

My eyes drift to a newspaper on the desk.

'Gowned in old rose cashmere, with deep black fringe, and wearing beads about her neck and chiffon twined about her head to represent a kerchief..'

'Oh, Puppa, me hand hurt me!
An' Annancy say.'

A voice from the page. English spoken in a West Indian dialect. Before my eyes type skims from paper to floor, writhing and sliding this way and that, word transmuted into form. '..Miss Smith sat flat upon a small round table with her feet tucked beneath her gown and a row of half a dozen short fat candles at her knees to represent footlights.'(Brooklyn Life, 1907)

'Drop den, drop! Death will know what to do wid you!'

Death sits cross-legged on the floor, utterly fixated by this strange performance. Giggling with childish glee he claps.

'This is my favourite part!'

'So de child drop, an' Death take him, an' put him in him bag. An' pretty soon anoder child cry out.' (Colman Smith, 1899 70)

'Bravo Pamela, bravissimo! Her Annancy stories. The consummate storyteller!'

He turns to me, tossing a bundle of newspaper clippings like confetti in the air.

'Isn't she magnificent? Performed all over the US, 'Fine Arts Club, Pratt Institute, the Pen & Brush' (Brooklyn Life, 1907) also 'the favorite reader of London drawing rooms'!' (Brooklyn Daily Eagle, 1907)

A clipping floats languorously into my hands. 'Washington Morning Times Jan 5th 1899 described her as 'An American Boutet de Monvel'.' (1899)

'Monvel you say, now that is intriguing.'

'Why?'

'Fourteenth shelf up, ninth from the right..'

'I'm sorry?'

He gestures irritatedly over my shoulder. Turning to face a towering bookshelf, I mount a precarious set of steps, gingerly retrieving the book. He flicks deftly through the pages.

'Ah, here she is! De Monvel's classic Joan of Arc.'

Emerging through a colourfully clad spear wielding army, Joan leaps into battle on her charger.

'Compare this to Pamela's Knight of Swords.'

he says throwing a card down next to the open book. The head and neck of the horse and pose of the rider strongly echo the De Monvel illustration. The banner is replaced with a sword. They look very similar.

'In discussing De Monvel's Joan, his biographer Addade wrote 'His admiration for the light and shadow modelling of Fra Angelico and the battle scenes of Paolo Uccello is expressed with grandeur here." (Addade n.d.)

'The afterlife of antiquity?

'Transmission of motifs?'

'Did she reference anybody else whilst drawing the cards?'

'Probably Howard Pyle. In 1898 she visited him at the Drexel institute wanting to enrol in his class. He looked at her portfolio. How did he describe your work Pamela?'

'Very ingenious and interesting!' (Colman Smith, 1898) she chirps.

'His image of Sir Pellias, from his The Story of King Arthur and his Knights is stylistically very similar. Other than that her inspirations have been described as Kate Greenaway, Walter Crane, William Blake and Japanese printmakers such as Hokusai. (Pyne, 2007, 48)

'Crane?.. I thought I saw his name somewhere?'

Death points to a clipping resting on my shoulder. I read. 'The likeness of her genius to that of Walter Crane is apparent. Whatever is quaint and old worldliest seems to find in her a natural affinity.' (*Morning Times*, 1899)

'So that would place her work within the Arts and Crafts movement?'

'She illustrated, wrote and was the subject of articles for Gustav Stickley's *The Craftsman* magazine.'

'American Craftsman style was an extension of the English Arts and Crafts style?'

'Affirmative! Her article 'Should the Art Student Think? (Colman Smith, 1908) is particularly enlightening!' Death looks me directly in the eye and winks.

'Though it has been suggested that her drawing style shows both the visionary qualities of fin-de-siècle Symbolism and the Romanticism of the preceding Arts and Crafts movement.' (Moore, 2014, 15)

'To me your card is a beautiful expression of both styles. The medieval, romantic and ruralism of the arts and crafts – Arthurian knight with heraldic rose set in a natural landscape with towering cliffs and river, incorporating figures in flowing dress wearing floral rings in their hair. Combined with the psychological and mystical elements of symbolism. Objects taking on more meaning than just their outward appearance. Figures from all walks of life succumbing to the skeletal knight of death with mystic quest, whilst the sun of eternal life rises in the background. '

'Ah, that reminds me! One of those articles discusses her synaesthesia. She had sound to colour synaesthesia. It talks about how the rhythm and harmonies of music stir her subconscious depths enabling her 'to enter the realm which lies beyond ordinary consciousness.' (MacDonald, 1912, 22) She really embodied the symbolist ideal in this area.'

Pamela hands me a drawing.

'Often when hearing Bach I hear bells ringing in the sky, rung by whirling cords held in the hands of maidens dressed in brown. There is a rare freshness in the air, like morning on a mountain-top, with opal-coloured mists that chase each other fast across the scene.' (Strand Magazine, 1908, 636)

'I imagine that Arthur was very particular about the colours used. Black symbolising death and white for life and purity?'

'Actually no, Arthur only mentions colour in his *Pictorial Key to the Tarot* once in relation to the red standard on the Sun card, so it is unlikely that the colour symbolism was of much concern to him.'

'So colour scheme would have been part of Pamela's design?'

'Yes, the cards were completed in black ink and then she probably coloured copies of these providing the scheme for the lithographic process.'

'Her style of illustration is very clean, favouring bold, bright colours with definite black outlines, but then I suppose she was an illustrator.'

'Ha! That's true, but she was also taught at Pratt by progressive arts educator Wesley Dow. His teaching incorporated the "putting together' of lines, masses and colours to make a harmony.' (1914, 1)
He thought Japanese *Ukiyo-e* style block prints were the perfect example of this. Look at this one!..Takiyasha the Witch and the Skeleton Spectre.'

He points to a page of his folio.

'What larks Kuniyoshi and I had…' he sighs poetically.

* * *

PART V: THE MOON

'Is this deck expressive of the time period it was created within?'

'Absolutely. Arthur and Pamela were very much actively engaged in the milieu of the time.'

'How so?'

'The end of the nineteenth century was a time of major social reform and the growing importance of rational science. During this period the Arts and Crafts movement flourished as a reaction to the industrialisation of Britain. Pamela was actively involved in these changes. As a member of the Suffrage Atelier she produced posters and postcards supporting social reforms. She also contributed articles to both *The Craftsman* and *New Age magazine*, which became a major channel through which these ideas were expressed. It featured a wide cross-section of writers with an interest in literature and the arts, economics, socialist politics, mysticism and spiritualism. Amongst them art theorist Herbert Read.'

'Who was Herbert Read?'

'Possibly one of the most important writers on modernism in England in the early twentieth century. A rise in rationalist thinking led people to question religious paradigms and explore alternative modes of thinking. It was within this environment that Arthur, according to his biographer Gilbert, was the 'first to attempt a systematic study of the history of western occultism - viewed as a spiritual tradition rather than as aspects of proto-science or as the pathology of religion'. (1987, 361) An intensifying interest in the occult, aided by the growth of the publishing industry led to the translation and reissue of important mystical and alchemical texts. Arthur was responsible for some of these. This led to reinventions or fabrications of medieval sects and secret societies such as the Knights Templar, Rosicrucian orders and the Hermetic Order of the Golden Dawn. As such Arthur's thoughts are an expression of the time period.'

'Why has the deck proved to be the most popular tarot deck ever produced?' (Winick, 2010)

'It may be down to its total visual aesthetic. Whilst Arthur focused on the Major Arcana and was very particular about how they were portrayed..'

'Pamela [...] had to be spoon-fed carefully over the priestess card, over that which is called the fool and over the hanged man.' (1936, 185)

'He was less interested in the Minor Arcana, and Pamela would have had more freedom with the designs. Kaplan says that the deck exemplifies what Pamela 'sought to express in all her paintings and drawings- mysticism, ritual, imagination, fantasy and a deep experience of the emotions felt, but not always understood, in everyday life.' (1990, 33) Not that she didn't find inspiration from the past for some of the designs. At the time it was created it was the only deck where both Major and Minor Arcana are fully illustrated, except for one other.'

'Which was?'

'The fifteenth-century century Sola-Busca deck. In 1908 the British Museum acquired black and white photographs of this deck. Pamela must have seen them.'

'How can you be sure of that?'

He throws two cards down on the table.

'The Sola-Busca three of hearts and Pamela's.'

'They are practically the same.'

He nods.

'The afterlife of antiquity indeed..'

* * *

The tomblike darkness of the room relents to the first rays of dawn. Giving my regards to both Arthur and Pamela I head out onto the foredeck. The skeletal silhouette of twin cranes grows on the horizon as the prow eases effortlessly towards the slip, the coruscate rays of the sun rising majestically between them. I turn towards Death.

'Thank you for being the consummate Virgil to my Dante..'

'Kind heart, you do flatter me so! It has been a true delight.'

Mounting his steed he pulls gently on the reins and wheels slowly around. Trotting calmly away into the dwindling darkness he calls out.

'Besides… I'll be seeing you again my dear!..'

A dusty chuckle rattles from deep within.

I smile and turn from death towards the light.

Reference Sources

- Addade, S.J. (No date) *Biography Maurice Boutet de Monvel.* [Online]. [Accessed 14 January 2018]. Available from: http://www.stephane-jacques-addade.com/en/maurice-boutet-de-monvel/biography

- Amir, D. (No Date). *'The Use of 'First Person' Writing Style in Academic Writing: An Open Letter to Journal Editors, Reviewers and Readers'.* [Online]. [Accessed 10 January 2018]. Available from: http://tiny.cc/amir2018
- Bar-Lev, Y. 1994. *The Song of the Soul: Introduction to Kaballa.* Israel:Petach Tivka
- Bible: King James version. 1855. Oxford: Oxford University Press.
- Boutet de Monvel, M. 1895. *Jeanne D'Arc.* Paris: Plon Nourrit & Cie (19 drawing)
- Bovino, E.V. (No date) *The Nachleben of Mnemosyne: The Afterlife of the Bilderatlas.* [Online]. [Accessed 14 January 2018]. Available from: http://www.engramma.it/eOS/core/frontend/eos_atlas_index.php?id_articolo=1618
- Brooklyn Daily Eagle. Sun Feb 24th 1907. [Online]. [Accessed 3 January 2018]. Available from: *https://marykgreer.com/2015/02/08/pamela-colman-smith-1907-story-teller/*
- Brooklyn Life. Sat Feb 9th 1907. [Online]. [Accessed 3 January 2018]. Available from: https://marykgreer.com/2015/02/08/pamela-colman-smith-1907-story-teller/
- Brooklyn Life. Sat Feb 16th 1907. [Online]. [Accessed 3 January 2018]. Available from: *https://marykgreer.com/2015/02/08/pamela-colman-smith-1907-story-teller/*
- Colman Smith, 1899. *Annancy Stories.* New York: R.H. Russell
- Colman Smith, *Colman Smith to Stieglitz,*, Jan 5, 1898. Letter. The Bryn Mawr College Library Special Collections. *Pamela Colman Smith Collection.* [Online]. [Accessed 3 January 2018]. Available from: http://www.brynmawr.edu/library/speccoll/guides/smithbox.shtml
- Crowley, A. 1911. *Wisdom While You Waite.* The Equinox. Vol 1. No 5., 135
- Court de Gebelin, A. 1781. *Monde primitif, Vol. 3.* Translated by D. Tyson [Online]. [Accessed 14 January 2018]. Available from: http://priory-of-sion.com/biblios/links/gebelin.pdf
- Dante and Longfellow, H.W. 1800. *The Divine Comedy.* Atlanta: Project Gutenburg Etext, 1997
- Davis, R. 1966. *Dedicated follower of Fashion.* Cambridge: Pye Records
- Decker, R., Depaulis, T. and Dummet. M. 1996. *A Wicked Pack of Cards: The Origins of the Occult Tarot.* London: Duckworth & Co
- Decker, R. and Dummett, M. 2002. *A History of the Occult Tarot.* London: Duckworth Overlook
- Dow, D. 1914. *Composition.* New York: Doubleday, Page & Co
- Farley, H. 2006. *A Cultural History of Tarot.* London: I.B. Tauris

- Fleming, I. 1954. *Live and Let Die.* Great Britain: Jonathan Cape
- Gilbert, R.A. 1987. *A.E. Waite: Magician of Many Parts.* Wellingborough: Crucible
- Higgins, S. 2013. *A.E. Waite and the Occult.* [Online]. Accessed 2 January 2018]. Available from: https://theoddestinkling.wordpress.com/2013/12/11/a-e-waite-and-the-occult/
- Giles, C. 1992. *The Tarot: History, Mystery and Lore.* New York: Paragon House
- Hurtig, M.A. 2013. *Antiquity Unleashed:Aby Warburg, Durer and Mantegna.* London: Paul Holberton Publishing
- Huson, 1972. *The Devil's Picturebook: The Compleat Guide to Tarot Cards: Their Origin and Their Usage.* London: Sphere Books Ltd
- Kaplan, A. 1997. *Sefer Yetzirah: The Book of Creation, in Theory and Practice,* revised edn. Maine: York Beach
- Kaplan, S. 1990. *The Encyclopedia of Tarot: Volume 3.* Connecticut: U.S. Games Systems
- Katz, M. and Goodwin, T. 2015. *Secrets of the Waite-Smith Tarot: The True Story of the World's Most Popular Tarot.* Minnesota: Llewellyn Publications
- Le Mieux, D. 1985. *The Ancient Tarot and its symbolism.* New Jersey: Rosemont publishing and printing corporation
- Lykke, N. 2012. *Feminist Studies: A Guide to Intersectional Theory, Methodology and Writing.* London: Routledge
- MacDonald, M. 1912. The fairy faith and pictured music of Pamela Colman Smith. *The craftsman.* Vol. XXIII, 1, pp. 20-34
- MacNeice, L. 1963 'Charon' in *The Burning Perch.*
- Markos, L. 2013. *Heaven and Hell: Visions of the Afterlife in the Western Poetic Tradition.* Oregon: Cascade Books
- Moore, C.L. 2014. *Unlocking the Tarot.* North Carolina: lulu.com
- Morning Times (Washington D.C.). Sun Jan 5th 1889. *A Jamaica Spider* [Online]. [Accessed 3 January 2018]. Available from: https://marykgreer.com/2015/02/07/pamela-colman-smith-1896-1899/
- Mosier, J. 2005. War Myths: An Exchange. *Historically Speaking: The Bulletin of the Historical Society*:VI:4 [Online] March/April 2005 [Accessed 14 January 2018].
- Available from: http://www.bu.edu/historic/hs/marchapril05.html#mosier1
- O'Neill, R. 2012. *Tarot Death Cards: The Iconology from 15/16th Century.* [Online]. [Accessed 11 November 2017]. Available from: https://www.tarot.com/tarot/robert-oneill/death-cards
- O'Neill, R. 1986. *Tarot Symbolism.* Lima: Fairway Press

- Paraskos, M. (Imperial), *'In Place of Facts: Creative Fiction as a Research Tool'* public lecture delivered at Imperial College London (CLCC Research Series Seminars), 18 January 2018. Available from: http://tiny.cc/inplaceoffacts
- Paraskos, M. 2016. *In Search of Sixpence.* Surrey: Friction Fiction
- Paraskos, M. 2018 *'The Ontology of Things'* in Joanna Barnes and Mark Stocker (eds.), A Festschrift for Ben Read. London: PMSA, 2018
- Prown, J. 1982. *'Mind in Matter: An Introduction to Material Culture Theory and Method,'* in *The Winterthur Portfolio No. 17*
- Pyne, K. 2007. *Modernism and the Feminine Voice: O'Keefe and the Women of the Stieglitz Circle.* Berkley: University of California Press
- Read, H. (No date) *'The Surrealist Object'* (CD recording), reproduced on LTM Recordings, *Surrealism Reviewed,* CD recording, LTMCD 2343
- Roob, A. 2015. *Alchemy and Mysticism.* Cologne: Taschen
- Shephard, J. 1905. *The Tarot Trumps: Cosmos in miniature.* Wellingborough: The Aquarian Press
- Simon, S. 1986. *The Tarot: Art, Mysticism and Divination.* London: Alpine Fine Arts Collection
- *Strand Magazine.* July, 1908. 634-638. [Online]. [Accessed 14 January 2018]. Available from: http://www.elfindog.sakura.ne.jp/strandstory.htm
- Tuve, R. 1966. *Allegorical Imagery: Some Mediaeval Books and Their Posterity.* New Jersey: Princeton University Press
- Waite, A.E. 1993. *The Brotherhood of the Rosy Cross.* New York: Barnes and Noble, Inc.
- Waite, A.E. 1909. *The Hidden Church of the Holy Graal: Its Legends and Symbolism.* London: Rebman Ltd.
- Waite, A.E. 1886. *The Mysteries of Magic: A Digest on the Writings of Eliphas Levi.* London: George Redway
- Waite, A.E. 1910. *The Pictorial Key to the Tarot.* Reprint, London: Rider Books, 1982
- Waite, A.E. 1911. *The Secret Tradition in Freemasonry.* London: Rebman Limited
- Waite, A.E. 1936. *Shadows of Life and Thought.* Reprint, Dublin: Bardic Press, 2016
- Warburg, A. 1929. *Mnemosyne. Grundbegriffe, II* London: Warburg Institute Archive, III.102.3–4
- Warburg, A. 1929 *Notes on Panel 50-51 Mnemosyne Atlas.* [Online]. [Accessed 3 January 2018]. Available from: http://www.engramma.it/eOS/core/frontend/eos_atlas_index.php?id_tavola=1050#

- Warburg, A. 1920. *The Renewal of Pagan Antiquity: Contributions to the Cultural History of the European Renaissance.* Reprint, Los Angeles: Getty Publications, 2006
- Winick, S. *Stephen Winick Interviews Stuart Kaplan.* July 21, 2010.

Step-by-Step: The Non-Figural Mosaics of Late Antique Cyprus

Jane Chick (University of East Anglia, UK)

MENTION CYPRIOT MOSAICS and the magnificent figural panels from Paphos or the beautifully executed pavements from Kourion will almost certainly spring to mind. These well-known pavements are widely admired and have, quite deservedly, received a great deal of scholarly attention. There is, however, another category of mosaics on the island that has largely been ignored, namely, the geometric and abstract mosaics that carpet many of the Late Antique basilicas and baptisteries. There is a tendency, and not just on Cyprus, to treat non-figural mosaics as secondary works; often abandoned to the elements, they are, at worst ignored altogether, at best recorded and compared to similar pavements from other parts of the Mediterranean. These productions, rarely considered worthy of interpretation, are generally dismissed as practical, albeit decorative, floor coverings—something to walk on like fitted carpets in modern houses.

By way of redress this chapter focuses mainly on pavements from four Cypriot ecclesiastical complexes, all dated between the late fourth and mid-sixth centuries: Agias Trias on the Karpas Peninsula, Agios Georgios at Pegeia, the basilica of Chrysopolitissa at Paphos and the basilica at Soloi on the gulf of Morphou (Figure 1). The first part of the chapter argues that many of the individual components from these floors were imbued with meanings which, although not immediately obvious today, would have been readily understood by Late Antique spectators. The second part considers the larger picture, suggesting a phenomenological relationship between viewers and the geometric mosaics underfoot.

Excavated mosaic pavements are notoriously difficult to deal with as studying them is problematic and how best to preserve them is a contentious issue. Once exposed, mosaics become very vulnerable and, if left unprotected, the tesserae are bleached by the sun and the mortar breaks down allowing the surface to disintegrate and vegetation to creep into the cracks causing further damage. This is evident at many archaeological sites where fragments of desecrated and sun-faded pavements can be glimpsed across walls and through fencing. Traditionally, one of the ways of dealing with this problem has been to lift selected sections of pavement—usually figural panels—and transfer them to local museums where they are hung like unframed pictures on the wall of a gallery. Stripped of their context the significance and function of these mosaics is largely lost. In addition, this strategy clearly favours the figural pavements and so promotes the idea that geometric and abstract mosaics are second-rate productions not worth preserving. A more recent approach has been to record, photograph and re-bury pavements, but inevitably only small sections of large fields of mosaics can be published, usually with no context or indication of doorways or openings and, again, it is usually figural panels that are privileged. At archaeological sites where funds have allowed for the construction of protective roofs and raised walkways, mosaics can often be viewed in their original contexts, but even this solution is not without drawbacks. The uninterrupted bird's-eye vistas offered from viewing platforms take in whole series of rooms, giving the false impression that no walls or doorways separated the spaces, and that no furniture, statuary, or indeed occupants, obscured any part of the mosaic. In an article addressing the issue of how best to illustrate Roman mosaics, Cosh and Neal suggest that, as it is almost impossible to photograph entire pavements and that, on the whole, only oblique views are attainable, scale paintings are a better option (Cosh and Neal 1998, 18). However, depictions of whole pavements, whether drawings, aerial photographs or computer generated images, can be misleading. Firstly, it is tempting, particularly if a pavement is comprised of a series of panels, to 'read' the imagery as one might read the page of a book, that is, from left to right and from top to bottom. Secondly, the inference of presenting a complete mosaic is that this is how the pavements would have been experienced when they were first made. In fact, Late Antique spectators would almost never have had complete uninterrupted panoramas of pavements. Perhaps rather ironically, it is only at the more neglected or ill-funded archaeological sites with little or no protective infrastructure, where mosaic pavements can be seen and experienced as they were intended—that is, as oblique and partial views which evolve as they pass underfoot. Such access, however, comes at a price and the poor preservation of the nave pavement in the basilica at Agias Trias is testament to this (Figure 2). Ideally then, to begin to understand the impact geometric mosaic pavements may have had on Late Antique viewers, they need to be put imaginatively underfoot.

It is easy to understand the temptation to treat figural mosaics, so-called 'paintings in stone' (Brilliant 1974, 140),[1] as works of art, as even in their original contexts they were almost always positioned and oriented to be admired and discussed. The pavement in the triclinium of the House of Aion at Paphos, for example, was positioned so that diners seated around the outside of the room could study the panels, read the inscriptions and no doubt show off their education—their paideia—by identifying the mythological protagonists and interpreting the narratives (Kondoleon 1995, 185-6). By contrast, carpets of geometric mosaics would not have held the attention of stationary viewers in the same way and panels of continuous and repetitive patterns are unlikely to have stopped visitors in their tracks demanding contemplation and interpretation. That is not to say, however, that non-figural imagery can simply be dismissed as insignificant or that visitors

---

[1] Brilliant discusses the idea that some mosaics imitated paintings, while others emphasized the nature of the material used.

were unaware of what was passing beneath their feet. The meanings associated with many of the commonly occurring motifs in geometric mosaics may no longer be immediately evident, but in Late Antiquity viewers were accustomed to 'reading imagery' (Onians 1980, passim), and even non-figural patterns and motifs carried multivalent meanings (Maguire 1987, 8-15; Elsner 1995, 220).

Despite Christianity being the mainstream religion at this time, the intervention of supernatural powers was accepted as part of everyday life and the observance of 'magical' practices was widespread (Russell 1995, 50). Personal amuletic devices, such as engraved gems, phylacteries and patches on clothing—orbiculi (roundels), tabulae (rectangles) or clavi (strips)—were part of everyday life; they were deployed as spiritual protection to repel evil and assure health, wealth and well-being. Public spaces, including streets and fora, were furnished with apotropaic devices at junctions and other vulnerable places, and buildings were safeguarded by spoliate elements included in the fabric of the structure and protective imagery in doorways and windows.[2] The early Christian basilicas on Cyprus were no exception and many of the motifs in the geometric pavements under discussion were actually well-established visual strategies designed to offer powerful protection against the unwanted attention of malevolent spirits and the envious glance of the evil eye.

Although this is not the place for an exhaustive study of protective motifs, it is worth singling out a few of the most popular for further consideration. The symbols and patterns found in the geometric mosaic pavements on Cyprus were, on the whole, not unique but drawn from an empire-wide repertoire of images, most of which had long-standing non-Christian origins. Despite regional trends and notable variations in the way imagery was presented and interpreted in different parts of the empire, certain designs were ubiquitous. For example,

---

[2] The term 'apotropaic' comes from the Greek *apotropaios*, meaning to avert or turn away evil.

cruciform designs and embedded cross motifs, evil-eyes, knots, and running borders of guilloches and swastikas can be found in Late Antique mosaic pavements as far apart as northern Italy to North Africa, and Portugal to Macedonia. It is partly the ubiquity of these designs that has led to them being dismissed as purely decorative—as compositions copied from so-called 'pattern-books' with no particular import or function.[3] However, I would argue that the commonality of these motifs, far from diminishing their importance, actually gave them added currency. The images were part of the Late Antique lingua franca and were universally understood as potent protective devices; there was no need for worshippers or visitors to pause and consider the meaning of individual motifs and patterns, they could simply pass over them confident in the knowledge that the necessary defences were in place to protect them.

One of the most common potentiated protective Christian symbols was the cross. A homily attributed to John Chrysostom lists the places where the sign of the cross was found, making it clear that its power to counter evil was readily understood.

> One can see [the cross] celebrated everywhere, in houses, in marketplaces, in deserts, in streets, on mountains, in valleys, in hills, on the sea, in boats, on islands, on beds, on clothes, on weapons, in chambers, at banquets, on silverware, on objects in gold, in pearls, in wall paintings, on the bodies of much-burdened animals, on bodies besieged by demons, in war, in peace, by day, by night, in parties of luxurious livers, in brotherhoods of ascetics; so much do all now seek after this

---

[3] The idea that mosaicists worked from pattern books is often used to explain how certain motifs, patterns or compositions moved from region to region. See for example, Dunbabin 1999, 97; Alföldi-Rosenbaum and Ward-Perkins 1980, *passim*. There is, however, no material evidence for the existence of such books and it is possible that designs moved with itinerant craftsmen or on small portable objects.

miraculous gift, this ineffable grace (Contra Judeas et Gentiles in Maguire et al. 1989, 18-19).

Despite the seemingly ubiquitous use of the cross to protect all manner of places and things, straightforward Latin crosses and Chi Rhos rarely appeared in mosaic pavements, possibly as a result of an edict issued by Theodosius II in 427 that forbade the representation of the sign of Christ on floors (Kitzinger 1970, 645).[4] Cruciform motifs, on the other hand, abound. Equal-armed Greek crosses, knots and swastikas present obvious cross-shapes, and once one has 'tuned-in' to seeing cruciate motifs they can be found in all manner of guises. For example, rosettes, quadrilobes, poised squares, the interstices of intersecting roundels and even the arrangement of objects—like the two crossed fish in the chancel pavement at Pegeia—all appear to form crosses (Figure 3). One of the most pervasive and apposite of the cross motifs is the knot of Solomon. The Latin word ligatura means both 'knot' and 'spell' and the image of a knot was therefore a symbol of both physical binding in the earthly world and spell-binding in the spiritual world (Maguire et al. 1989, 3; Trilling 2003, 98). The irresolvability of the knot of Solomon, together with its association with Solomon, master of demons, made it a particularly potent tool against evil.[5] Simple Solomon's knots are ubiquitous in early Christian floor mosaics, and can be found in all four basilicas under discussion (Figure 4). More complicated and aggrandised versions of the knot appear in the atrium of Chrysopolitissa and in the south aisle at Agias Trias (Figure 5).

---

[4] Although rare, Latin crosses did sometimes appear in floor mosaics, for example a recently excavated sixth-century pavement in a church near Tel Aviv in Israel includes a cross in a roundel adorned with *Alpha* and *Omega, pers comm.* Erga Schneurson March 2016.

[5] The Archangel Michael is said to have given Solomon a seal-ring which was empowered to control all evil spirits, Mitchell 2007, 290.

The swastika, an ancient symbol with long-standing auspicious associations, is another much-favoured cruciform motif.[6] Although sometimes appearing as a stand-alone image, often framed by a circle or polygon, in early Christian contexts the swastika is probably more often seen in the form of a meander, as found, for example, in both the nave at Soloi and the nave at Agias Trias (Figure 6).

Another commonly used protective symbol, which appeared in a variety of forms and in many different contexts, was the pelta. Although this motif may seem a long way removed from the exotic Amazonian shield it was named after and took its amuletic properties from, in the Villa of Theseus at Nea Paphos on Cyprus, peltae and battle-axes appear side by side in all four corners of a room—an arrangement that makes a clear reference to both the origin of the motif and its protective function (Daszewski & Michaelides 1988, 52-63) (Figure 7).[7] In the narthex at Agias Trias, elaborated peltae fill the interstices of a strangely off-centre eight-pointed star which guards the main entrance to the basilica, and at Chrysopolitissa peltae with crossed or stepped tops are found in fragments of the pavement from the north aisle (Figure 8).

Roundels and concentric circles were also understood as apotropaic devices; the infinite circularity of these propitious motifs was believed to create an inescapable trap. Henry Maguire has also noted that roundels may have been ciphers for mirrors, objects believed capable of reflecting evil back on itself (Maguire et al. 1989, 5-7). A particularly pertinent example can be seen in the basilica of Chrysopolitissa where the east court is protected by an array of apotropaic motifs, including a trio of images by the centre of the shallow apse; a Solomon's knot, a Chi-Rho—or Christogram—and a

---

[6] The word 'swastika' comes from Sanskrit origins and means good fortune or well-being.

[7] Another example of an axe and a pelta-shaped shield appearing together is in a second-century black and white mosaic, now in the museum at Conimbriga, Portugal.

circular, lollipop-like motif, which, given the well-attested protective qualities of its companions, is likely to represent a mirror (Figure 9). In other pavements, roundels were depicted as though in perpetual motion —the idea of movement imbuing the motifs with added efficacy. Spinning objects were believed to have the power to fascinate and avert evil,[8] and were therefore used to protect liminal or transitional spaces from malevolent spirits (Johnston 1991, 217-8). The perceived power of these motifs is attested to by graffiti of conical shapes, interpreted as spinning-tops, on a street corner in Pompeii (Kellum 1999, 285), and by carvings of whirling roundels on lintels above doorways and windows, a tradition that was practised throughout the eastern Mediterranean but which was particularly prevalent in Syria (Figure 10). Multi-coloured spinning roundels can be seen in the atrium pavement at Chrysopolitissa (Figure 11), and in the south aisle at Soloi, roundels constructed from fragments of terracotta set on end give a sort of radiating sunburst effect suggesting a constant spinning movement (Figure 12). And roundels were not the only motifs set in motion, in the nave at Soloi, Solomon's knots were combined with peltae to create enigmatic motifs resulting in an illusion of whirling, the movement presumably making the carpet more powerful than the sum of its parts (Figure 13).

  The so-called 'much-suffering' eye—an imitation of the evil eye —was another powerful apotropaic symbol with a long history. According to the Testament of Solomon, the thirty-fifth demon summoned by Solomon was responsible for the evil eye and when forced to reveal its identity and charm effective against its evil, it announced: 'I am called Rhyx Phtheneoth. I cast the evil eye on every

---

[8] The modern word 'fascinate' comes from the Latin term *fascinum,* the term for an object that would avert evil by distracting, confusing, attracting, or repelling a demon, Clarke 2007, 69.

man. But the much-suffering eye, when inscribed, thwarts me'.[9] Pre-Christian examples of the 'much-suffering' eye fighting off all manner of evil can be seen carved in stone on a street corner in Leptis Magna (Figure 14), and in a second-century mosaic doormat from the House of the Evil Eye in Antioch, Syria (Cimok 2000, 36-7). Stylised versions of the 'much-suffering' eye found their way into Christian contexts. Sometimes they appeared as a roundel set within a lozenge, for example, in the intercolumniations of the Church of Al-Khadir in Madaba, Jordan (Piccirillo 1997, 129-31), at the threshold to the south aisle in Basilica A at Amphipolis, Greece (Zikos 1989, 7-12), and, on Cyprus, in the main doorway of the Basilica at Alassa.[10] In other instances, the motifs were more eye-shaped, for example in the peristyle of the fourth-century triconch palace at Butrint in Albania (Bowden and Hodges 2011, 264), and in the nave of the basilica at Soloi, where motifs, although not quite eyes, are similar enough in shape to have been recognised as protective emblems (Figure 15).

It was not only individual stand-alone elements that were deployed to safeguard Christian buildings. In the baptistery at Pegeia, for example, baptisands, in their transitional and vulnerable state, were offered extra protection by an expansive carpet of overlapping and intertwining motifs along the east side of the font (Figure 16). The pattern created a delicate latticework structure that appeared to be stretched, snare-like, above a lower base giving an illusion of depth and

---

[9] Duling 1983, 981. The *Testament of Solomon*, a treatise falsely ascribed to King Solomon, is generally thought to date from somewhere between the first and fifth centuries AD. It contains both Jewish and Christian elements and details the forms and activities of demons and effective charms against them.

[10] The mosaic is now on display in the Limassol Museum. For The Basilica of Alassa see, Flourentzos 1996.

fragility.[11] A similar effect was achieved in two sections of pavement in the atrium of the basilica of Chrysopolitissa (Figure 17). Running borders of simple or multi-stranded guilloches, compelling and continuous patterns with no obvious beginning or end, were often used to frame panels or to border entire pavements. Although such borders were ubiquitous in Late Antique pavements, in certain instances they too may have served a beneficent function and should not be dismissed as simply decorative. At Agias Trias, for example, a panel of interlocking swastikas formed from a simple guilloche, borders an inscription, now lost. To the human eye the pattern appears labyrinthine and impenetrable and to the evil eye its indeterminacy and intrinsic brilliance would have been mesmerising and therefore distracting enough to protect both the inscription and the entrance to the atrium from unwanted attention (Figure 18).

The patterns and motifs discussed above have well-attested and easily recognisable protective attributes. However, given the Late Antique preoccupation with all things apotropaic, it is possible that it was not only the imagery that gave the mosaic pavements potency, but also their actual construction—the fact that each pavement was made from thousands of tiny pieces. Indeterminable numbers were considered captivating, and small bags filled with seeds were often attached to bedposts in the hope that the impossibility of counting them would divert the attention of evil and so protect the occupants (Hildeburgh 1944, 135-6; Trilling 2003, 98). In the same way, the innumerability of the tesserae that made up a mosaic pavement may have added to the protective mantle enveloping the building.

The first part of this chapter focuses on some of the commonly occurring motifs found in the geometric mosaics carpeting the early Christian basilicas on Cyprus. It argues that, although not as imposing

---

[11] Richard Brilliant discusses the Romans' pleasure in playing with perspective in internal decoration and highlights their 'peculiar perception of an irresolute, active boundary between solid and void', Brilliant 1974, 136.

or arresting as many of the figural panels, these pavements were, nonetheless, more than mere decoration and that they played an important role in protecting transitional and sacred spaces and offering reassurance to worshippers. Thus far, however, only individual elements of the pavements have been singled out for attention—small details or discrete sections from large fields of mosaics—but visitors moving through the buildings would have seen expansive swathes of mosaics, albeit only fleetingly. In his book on black and white figural mosaics from Ostia Antica, John Clarke has proposed a so-called 'kinaesthetic address' between viewers and pavements, suggesting that the placement of figures in some pavements would have prompted visitors to walk in a certain direction or to turn one way or the other (Clarke 1979, 20-21, 33). I would argue that this kinaesthetic address need not be restricted to figural mosaics, but could equally be applied to geometric pavements in which patterns can be understood as signposts to guide visitors and direct the flow of traffic. A particularly good example is the sixth-century pavement of a basilica at Bir Messaouda in Carthage. Constructed over an earlier north-south orientated building and squeezed between existing structures and roadways, only the westernmost columns of the basilica and the mosaic pavement defined the narthex of the basilica. Panels of overlapping scales, alternately inverted triangles and rows of peltae were all oriented north-south marking out the narthex and encouraging visitors to turn either left or right, rather than walk straight ahead into the nave. On reaching the inner north or south aisles, continuous carpets of undulating scallop-shells rolling from west to east along the whole length of the aisles carried visitors eastwards (Chick 2019 forthcoming, passim). The pavement carpeting the south aisle at Agias Trias worked in a similar way; the imagery may have been polyfocal rather than directional, but the repetitive pattern of squares containing a limited repertoire of designs running the length of the aisle. With no visual obstacles impeding progress, the imagery would have urged visitors onwards (Figure 19). This is particularly pronounced when the imagery is compared to that in the north aisle of the same church, as a panel of motifs presents a barrier or 'Stop Here' sign half way along the aisle (Figure 20).

The geometric mosaic pavements carpeting the basilicas on Cyprus served several practical functions; they provided a hard wearing yet decorative surface to walk on, they added a layer of spiritual protection to the ecclesiastical buildings, and they helped visitors navigate their way around the complexes. But how did Late Antique viewers react to these productions that were not only visible, but also tangible? That were not only works of art, but also supporting surfaces over which they moved? When seen from a doorway or stationary viewpoint, the geometric motifs and patterns appear static and lifeless but as they pass underfoot they are transformed—the forward movement of the viewer animates them giving them momentum. Individual components, indecipherable from a distance, come into focus, arbitrary units join to form scintillating constellations, and complex patterns emerge. However, no sooner has one section of pavement come into view—the discrete elements of the design revealed and the patterns resolved—than it disappears again, obscured by the very person who, just seconds earlier, had brought it to life. And it was not only the imagery that was transformed by the passage of visitors. The surface of the pavement, seemingly so sturdy and immovable when seen stretching ahead, continually disintegrates into hundreds of tiny pieces beneath the feet of visitors, revealing an apparent contradiction between the solidity of the material—stone—and the fragility of a fragmented surface. The perceptual uncertainty this creates is disorientating; to the human eye the surface appears to shift and change, taking on an ephemeral quality and giving the impression that it has become insubstantial, almost as though one is walking on water, and yet, underfoot, the floor is still stable.[12] This 'intentional ambiguity'

---

[12] The idea of solid pavements representing water is discussed in Barry 2007, *passim*.

lent mosaic pavements an almost magical quality and gave agency to the flat two-dimensional symbols etched on their surfaces.[13] In the same way that some apotropaic objects, for example, tintinnabula—bells hung by doorways—needed a breeze to breathe life into them, these fields of tessellation needed the movement of visitors to unlock their dynamism. Like an empty stage awaiting the entrance of actors to bring it to life, geometric pavements were reliant on the presence and intuition of viewers who, by populating these previously uninhabited visual fields metamorphosed into protagonists and, step-by-step, set the imagery in motion. The synergy between viewer and pavement prompted a kind of phenomenological response—visitors not only reacted to the imagery beneath their feet, but also interacted with it.

The geometric pavements in the early Christian churches on Cyprus may not have the same immediate wow factor or universal appeal of the splendid figural panels from Paphos or Kourion, and they may not warrant hanging space on the walls of museums. They do, however, deserve more than a second glance, and should not be dismissed as simply decorative floor coverings devoid of meaning. These pavements played an integral role in the overall experience of those visiting the ecclesiastical complexes on the island during Late Antiquity.

---

[13] Richard Brilliant discusses the use of decoration in Roman interiors to transform apparently stable surfaces into energised fields, Brilliant 1974, 136.

Reference Sources

- Barry, F. 2007. 'Walking on Water: Cosmic Floors in Antiquity and the Middle Ages.' *The Art Bulletin* LXXXIX (4): 627-656.
- Bonner, C. 1950. *Studies in Magical Amulets: Chiefly Graeco-Egyptian.* Ann Arbor: University of Michigan Press.
- Bowden, W. and R. Hodges. 2011. *Butrint 3: Excavations at the Triconch Palace.* Oxford: Oxbow Books.
- Brilliant, R. 1974. *Roman Art: From the Republic to Constantine.* London: Phaidon Press.
- Chick, J. 2019 (forthcoming). 'The Mosaic Pavements of Bir Messaouda.' In *The Bir Messaouda Basilicas: The Transformation of an Urban Landscape in Late Antique Carthage*, ed. R. Miles, Oxford: Oxbow Books.
- Cimok, F. 2000. *A Corpus of Antioch Mosaics.* Istanbul: A Trurizm Yayinlari
- Clarke, J. 1979. *Roman Black and White Figural Mosaics.* New York: New York University Press.
- ---. 2007. *Looking at Laughter: Humour, Power, and Transgression in Roman Visual Culture, 100 B.C.-A.D.250.* Berkeley: University of California Press.
- Cosh, S. and D. Neal. 1998. 'Roman Mosaics.' *Current Archaeology* 157 (March): 18-25.
- Daszewski, W. and D. Michaelides. 1988. *Guide to Paphos Mosaics.* Nicosia: Bank of Cyprus Cultural Foundation.
- Duling, D. C. Trans. 1983. 'The Old Testament Pseudepigrapha.' Volume 1. In *Apocalyptic Literature and Testaments*, ed. J. Charlesworth, 935-987. New York: Doubleday.
- Dunbabin, K. and M.W. Dickie. 1983. 'Invida Rumpantur Pectora.' *Jahrbuch für Antike und Christentum* 26: 7-37.
- Elsner, J. 1995. *Art and the Roman Viewer: The Transformation of Art from the Pagan World to Christianity.* Cambridge: Cambridge University Press.
- Flourentzos, 1996. *Excavations in the Kouris Valley: II. The Basilica of Alassa.* Nicosia: Department of Antiquities, Cyprus.
- Hildeburgh, W.L, 1944. 'Indeterminability and Confusion as Apotropaic Elements in Italy and Spain.' *Folk-Lore* 55 (4): 133-49.
- Johnston, S.I. 1991. 'Crossroads.' *Zeitschrift für Papyrologie und Epigraphik* 88: 217-224.
- Kellum, B. 1999. 'The Spectacle of the Street.' In *The Art of Ancient Spectacle*, eds B. Bergman and C. Kondoleon, 283-99. Washington: Yale University Press.

- Kitzinger, E. 1970. 'The Threshold of the Holy Shrine. Observations on Floor Mosaics at Antioch and Bethlehem.' In *Kyriakon, Festschrift Johannes Quasten*, eds J.A. Jungman and Greenfield, 639-647. Münster: Verlag Aschendorff.
- Kondoleon, C. 1995. *Domestic and Divine: Roman Mosaics in the House of Dionysos*. Ithaca: Cornell University Press.
- Maguire, H. 1987. *Earth and Ocean: The Terrestrial World in Early Byzantine Art*. Pennsylvania: Pennsylvania State University Press.
- ---. 1995. *Byzantine Magic*. Washington: Harvard University Press.
- Maguire, E. D. and H. Maguire. 2007. *Other Icons. Art and Power in Byzantine Secular Culture*. Princeton N.J: Princeton University Press.
- Maguire, E.D., H. Maguire and M. Duncan-Flowers. 1989. *Art and the Holy Powers in the Early Christian House*. Chicago: University of Illinois Press.
- Mitchell, J. 2007. 'Keeping the Demons out of the House: The Archaeology of Apotropaic Strategy and Practice in Late Antique Butrint and Antigoneia.' In *Objects in Context. Objects in Use. Material Spatiality in Late Antiquity*, eds L. Lavan E. Swift and T. Putzeys, 273-310. Leiden: Brill.
- Onians, J. 1980. 'Abstraction and Imagination in Late Antiquity.' *Art History* 3 (1): 1-24.
- Piccirillo, M. 1997. *The Mosaics of Jordan*. Amman: American Centre of Oriental Research Publications.
- Russell, J. 1995. 'The Archaeological Context of Magic in the Early Byzantine Period.' In *Byzantine Magic*, ed. H. Maguire, 35-50. Washington: Harvard University Press.
- Trilling, J. 2003. *Ornament: A Modern Perspective*. Washington: University of Washington Press.
- Zikos, N. 1989. *Amphipolis: Early Christian and Byzantine Amphipolis*. Athens: Archaeological Research Funds.

Illustrations

Fig. 1 Map of sites on Cyprus mentioned in text.

Fig. 2 Agias Trias. (Author)

Fig. 3 Crossed fish in the chancel at Pegeia. (Author)

Fig. 4 Solomon's knots at Pegeia, Chrysopolitissa, Agias Trias and Soloi. (Author)

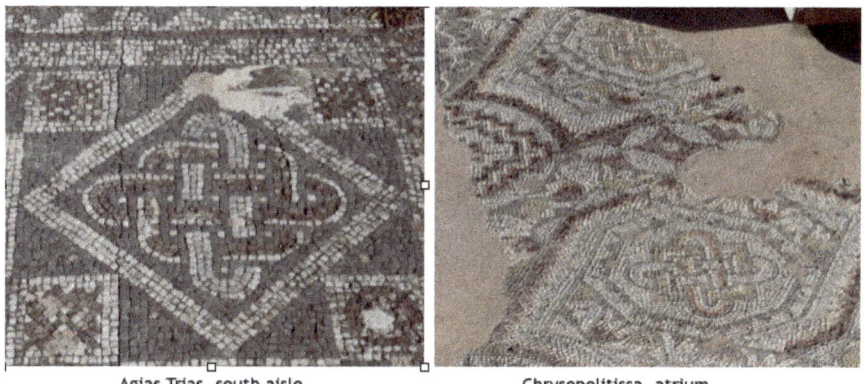

Fig. 5 Elaborated knots at Agias Trias and Chrysopolitissa. (Author)

Fig. 6 Swastika meanders at Soloi and Agias Trias. (Author)

Fig. 7 Villa of Theseus, Nea Paphos – battle axes and shields. (Author)

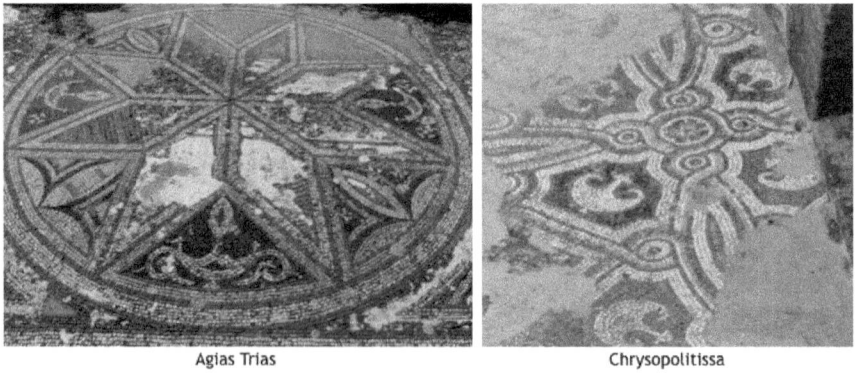

Fig. 8 Peltae at Agias Trias and Chrysopolitissa. (Author)

Fig. 9   East court apse, Chrysopolitissa. (Author)

Fig. 10   Carved doorway, Serjilla, Syria. (Author)

Fig. 11 Spinning roundels, Chrysopolitissa. (Author)

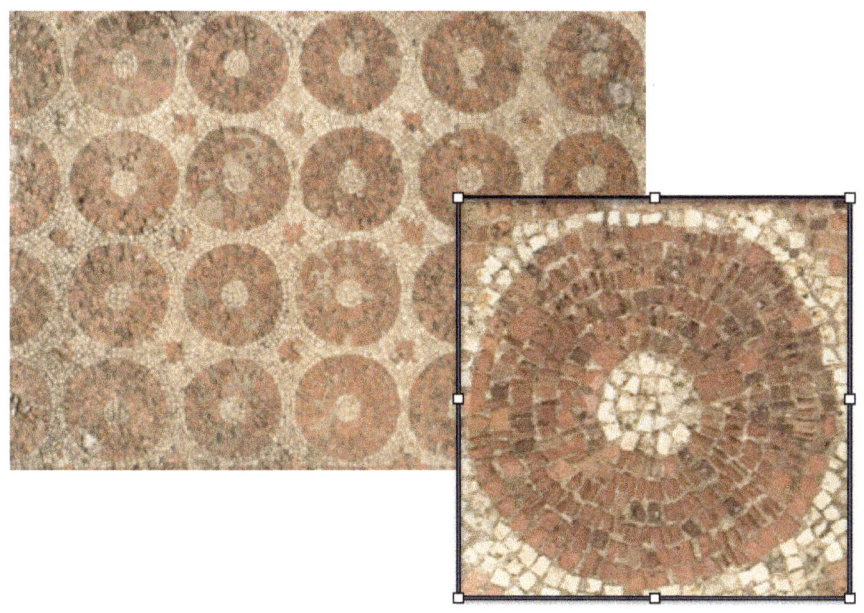

Fig. 12 Spinning roundels, Soloi. (Author)

Fig. 13 Swirling Solomon's knots with attached peltae. (Author)

Fig. 14   A 'much-suffering' eye at Leptis Magna, Libya. (Author)

Fig. 15   Eye motifs at Soloi. (Author)

Fig. 16 Net-like carpet of mosaics in the baptistery at Pegeia. (Author)

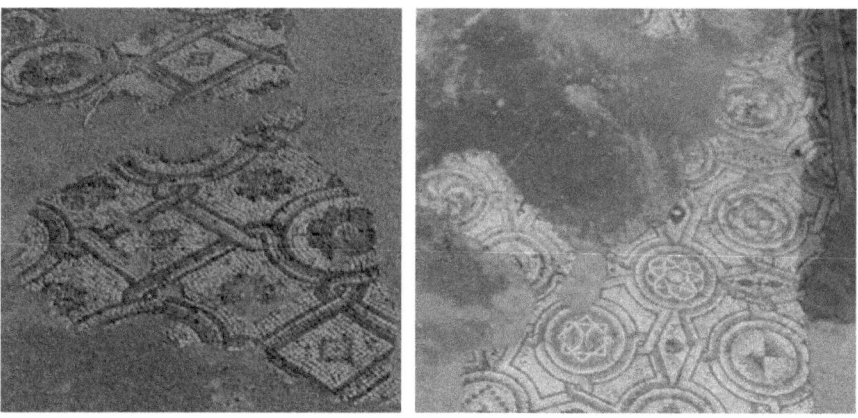

Fig. 17 Net-like carpets of mosaic from the atrium at Chrysopolitissa. (Author)

Fig. 18   Protective doormat at Agias Trias. (Author)

Fig. 19 South aisle at Agias Trias, looking west. (Author)

Fig. 20   North aisle at Agias Trias, looking east. (Author).

Mens sana in sano corpore: The nobility of Grand Duchy of Lithuania travels to spa from 16th to 18th centuries

Milda Kvizikevičiūtė *(Vilnius University, Lithuania)*

Introduction

THE ROMAN POET Juvenal once told that a healthy mind lives in a healthy body. Health and health repair was always a very important, if sometimes very tiresome, process. There were no exceptions among noblemen from Grand Duchy of Lithuania – they were anxious to try new methods of treatment and tried to fix their health problems in every possible way. One of the most popular methods in early modern period was taking the water, going to the baths, and so on.

The most informative sources for personal experiences at the hot spring resorts, terme or spas—two terms used synonymously in the paper—are personal writings, such as diaries and correspondence. In the context of the Grand Duchy of Lithuania, the most appropriate chronological frame is the period between the sixteenth and eighteenth centuries. The sixteenth century marks the beginning of personal writing, which was not common until the mid-seventeenth century, when writing was understood as a means for personal expression (Tereškinas 2002, 175). From that point on, the number of diaries, memoirs, autobiographies grew, albeit gradually. Consequently, part of medical tourism found its place in personal writing.

The aim of this paper is to analyse the perceptions of the nobility of the Grand Duchy of Lithuania towards health and sickness, as well as treatments and their success, through personal writings. This will be explored through two main perspectives. Firstly, medical geography, looking at the most visited regions and resorts, and then considering the reasons for those choices. Secondly, the treatments themselves, including the medical procedures and their descriptions, and the success or failure of the treatment.

The noblemen of Grand Duchy of Lithuania will often be referred to as patients in the paper, but it is important to introduce them for better understanding of their background, and social and political positions. In this paper I have kept the names of the nobility in the way they appear in the sources which is usually in the Polish language. Most of the nobility who could afford the luxury of going abroad for medical reasons came from the higher to highest social ranks. For example, Mikołaj Krzysztof Radziwiłł Sierotko (Michael Christopher Radziwill the Orphan) 1549–1616, was a highly educated person, who was not only able to carry on with high-level political duties, but also managed to write a very interesting account from his pilgrimage to Jerusalem, which was published in 1601. But he had weak health, and had visited hot springs several times in Poland (Jelenia Góra) and Italy (Lucca).

Another patient was Krzysztof Dorohostajski (Christopher Dorohostajski), 1562– 1615, who was educated in Strasbourg and Fribourg. Even though his career took him into the military, he was well known for his book, Hipika, to jest o koniach księgi, published in 1603. He had even more experience of medical tourism, having visited Jelenia Góra, and Austrian and Italian resorts. In 1605 Dorohostajski went to the Polish resort with his wife Zofia z Radziwiłłów Dorohostajska (Sofia from Radziwill Dorohostajska), 1577–1614.

Albrecht Stanisław Radziwiłł (Albert Stanislav Radziwill), 1593–1656, also travelled to the resort of Teplice with his wife Anna Krystyna Lubomirska (Ann Christine Lubomirska), 1618-1667. A. S. Radziwiłł was in charge of foreign policies and internal affairs for the Grand

Duchy of Lithuania and he too wrote his memoirs, which included not only political affairs, but also some personal information. The most elaborate diary on medical matter was left by Michał Butler, 1715 – 1782. Not much is known about Butler, except that his family originated in the German lands. It is possible that his wife, Marijana Markowska, also travelled with him to spas, but if so she did not take any recorded cures.

Others visitors to spas were from the clergy, including Mikołaj Pac (Michael Pac), 1570-1624, Bishop of Samogitia; Benedykt Woyna (Benedict Woyna), ? - 1615, Bishop of Vilnius; Józef Stanisław Sapieha (Joseph Stanislav Sapieha), 1708 – 1754. These are only a few figures who took treatments abroad at hot springs resorts. They were highly educated and wealthy people, who had expectations and possibly some knowledge of the treatments. Moreover it is interesting how their expectations were met and what parts of the whole experience left them excited or even confused.

Medical Geography and Seasonality of Treatment

'He never can go to Italy, except for health'

Testament of Christopher Radziwill the Thunder (1608)

There were many different spa resorts in Europe during the early modern period, however, the nobility of the Grand Duchy of Lithuania, went only to a few of them. The geography of medical tourism was not very wide and some places were more popular than the others. The most popular region was Italy, especially Abano Terme near Padua, as well as Lucca and Pozzuoli. Two other popular resorts were Teplice and Karlovy Vary in current Czech Republic, as well as Yavoriv, in what is now Ukraine, and Jelenia Góra in what is now Poland. The list of the most visited resorts is quite predictable, as those countries and regions were often travel destinations for the nobility of Grand Duchy of Lithuania in any case. Yet, it is interesting to question why those regions and those particular resorts.

Hot spring resorts were in some ways a controversial form of treatment amongst medical professionals at the time. On one hand, it was suggested that going to a hot spring was a last option for when nothing else could help or improve the health of a patient (Palmer 1990, 21). But evidence suggests some patients who went to the hot springs were those unwilling to take advice from medical professionals in any case. Consequently, the Italian physician, Andrea Bacci, who wrote several books on thermal waters, suggested doctors should be more involved in the treatment processes at the springs. He noted three types of patient who tended to visit them: 1, thoughtless people, who did not use a doctor; 2, people whose lives were despaired of by doctors and who usually died, either blaming the doctors, or the hot springs; 3, patients who consulted doctors and obediently carried out their instructions (Palmer 1990, 22).

Almost every time Lithuanians fell into the third category, as most of them mentioned their doctors or medical consultations in their travel diaries or correspondence. An example is Michael Butler who went on a trip to Abano Terme in Italy and consulted a doctor there and the doctor gave him a brochure, in Italian, about Abano Terme. Next day Butler had read the book and, after a couple of months, came back for a whole month for treatment. Butler also mentioned that he bought several different medicines, recommended by a doctor, to help with his leg pain (Butler 2013, 293). M. K. Radziwiłł Sierotko, had spent all summer in 1580 in Italy at hot springs under medics instructions (Radziwiłł 1990, 37).

Another important factor in making the decision as to whether to go to a resort could depend on a close personal connection, leading to a recommendation. Sadly, this type of information is extremely rare and can be found only in personal correspondence. In 1593 Leon Sapieha, who was an important person in the political life of the Grand Duchy of Lithuania, wrote to Krzysztof Radziwiłł (another highly valued person in the Duchy's political life) that, 'I contacted with my doctor about your illness, and he says that you have liver inflammation, which can be lit ever more in Teplice' (Archiwum domu Radziwiłłów 1885, 213). There is no further information about this particular case, and it is unknown which recommendation was taken: the doctor's or the political comrade's.

Italy was the most common destination for travelling for a variety of purposes—education, religion, social engagements, and so on. Consequently it was a well-known culture, and possibly people heard much about it from other travellers. Also, there were several guidebooks for Italy circulating in Grand Duchy of Lithuania written in both Latin and Polish. Italy was, of course, religiously compatible for the mostly Catholic nobility of the Grand Duchy of Lithuania, and this was an important factor for a number of early modern travellers from the Grand Duchy, and many travellers felt relieved when they finally reached Italy. Kazimierz Woysznorowicz was traveling throughout Europe in 1667–1669 with Italy as his final destination after travelling through predominantly Protestant territories north of the Alps. Religious conflict was felt through the whole journey, with people described as dressing in a hideous way, churches not being beautiful enough and the architecture disappointing. This mood finally ended as he crossed the Alps into Italy (Vaišnoravičius 2009, 200).

Looking from the Protestant perspective, on the other hand, Italy was the least desirable country to visit. M. K. Radziwiłł the Thunder in determining the educational framework of his youngest son in his testament (1608), included schooling in Leipzig or other German lands, but Italy was ruled out as a religiously dangerous country due to its Catholicism. This attitude went from one testament to another, with several other Radziwiłłs writing on Italy, using almost the same phrases. The only exception to this general rule was M. K. Radziwiłł the Thunder giving his permission to visit Italy in cases of weak health (Augustyniak 2014, 96). As this seems to show, Italian hot springs were thought to be the best in Europe, being recognised as having the highest quality standards. Even doctors from other hot spring resorts around Europe agreed that Italian terme were the most effective. K. Dorohostajsky was advised in 1608, by doctors from an Austrian resort, to go to Padua, as the springs there were much stronger, and the chance of a cure was higher (Seredyka 2010, 144).

Not only was there a geographical connection between regions, there was also a clear seasonality of the treatments, which usually took place in late spring and summer, with treatments usually taking from two to three months. M. K. Radziwiłł spent two months from August to September in Yavoriv in 1576 (Radziwiłł 1990, 35), and three months from June to September in Lucca and Pozzuoli in 1580 (Kempa 2000, 330). There is no single explanation for this pattern of visits as the early modern nobility did not have modern work or leisure patterns. According to brochures the period from May to August was the best time to receive treatment, even though they do not go into details or explanations as to why. Possibly those months were selected according to the hippocratic four humours theory, which was elaborated through the surviving works of the Roman physician Claudius Galenus (AD 129– 200 / 216). This theory relied on the thought that every person had four humours – blood, yellow bile, black bile and phlegm – and posited that if any one of the humours were not intact sickness ensued. Consequently, the main principle of the treatment was to maintain the balance of the four humours, using processes such as blood-letting, sweating and vomiting, amongst others. The humours were believed to exist in cycles according to the seasons and constellations, revealing the strong influence of astrology on the theory (Hope 2014, 72), so different diseases were seen as being caused by the imbalance of the different humours, and they were treated accordingly (Pietrzak 2012,32). For example, over-saturation of phlegm, which was associated with coldness of winter, would be treated with the application of hot substances. Many patients from Grand Duchy of Lithuania travelled to spas for the treatment of arthritis, gout, headaches or stomach problems which it was believed could be treated through the hot springs.

These were not the only reasons why people might opt for treatment during the spring and summer months. Logistical factors had to be taken into account as an important part in travelling. The best time to travel in the early modern period was, unsurprisingly, summer and winter, when the ground would most likely be solid underfoot. The journey from the Grand Duchy of Lithuania to Italy could take up to a month, depending on the urgency of the patient, and most resorts were in mountainous regions, relatively difficult to reach. Almost every traveller to a spa mentions the mountains and the sense of gloominess while traveling through them. Teodor Billewicz even compared the Italian Alps with hell and mentioned that after the mountainous road section you felt like you had entered the heavens (Billewicz 2003, 51).

Reflections on treatment and its success in personal writings

If you want your wife to conceive, send her to the baths, and stay at home yourself (Italian proverb) (Palmer 1990, 19).

Interest in 'balneology' began to rise in sixteenth-century with a questioning of the Galenic attitude towards 'medical waters' (Palmer 1990, 14). A. Bacci suggested it was a serious form of treatment that should be supervised only by professionals as it was something requiring knowledge and practice. Therefore, it was important to analyse the waters themselves – their mineral content, the features of each element, etc.– and their impact on the human body – heating, cooling, drying, purging, softening etc. (Palmer 1990, 16). Of course, the analysis part of this equation was extremely complex and every physician tried to do their research in their own way, leading to results that could be somewhat different. Most analysis was based on determining the colour of the water, its taste, the distillation of the water and processes to determine the presence of the four main elements – earth, water, air and fire (Coley 1982, 123-125). At least in theory it was believed that physicians had to know both the ailment of the patient and the nature of the waters in specific hot spring resorts in order to pick the right treatment. Failure to do so correctly could prove to do more harm than good. T. Billewicz while traveling through Teplice, described hot springs that he had seen and mentioned that they could prove very harmful for some people, especially for thin people (Billweicz 2003, 31) as it was thought that hot springs could prove too efficacious on thin people.

The analyses made by physicians went straight on brochures of specific resorts, so that M. Butler mentions that doctors in Abano Terme gave him a little book on the treatments that could be given there (Butler 2014, 294). This booklet or brochure also included examples of successful treatments, acting as an advertisement for the variety of different ailments that could be treated in the resort with different medical methodologies.

At the same time that physicians were focused on the curative properties of hot springs, others were much more interested in the social life and scandal of what happened in the resorts. Throughout the period a large number of comic texts were written, often with sexual connotations (Gomez 2000, 228), and these helped build interest in the social aspects of the resorts. It has been noted that resorts in different countries varied in their organisation, so that Italian baths were, for example, segregated by gender, while the Swiss resort at Leukerbad was mixed (Palmer 1990, 19). French resorts were very strict in the application of timetables, with clear regimes of leisure time, medical procedures and nutrition, which had to be designated by the consulting physicians (Brockliss 1990, 43-44). But sometimes there was a circularity in the social life of a resort and the curative properties of the springs. The springs at Aachen were considered particularly effective in treating venereal disease, especially syphilis, despite the irony of Aachen being, until the nineteenth-century, a major centre for prostitution, which often caused those diseases (Czelllec; Petrea 2013, 68).

Although patients from Grand Duchy of Lithuania travelled to improve their health, they could not leave out the social element from their accounts. In 1740 the Bishop of Vilnius, J. Sapieha, was advised by doctors to go to Aachen for treatment of rheumatism and gout. Once there he was surprised to find men and women bathing together, and he noted that the women were exceptionally lightly clothed (Kucharski 2013, 39). Other writers were not so much concerned about these particular matters, but they did notice that people went into the waters fully dressed, even though the water would ruin their clothes (Billewicz 2003, 32). A few travellers also tried to explain the dynamics of social class at the resorts. In most cases the baths were a privilege for wealthy people, but in a few places poor people could attend for treatment (Palmer 1990, 22), M. Butler mentioned, while visiting Abano Terme for the very first time, that there was an area for common people, as he called them, located in a small separate annex (Butler 2014, 282).

The treatments themselves could involve very complex processes, and included not only the water procedures. A. Bacci notes that a positive frame of mind, good rest and physical activity were extremely important for good results (Tubergen & Linden 2002, 274). The doctor L. Rowzee went even further in his book The Queens Wells: That is a Treatise of the Nature and Virtues of Tunbridge Water (1632) by advising patients to leave melancholy at home as it was the enemy of a successful treatment (Gomez 2000, 225). To aid this he suggested his patients engage in physical and social activity. In all this, different resorts based their treatment methodologies more or less on the same philosophy, and the daily life of patients during the treatment was quite similar throughout the period, regardless of country or resort.

The nobility of Grand Duchy of Lithuania was not very eloquent in writing about the treatment regimes and descriptions were especially vague in their correspondence. It is known that S. Dorohostajska discovered that she had arthritis having arrived at a spa to recover from tuberculosis (Seredyka 2010, 57). M. Butler spent one month in Abano Terme hoping to overcome leg pain, possibly gout, (Butler 2014, 536), while M. K. Radziwiłł Sierotko sought frequently to improve his health as he was often sick and would seek out any kind of medicine (Kempa 2000, 87). The most elaborate Lithuanian descriptions of the treatment process were given by two noblemen, M. Butler and J. Sapieha. They each left diaries which described the organisation of the daily life for patients in hot spring resorts. These show that there were two main courses of treatment – bathing in the waters and drinking the water. M. Butler appears to have had more bathing procedures, while J. Sapieha focused his descriptions on the procedure for drinking the mineral water.

There were several options for how a person could take the bathing treatment – in baths at the specific resort, or at their own temporary residence. Of course, the latter option was much more expensive, but M. Butler decided to have the water brought to his residence, with a servant carrying water from the resort every morning for him to bathe in. Usually his day would start with bathing and be followed by the consumption of mineral water, the quantity of which grew gradually greater as the days went by. From several cups a day, his intake grew to around 20 cups per day. Often Butler would divide his daily treatment into two parts by going to the church in the middle of them and making sure he only drank his daily dose of mineral water after attending the church service (Butler 2014, 328).

As has been mentioned, J. Sapieha was more interested in the consumption of the mineral waters than he was in bathing. He wrote: 'We started [drinking] medical water of Aachen, drinking 12 glasses of it on an empty stomach in the morning, [and] 15 glasses in the middle of the day without any preparation' (Kucharski 2013, 38). Sapieha was very precise on the quantities consumed and the effects so that on one occasion he wrote that he felt a 'noise in his head'. This was accompanied by a feeling of breaking bones and inner fever, which resulted in his doctor prescribing him at least 10 glasses of water per day, or even more, for recovery. Sapieha also added that for the full treatment he went every day to the public hall and only in the evening would he take the baths (Kucharski 2013, 39).

Even though physiological effects of taking waters was an important part of the treatments, it was also the one that led to the most humour in diaries and satires. One patient visiting Epsom in 1663 wrote in his diary: 'We drunk each of us two pots and walked away – it being very pleasant to see how everybody turns up his tail, here one and there another, in a bush, and the women in their Quarters the like' (Gomez 2000, 230). In 'A poem on the New Wells at Islington', published in 1684, the physiological effects of the waters was also stressed:

> How does your waters pass to day? Says Jenney,
> I've drank six Pints that are well worth of Guinney,
> They come so freely from and so cool,
> I vow to you this is the seventh Stool (Gomez 2000, 230).

From a researcher's point of view, it is sad that Lithuanian patients were not so very interested in describing this somewhat humiliating part of their treatment. They appreciated far more activities such as strolls in the parks, gardens and palaces. Patients had lived socially active lives during the treatment – visiting friends and acquaintances, or organising little parties for themselves. For example, dining with other Polish and Lithuanian noblemen is often mentioned in the diary of M. Butler. All kept up the act of correspondence, in part because they tended to be active in the political life of the Grand Duchy of Lithuania, and even when in weak health there was a need for them to maintain communication with political allies and members of their families.

As Lithuanians were not very keen on explaining the treatment routines and detailed medical procedures that they received at resorts it is difficult to know whether they were successful. Obviously they travelled with hope and the expectation that they would get better, and it is only occasionally that a patient confesses that their condition did not improve. An exception to this is A. S. Radziwiłł, who travelled to Teplice with his wife, writing that its waters 'were not effective neither for me nor for my wife' (Radziwiłł 1980, 392). In the case of K. Dorohostajsky, who went to different resorts six times in a seventeen-year period, it is hard to tell whether he was desperate for a cure, or whether the hot springs really helped him, but he wrote on occasion that his health got even worse after some treatments and it looked like nothing could help. He described feeling dizzy, and noted that he had a high fever (Seredyka 2010). Despite this, some cures were reported. In September 1605, Dorohostajsky wrote to M. K. Radziwiłł Sierotko that the condition of his wife had improved. Her colour and vitality had returned: 'She had strengthened her nerves and vincula resolute [joints were loosened], and she walked almost good, and that could manage [her] limbs' (Seredyka 2010,57).

If attitudes towards hot springs were not always positive it was perhaps due to occasional deaths during treatment. The author of the M. Butler diary left a note on 9 August 1780 on rumours that had came from Grand Duchy of Lithuania: '[Mister Commissioner] wrote, that Mister Postmaster in Koenigsberg told that Mister [Butler], had died, God give him as many decades to live as many times he was mortified' (Butler 2014, 418). The Bishop of Vilnius, B. Woyna, also died whilst seeking the curative powers of water treatment, in his case in Padua, a fact even noted on his memorial stone in the Cathedral at Vilnius:

> Vilnius Bishop Benedict Woyna wanted to be buried
> In this grave [….]
> Finally,
> When he was planning to gain strength for his weak body
> He came to Italian waters. God of life and death
> Was preparing infinite life for him
> Instead of temporary one, with mediation of death,

And he – honoured for faith and country, in old age and weak health,
was called for the end of misery in Padua in 1615.

A similar fate befell the Bishop of Samogitia, M. Pac, who died in Padua, aged 56. He began by seeking treatment in Austria, before moving on to Padua, where he resigned from his episcopal duties and died in 1624.

Overall the Nobility of Grand Duchy of Lithuania was not very forthcoming about the treatment or its success, but in general it appears they were more skeptical than satisfied by the efficacy of the hot springs. Only a small number of them had full confidence in doctors, even when they carried out the doctors' recommendations very closely.

Conclusions

The nobility of the Grand Duchy of Lithuania were frequent visitors to hot spring resorts. Interest in them began to grow in the 16th century and they attracted the wealthy part of society that could afford to travel to the resorts and take this type of treatment. The nobility was also well educated, and so trips to hot spring resorts were relatively well-documented in diaries and correspondence.

Even though there were many different possible regions to visit for water treatments, only few were distinctly popular among the noblemen: Jelenia Góra in modern-day Poland; Teplice and Karlovy Vary in modern-day Czech Republic; a number of resorts in modern-day Germany (Aaachen); and several of the Italian terme (Abanno, Lucca and Pozzuoli). The decision making process on where to seek treatment was not clarified by the nobility itself, and it is likely there was no single reason. Italian terme had a quality 'brand', as they were recommended by physicians, and it was believed they were more effective. Others were probably chosen because of the distance, with Jelenia Góra much closer than other resorts, and possibly also because it was less expensive. Treatment seasonality was also a factor, with the late spring-summer months being recommended, even though it was possible to go all year round. Gallenic theory suggested that spring and summer was the most effective and appropriate period for the treatment, and this tied into the fact that the summer period was much better logistically, due to the generally better road conditions.

Lithuanian patients were not very forthcoming when talking about the details of the treatments they received, possibly because they were too personal, or considered unsuitable to share in correspondence. Yet it is clear that they had the same treatments as other visitors to the resorts and, like other visitors, they shared many of the same responses to the resorts - from the shock over social arrangements, such as men and women bathing together, or excitement about the environment. The Lithuanians tended to be obedient patients when it came to carrying out their doctors' orders, whether it was the regime for bathing, drinking the necessary amount of water, or taking exercise. In this it is clear that patients were usually happy about the arrangements in the resort, and to some extent about the treatment that they were getting. Indeed, many came back several times. But not all patients saw the treatments as worthwhile, with some even noting their conditions seemed to get worse. Overall Lithuanian society was not against the hot spring resorts, but it is fair to say that they were sceptical about their value, an attitude that was only reinforced by occasional reports of deaths, albeit through natural causes, rather than the treatment itself, during visits to spa resorts.

Reference Sources

- Archiwum domu Radziwiłłów: listy ks. M. K. Radziwiłła Sierotki, Jana Zamoyskiego, Lwa Augustynia, Urszula. 2014. Testamenty ewangelików reformowanych w Wielkim Księstwie Litewskim. Warszawa: Semper.
- Bilevičius, T. 2003. Kelionės vokiečių, čekų ir italų žeme dienoraštis. Vilnius. http://www.epaveldas.lt/recordText/LNB/C1B0003021909/T.Bilevicius_Keliones_vokieciu_italu_ir_ceku_zeme_dienorastis.pdf?exId=317117&seqNr=5
- Brockliss, L. 1990. 'The Development of the Spa in Seventeenth-century France'. *Medical History*, 10: 23-47.
- Butleris, M. 2014. Butlerio kelionės į Italiją ir Vokietiją 1779-1780 dienoraštis. Vilnius: Vilniaus universiteto leidykla.
- Coley, N. G. 1982. 'Physicians and chemical analysis of mineral waters in Eighteenth-century England'. *Medical History*, 26 (2): 123-144.
- Czellecz B. and D. Petrea. 2013. 'Mineral Water For Treatments: Summarized presentation of the Bathing Culture'. *Studia UBB Geographia*, LVIII(1): 63-74.
- Epitaphy for Benedikt Woyna. http://www.katedra.lt/epitafijos/22/
- Gomez, L. M. J. 2002. 'Trotting to the waters: Seventeenth century spas and cultural landscapes'. In *Sederi XI: Revista de la Sociedad Espanola de Studios Renascentistas Ingelses*. Huelva, Universidad de Huelva
- Javier. 2014. 'The Four Humors Theory'. *ESSAI*, 12 (Spring): 72-74.
- Kempa, T. 2000. *Mikolaj Krzysztof Radziwill Sierotka (1549-1616)*, Warszawa: Semper.
- Kucharski, A. 2013. 'Sarmaci u wód. Podróż biskupa Józefa Sapiehy oraz Ignacego i Jana Lopacińskich do cieplic akwizgrańskich w 1740 r.'. In *Klio. Czasopismo poświęcone dziejom Polski I powszechnym 1643-1891*, 24 (1): 17–45.
- Pacevičius, A. 2014. 'Pratarmė', *Butlerio kelionės į Italiją ir Vokietiją 1779-1780 dienoraštis*, 7-14. Vilnius: Vilniaus universiteto leidykla.
- Palmer, R. 1990. ''In this our lightye and learned tyme': Italian baths in the era of the Renaissance,' *Medical History*, 10:14-22.
- Pietrzak, J. 2012. ''Jaka woda pomocna?' – uzdrowiskowe wojaże rodziny Sobieskich na tle wyprawim współczesnych i wiedzy medycznej'. *Acta universitatis Lodziensis, Follia Historica*, 88: 17-42.
- Radvila, M.K.N. 1990. *Kelionė Į Jeruzalę*. Vilnius: Mintis.
- Radziwiłł, A.S. 1980. *Pamiętniki o dziejach w Polsce* (1647–1656). Vol. 3. Warszawa: PIW.

- Seredyka, J. 2010. *Kunigaikštytė ir plikbajoris Zofija Radvilaitė – Dorohostaiska ir Stanisławas Tymińskis.* Vilnius: Vilniaus Pedagoginio Universiteto Leidykla.
- Tereškinas, A. 2002. 'Bajoriškojo 'aš' retorika XVII a. Lietuvos Didžiojoje Kunigaikštystėje'. In *Tipas ir individas Lietuvos Didžiosios Kunigaikštystės kultūroje*, 171-200. Vilnius: Vytauto Didžiojo Universiteto Leidykla.
- Tubergen, van A., and, S. van der Linden. 2002. 'A Brief History of Spa Therapy'. *Annals of the Rheumatic Diseases.* 61 (November): 273-275.
- Vaišnoravičius, J.K. 2009. *Kelionė po Europą su jaunuoju kunigaikščiu Ostrogiškiu:* 1667-1669 metų dienoraštis. Vilnius: Lietuvos Literatūros tautosakos institutas.

The Setting of Shakespeare's Othello: Its Symbolic Significance

Jamal Subhi Ismail Nafi' (Al-Quds University, Palestine)

INTRODUCTION
Historical Background

BOTH EXTERNAL AND internal evidence indicates that Shakespeare's play Othello must have been composed about the year 1604. It must have been written after Hamlet (1603). It is mentioned in the Revels book, which records that a play called Othello was staged in 1604. Its workmanship also indicates that it must have been composed about this year.

It is a well-established fact that Shakespeare did not invent his own plots. He borrowed his plots from a variety of sources. But what he borrowed, he transformed into something new and far superior. Othello is no exception in this respect. Its story is borrowed from a novel The Moor of Venice written by a Sicilian novelist by the name Giraldi Cinthio. Even though in the main outline Shakespeare has followed the original, he has handled it with perfect freedom. He has omitted several incidents which he could not utilize and added a few characters—Barbantio, Roderigo, Montano and others—all for well-defined dramatic purposes. He wove the threads of the plot far more closely together than did Cinthio, making Iago responsible for Cassio's disgrace, and Iago's wife for the final resolution of the intrigue. And he quickened the speed of the action until, once the plot is fairly started, it seems to sweep before us in one unbroken succession of events. In this way, he imparted speed and intensity to the action.

Othello is a tragedy with a number of distinctive features of its own. It is in many ways the most perplexing of the tragedies and the most productive of conflicting critical interpretations. It is generally accepted as one of Shakespeare's great tragedies. Bradley (1905) is of the opinion that it was the tragedy written immediately after Hamlet, according to him, '[d]espite its lingering exposition and its division between the affairs in Venice and the later events in Cyprus, it has an almost classical unity of construction without any subordinate theme' (Bradley 1905, 201). As we see, setting and theme cannot be separated, for setting is linked to theme. The locations of a story are important in the sense that they enable the author to communicate his ideas clearly, when setting is well-chosen. The subject of the play is narrowly domestic, involved only in a marginal way with the affairs of the state. Unlike Hamlet and King Lear, it has but three characters of major interest. Hazlitt (1818) noted that few of its lines have passed into popular quotations, and the main parts of the text contain characterisation, and this suggests the writer's skilful handling of characters in his plays, especially in Othello.

In the characterisation of Othello, Iago and Desdemona, Johnson (1765) finds 'such proofs of Shakespeare's skill in human nature, as is vain to seek in any modern writer' (Johnson 1765, 11). While Drakakis (1980) is of the view that Othello is one of Shakespeare's most unusual heroes in the sense that he is a 'black' man with a 'perfect soul.' In this way the theme of appearance and reality is stressed from the very beginning. So long as his perfect soul rules his actions, he is the noble Moor, but once he falls a victim to his passions then this relationship is reversed, and he seems to be as black in his soul, as he seems to be in appearance, this contrast in the character of Othello correlates to the contrast between Venice and Cyprus. Bradley's view is that Othello 'is by far the most romantic figure among Shakespeare's heroes' (Bradley 1905, 200). What makes Bradley hold this opinion is that Othello has not been born and bred in familiar, prosaic England, but comes from a remote, wonderland-the distant, unknown Morocco. He has always lived a life of adventure and romance. He has travelled to distant lands and strange are the tales of his travels which he relates; this made Desdemona fall in love with him. She was attracted by his adventures, and being an adventurer, he was chosen to travel to Cyprus to fight the Turks, for he is used to travelling to distant lands. And Cyprus seems a place that fits his character. There, he can act wildly and adventurously, but Cyprus, a distant island, separated from what is called civilization had an adverse effect on his character; it's there that Iago manages to convince him that Desdemona is unfaithful to him, and thus brings about the break-up of their marriage. While Venice, a city inhabited by the whites, made Othello exceptional with regard to his colour, and is therefore connected to the theme of race, and appearance versus reality.

Shakespeare's Violation of the Classical Rules

According to Johnson, Shakespeare's neglect of the unities of time and place 'is not really a fault' (Johnson 1765, 12). In his disregard of these two unities, Shakespeare believed to have violated a law which had been established and recognised jointly by dramatists and critics. What Aristotle meant by the three unities of action, time and place is that a play should contain one main plot, instead of two plots; unity of time limits the time of action to 12 or 24 hours (a single revolution of the sun); while unity of place dictates that the action of the play should take place in one location, and there should be no shift of scene (Butcher, 1905).

But Johnson defends Shakespeare in this matter. Shakespeare's history plays do not, of course, come under the purview of the law of the three unities because of their very nature, and because time and place must keep changing in plays of this kind. In his other plays, Shakespeare has largely preserved the unity of action. Although, being the dramatist of nature, Shakespeare does not unfold any hidden design of the story in his plays; his story has generally a beginning, middle, and an end, as required by Aristotle. There is a logical connection between incident and incident, and the conclusion follows naturally. Some incidents may be superfluous, but the plot as a whole develops gradually and naturally, and the end of the play marks also the end of our expectation. While the nature of Othello requires the shift of location (scene) to suggest the shift in Othello-Desdemona relationship. Hatred and love is what characterises this relationship. It's in Venice where their love flourishes, and it is in Cyprus that this same love withers.

Concluding this part of the discussion, Johnson believes that the unities of time and place are not essential to a good play, if the author copies life and instructs nature in his plays. If we consider Shakespeare's Othello, we realise that the author has violated the unity of place by making the action of this play extend over two countries, Venice and Cyprus. This cannot be considered a fault either, for Shakespeare aimed at using these two places symbolically and to show how characters' behaviors are influenced by setting, or how a setting might give importance to a certain character like that of Othello, who is considered important because he travelled to Cyprus to fight against the Turks. As for the violation of the unity of action, Shakespeare, as a realist dramatist, mingled between emotions and did not separate tragedy from comedy, in a comedy, you find tragic scenes, and vice versa. This act on the part of the dramatist imparted realism to his plays.

This paper focuses on Shakespeare's play Othello with a special reference to its setting, some major themes and characters are also emphasised in order to highlight the relationship between these elements, and to see how they affect and are affected by each other. The analytical and psychological approaches are adopted throughout. The setting of the play has a symbolic significance, and characters' actions are determined to some extent by where the actions take place. Venice and Cyprus are the two locations where the action takes place. Certain things are tested in these two places, and one cannot deny the fact that characters are very much influenced by the place(s) where they live.

DISCUSSION

The Setting of the Play and the Dramatist's Concern

In Othello the dramatist is not concerned with current political affairs as he was in Hamlet. He has distanced the action of the play by making distant Venice and Cyprus its setting. According to Skiba et al. 'The setting of Othello must have seemed very exotic to Shakespeare's audience in London' (Skiba et al. 2004, 16). Venice is where the action is set in Act I, while the following acts are set in Cyprus, which is today a part of modern Italy. Venice is linked with Cyprus because the latter was controlled by the earlier economically, added Skiba. This setting can be said is related to the theme of conflict in the play, the conflict between barbarity and civilization, barbarity represented by the Muslim Turks and civilization represented by the Christian Venetians, who considered the earlier people as their bitter enemy.

Shane, Kupis and Liang argue that 'The literary sociologist regards all literature as being only a product of the writer's conscious creative mind or based upon certain social and political creative mind or based upon certain social and political determinants of his particular cultural setting' (Shane, Kupis and Liang 2015, 11). This dichotomy can be applied to Shakespeare's Othello in the sense that Shakespeare was inspired to write the play by the wars between Venice and Turkey which took place in the 16th. Century.

Othello is not a historical figure, but the Turkish attack on Cyprus is a historical event. In 1487 Cyprus came to Venice from the Turks by right of conquest. Ever afterwards, the Turks tried to regain it, till it was taken by them during the reign of their glorious King Salim II, about the year 1570. We learn from the play that there was a junction of the Turkish fleet at Rhodes, for the invasion of Cyprus: that it came sailing to Cyprus, and then went to Rhodes, there met another squadron, and then resumed its way to Cyprus. These are real historical events which happened when Mustapha, Salim's General, attacked Cyprus in May 1570. Therefore, this is the date of the action of the play. Dispatching Othello to fight against the Turks in Cyprus could be explained by the fact that this man can act barbarically; therefore, his character can be linked to the setting where he finds himself. Kale declares that 'Iago's poison serves only to evoke Othello's innate barbarism' (Kale 2015, 2). Therefore this barbarism, represented by Othello, is placed by Shakespeare in the right place in order for it to sprout and choke the one that harbours it.

Double-Time Scheme

Shakespeare has followed in Othello what has been called a double-time scheme. There is both a long time and a short time. The action of the first three scenes is continuous throughout one night, after which an unspecified interval allows for the voyage from Venice to Cyprus. The three ships all arrive on the same day, some time before five o'clock, when Othello's proclamation is read, and between ten and eleven, Iago involves Cassio in the quarrel with Roderigo. By the end of this scene (II, iii), it is morning and Iago proceeds without sleep through the following day until the attempted murders of Roderigo and Cassio, which take place between twelve and one at night, and the final scene is enacted later the same night. This suggests that there is not much time dedicated to the shift of location; therefore, actions need to be swift. It is impossible to suppose any interval, of more than one hour or two, during the whole of the action of Acts II to V, without doing violence to the effect in the theatre and to Shakespeare's intention.

Superimposed on this continuous action, however, are many references designed to give the impression of a much larger period of time during which Desdemona's supposed adultery might have occurred, for it clearly could not have taken place within the period represented by the play. A few of the more important references will suffice as illustrations of the long time. Emilia, finding the handkerchief, says: 'My wayward husband hath a hundred time / Woo'd me to steel it' (3.3.292-94). Later in the same scene, Othello cries:

> What sense had I of her stol'n hours of lust?
> I saw't not, though it not, it harm'd not me,
> I slept the next night well, was free and merry;
> I found not Cassio's kisses on her lips. (3.3.338-41)

Again in the following scene, Bianca accuses Cassio, who had arrived from Venice only the previous day, of keeping away from her for 'seven days and nights' (3.4.174) When Othello is fallen into his trance, Iago tells Cassio 'This is his second fit, he had done yesterday' (4.1.62) although he cannot possibly mean the 'yesterday' of their arrival in Cyprus; and in the final scene even the language of hyperbole cannot justify Othello's charge: 'That she with Cassio hath the act of shame / A thousand times committed' (5.2.244-45). Here Cyprus creates a kind of confusion in the minds of character, and this is one of the adverse effects that it has on characters.

According to Wakefield (1968): The employment of both a 'short' time-scheme, essential for the fulfilment of Iago's aims before his plot revealed, as it would certainly be of any delay were admitted, and for a 'long' time-scheme without which his allegations of adultery would be ludicrous, has been considered a fault. But it is not a fault in the context of Shakespeare's theatre, and although this deliberate ambiguity is unique in his plays, his treatment of dramatic time and that of his contemporaries, was always somewhat vague and flexible, simply because theatrical convention allowed it to be so. It had many advantages and caused the audience no uneasiness (Wakefield 1968, 30).

It is not to be supposed that Shakespeare failed to give Othello a universality that he had aimed at and achieved elsewhere. Wakefield

(1968) is of the view that the theme of the play is universal because of the intensely passionate character of the play itself, and by the need for Iago to act swiftly before his machinations are revealed and disclosed to others.

The double-time scheme, important in this rapid movement, is unique in Shakespeare. No part is played by supernatural forces, or by mental disturbance. Othello's fit, of what Iago calls epilepsy, is a device for arranging Iago's later conversation with Cassio, to be observed but not overheard by Othello; and for 'showing the awful domination of the Moor's passion over his body and soul' (Campbell 1930, 16). No special effect of setting or of the elements is used to heighten the dramatic intensity; the events are more terrible in the sense that they occur in ordinary surroundings. There is little wit and humor. Finally, there is no other hero whose tragic fall is contrived, whether by one man or several. Claudius' attempts on Hamlet's life, the cruelty of Goneril and Regan to Lear, and Macduff's over-throwing of Macbeth, are each of entirely different order of things. As a consequence, Othello is the only hero who has to command the audiences' attention in rivalry with another, added Wakefield (1968).

Othello as a Domestic Tragedy

A domestic tragedy is a tragedy which deals with the married common people. It shows that jealousy or unfaithfulness or any other fault on the part of anyone of the married couple, leads to the disintegration of family life, and it results in much suffering. In this connection, Iago, in Act III, Scene iii, utters few words that warn against this disease called jealousy; he says: 'O, beware, my lord, of jealousy! / It is the green-ey'd monster which doth mock / The meat it feeds on' (165-67). Jealousy here is likened to a monster that feeds on its prey; Othello may not have understood the connotation of these words, but he did understand them when it was too late.

Othello has certain features of a domestic tragedy. Its theme is also the impact of jealousy on the domestic life of Othello and Desdemona. Othello is not jealous by nature, but he is made jealous by the machinations of Iago. Iago, through his machinations, makes Othello jealous of Cassio and suspicious of Desdemona. He begins to doubt his innocent wife of having immoral relations with Cassio.

Kitishat and Alzu'bi (2013) hold the opinion that 'Othello is seen as not deserving the noble fair Desdemona because he does not know how to deal with Venetian women, mainly because he 'is not Italian, nor even European; that he is totally ignorant of the thoughts and customary morality of Venetian women' (Bradley 1905, 186, as cited in Kitishat & Alzu'bi 2013, 43). Another hateful quality that Othello develops is his jealousy. 'Jealousy is another negative representation of the Oriental figures in general and the Arabic in particular' (Kitishat and Alzu'bi 2013, 43). This hateful quality can be considered normal among Arabs, but it is dangerous and has dire consequences when it surpasses its limits. Although Othello is a black Moor, he is still considered worthy of Desdemona because of his high rank in society. He suffers hellish tortures; and, spurred on by Iago, ultimately destroys, first, Desdemona and then himself.

Ragland (1888) points out that: As in Lear the play turns upon the breaking of the tie, which binds father and children, in Macbeth, the tie which binds subject and sovereign, so in Othello we have the breaking of the tie between husband and wife, of the most sacred of all sacred ties. There is also the breaking of the tie between father and daughter. (n.)

Othello may have the impact of jealousy on married life as its theme, but it differs from a domestic tragedy in many respects. For one thing, Othello is not a common individual. He comes from a royal family and is an able General, considered indispensable for the defense of the State of Venice. He is appointed to the post of the Governor of Cyprus, and on his ability hangs the fate of the nation. He is not a common individual as the hero of a domestic tragedy usually is.

Not merely is Othello placed highly in society, he also has exceptional qualities of head and heart. Even his enemies acknowledged that he is of a frank, generous and noble nature. He is a courageous and skilled warrior. By his tales of travel, he is able to win the heart of Desdemona, a woman of exceptional beauty, much sought after by the gallants of her own country. Her decision to wed a black Moor is an act of disobedience at that time when girls were expected to obey their fathers. Rahmani and Khodamoradpour commented on her decision to marry Othello saying: 'Her decision to marry Othello is both a violation of her father's expectations and those of her society that disapproves of marriage between different races and ethnic groups, i.e. by marrying Othello secretly' (Rhamani and Khodamoradpour 2015, 24). Thus it can be deduced that there was a kind of discrimination in Elizabethan England which prohibited this kind of marriage. Desdemona's marriage to Othello aggravates the situation, especially for the fact that her father doesn't approve of him. Mutlu stresses the fact that 'Desdemona's marriage to a man that he does not approve is more acceptable than her marriage to a black Moor' (Mutlu 2013, 137). Later on in the play, Iago uses her violation of patriarchal rules to manipulate Othello and give the impression that his wife may prove unfaithful to him, in this connection he says: 'Look to her, Moor, if thou hast eyes to see. She hath deceived her father and may thee' (1.3.294-95).

Moreover, the Moor's marriage to a Venetian may have incurred the wrath of some characters in the play. By marrying Desdemona, according to Ruma 'Othello incurs the wrath of Brabantio, Iago, and Roderigo. And if it were not for the war imminent between Venice and the Turks at this particular moment, it is doubtful whether the senate of Venice will bless the marriage' (Ruma 2014, 35). It's only the need for Othello to protect his religion and to fight against the Turks that made the senators of the state forgive him or at least not act against his deed by marrying the fairest Venetian. In this regard, it is worthy to quote the words of Ruma who states that the State of Venice 'depends mostly on the services of mercenaries in defending itself against external enemies. That clearly explains how Othello, Cassio, and Iago find themselves in the Venetian militia that is sent to fight the Turks in Cyprus' (Ruma 2014, 36). These three characters found themselves a place in a city that needed them for protection and support.

Therefore, we get astonished when Othello realises that his wife might have been unfaithful and is hiding something from him. Adade-Yeboah and Amankwaah are of the view that 'His noble speech which he uses to woo Desdemona deserts him and his fury betrays his emotional imbalance' (Adade-Yeboah and Amankwaah 2012, 121). This sudden change in the character of the noble Moor is unexpected, especially when his love for Desdemona is deep and should be unshakable. Othello is honest, frank and confiding. He can command and inspire confidence, and he is conscious that he can do so. When such an exceptional individual falls, his fall produces the pity and terror proper to true tragedy, for Catharsis is best created when a man of eminence, but has a tragic flaw, falls.

In a Domestic Tragedy, the action of the drama moves on a common everyday level. The characters are near to us and so is the action. There is no remoteness and no suggestion of mysterious fatal forces working against mankind. All this cannot be said of Othello. Its action does not take place in familiar England, but we are transported to romantic Venice and from there to the remote, unknown Cyprus. Although there are no ghosts or witches as in other tragedies, there is never the less a very strong sense of some hidden forces, malignant and hostile. Iago, the embodiment of Evil, appears in the very first scene, and his appearance with all his evil designs fills us with foreboding. Djundjung states the reasons behind Iago's machinations, saying 'At first, his grudge against them is based on his lack of promotion, then on sexual jealousy and finally on the belief that his own made up affair between Cassio and Desdemona is true' Djundjung 2002, 4). The impression of some fatal force working against the hero and driving him to an inevitable doom is further strengthened by the preponderance of the Chance element. Traub (1992) is of the opinion that sexuality might be the predator which compelled Othello to murder Desdemona and bring about an end to their enduring love.

Therefore, it can be assumed that Othello is unlike other domestic tragedies set in England, it is a tragedy set in far off lands which affect the behaviour of characters. Had the play been set in England, the action would have taken a different course, and Othello's marriage to Desdemona would have not ended the way it ended in remote Cyprus.

The Operation of Fatal Forces

In a Shakespearean tragedy, the suffering and calamities do not simply happen; they are the result of the action of men. Men are thus the authors of their own destiny. The tragedy arises from action caused by character, or character issuing action. The dictum 'character is destiny' (Taylor 2001, 17) is true of a Shakespearean tragedy also, though only in a limited sense. The final impression which a tragedy must create is that of an awe and terror. Hence the final catastrophe cannot be attributed solely to the action of the hero, for in that case the impression would be different. Other factors, besides character, are, therefore, always made responsible to some extent for the tragic fate of the hero. Shakespearean conception of tragedy involved, over and above character, the suggestion of fatal forces operating on the action of mankind.

The Handkerchief Episode: Its Crucial Role

In Othello this suggestion of fatal forces is created by chance happenings. While tragedy issues of the character of the hero, chance plays a prominent part in bringing about the fall of the hero. It intensifies the tragedy and fills the reader with fear and terror. At every turn of the road, they are made conscious that there are certain forces of powers working above and sending puny mortals to their doom. In the play, chance is at the very centre of the action, and the tragic action would not have been possible without its operation. Numerous instances can be sighted to illustrate the point. It is by chance that Desdemona drops her handkerchief and does not pick it up, in spite of its being her first present from Othello. It is also by chance that Emilia finds it. Iago seizes it from her hands and plants it in the room of Cassio. It is by chance that Othello sees it in his hands, and thus Iago succeeds in providing him with that ocular proof which is necessary for the success of his plot. Again, it is by chance that Cassio arrives on the scene when Othello is having a fainting fit. By a brain wave, Iago arranges the eavesdropping scene. It is again by chance that Bianca arrives at the proper moment and Othello is horrified to find that he has given the handkerchief to this whore. His passions grow uncontrollable and he decides then and there to murder Desdemona (Schlegel 1965), while Iago is to be the undertaker of Cassio. All these chance happenings have been introduced by the master craftsman in a way that they appear quite natural and proper to the occasion.

Chance: Its Crucial Role

Thus in the play chance events play a crucial role. That's why Herford remarks 'The great distinctive feature of the drama among the mature tragedies lies not in the hero, magnificent creation as he is, but in the external agency by which the tragic situation is brought about' (Herford 1920, 15). These words illustrate the idea that man is not a free agent, and that some chance happenings control his actions.

Brooke stresses the point that: The writer who devised all this, was in doubt, while he wrote, that any rational will or justice, or even a fixed destiny was at the helm of the universe; but a general unreason which one might call chance, and which made a mere muddle of the course of humanity or of our personal lives (Brooke 2013, 173).

Chance: Its Symbolic Significance

In short, chance is symbolic of fate or supernatural powers which govern the human destiny. There this supernatural power is shown to be in league with the villain. It favors him, helps him in his intrigues and thus brings about the downfall of the hero and heroine. Chance has not been assigned such a crucial role in any of the other great tragedies' (Greenblatt 1988, 29). Othello may have the impact of jealousy on married life as its theme, but it is not a domestic tragedy. It moves on a much higher plane, and its effect is Cathartic in the true sense of the word.

The Dual Setting

Othello is unique among Shakespearean tragedies in as much as its action is not all confined to a single place or to places which are near to one another. Its Act I takes place in Venice and then Act II moves on to Cyprus where the rest of the action takes place. This choice of setting by Shakespeare made 'Othello sees his blackness and his age as weaknesses in the cultural world of Venice/Cyprus. His self-deprecation is seen when he bemoans his blackness and age' (Rose n. d., 28). The following words from the play illustrate this point:

> Haply for I am black
> And have not those soft parts of conversation
> That chamberers have, or for I am declined
> Into the vale of years. (3.3.265-68)

There is no violation of the unity of atmosphere because the tumult and bustle of Act I is carried over to scene I of Act II, which takes place in Cyprus. Moreover, the marriage of Desdemona takes place in Venice, but it is tested with such horrible consequences in Cyprus. Elroy (1973, Chapter 1) is of the opinion that 'The world of Venice has its problems—impending war, midnight elopements, and outraged fathers —but it also has institutions capable of dealing with them' (5). Both Venice and Cyprus have symbolic significance. Venice symbolises civilized behaviour, law and order, while the reverse is symbolised by Cyprus. The point would become clear when both locations are examined in some detail.

Othello as an Elizabethan Tragedy

Before we consider Othello's setting, it is worthy to consider it with regard to being Elizabethan, not classic. The establishment of romantic drama in England was the work of Shakespeare's immediate predecessors known as the university wits (Kyd, Lyly, Greene, Peele, Marlowe, etc.) Shakespeare's plays follow the example set by these men. In other words, he is a romantic dramatist as distinguished from the classical dramatists of ancient Greece and Rome. Briefly speaking, the classical drama of antiquity was supposed to observe the following principles: First, it rigorously maintained a unity of subject and tone. As a result, it kept the spheres of tragedy and comedy entirely separate. A tragedy had to be a tragedy from first to last; it had to maintain the proper tragic pitch and no humorous episode was permitted in it. A comedy, on the other hand, had to be a comedy from first to last and no tragic element was allowed to enter into its composition. Second, there was little or no dramatic action on the stage. The incidents composing the plot took place off-stage and were reported to the audience in dialogue. Third, the three unities of time, place and action controlled the writing of drama. The entire story of a play had to be confined to a single day; the scene of the entire play remained the same throughout; the plot was to be one, and no sub-plots or minor episodes were permitted.

The Elizabethan drama of Shakespeare and his immediate predecessors departed from all the above principles. Romantic drama makes free use of variety in theme and tone, often mixing tragic and comic scenes in the same play. Romantic drama, again, is essentially a 'drama of action, nearly every incident of the play being exhibited on the stage' (Holloway 2005, 16). Romantic drama violates also the three unities. It allows the story to extend over months, and even years. It changes the scene as often as necessary, sometimes from one town or country to another. It employs sub-plots and under-plots, besides the central theme.

In light of the above, one can say that Shakespeare's Othello is purely romantic in the sense that it violates those principles, which were set by the ancient Greeks (Knight 1972). The play contains action that takes place on the stage. The action extends over a long period of time. It explores more than one theme; its action extends over two different locations, Venice and Cyprus. The two locations are different and each has a symbolic significance. Thus we can say that Othello is not confined to a single place, but its incidents and the action shifts from one place to another. An examination of the symbolic significance of the two locations would reveal the relationship between theme and setting and would show how characters are affected by place and environment.

Venice: Its Symbolic Significance

It is in Venice that the play opens. In the very opening scene, Iago and Roderigo awaken Barbantio and he says angrily: 'What, tell'st thou me of robbing? This is Venice / My house is not a grange' (1.1.101-102). Barbantio's surprise indicates that robbery and law-breaking in Venice are unusual. Even after having established to his limited satisfaction that Iago's and Roderigo's story has some truth in it, he goes to confront Othello with the Venetian law: 'To prison, till fit time / Of law; and course of direct session / Call thee to answer' (1.2.87-88). These words suggest the idea that law and order are so much respected in Venice.

In the scene which follows this confrontation, we observe the workings of the Venetian law at two levels. First, the Duke of Venice, in whose authority the law is vested, has to deal with an external threat to the stability and peace of Venice. But he methodologically gathers evidence from his advisers, weighs different possibilities and only sanctions action when he is certain of the direction in which the enemy fleet is traveling. Secondly, he deals with the internal problem of Barbantio's intemperate accusation, but he uses the same method allowing both Othello and Desdemona to speak before deciding on a course of action. That the Duke is persuaded by Othello's story is vital in establishing the hero's worth according to the standards of Venice: 'If virtue no delighted beauty lack / Your son-in-law is far more fair that black' (1.3.290-91).

According to Christofides the Cyprus wars also haunt Venice as represented in the play: at a time when Venice was host to a diversity of foreigners and its dominions were threatened by a more powerful empire, this deconstruction of the opposition between outsider and insider allegorizes the contemporary struggle between Venice and the Ottoman Empire for control of the eastern Mediterranean, a historical event that provides the backdrop for Othello (Christofides 2008, 85).

In Venice, at any rate, the more cynical view of human nature which Iago and Roderigo express, and to which Barbantio, and later Othello, fall prey, is held firmly in check by the judicious judgment of the Duke.

It is upon the foundation that Othello's 'reputation' rests, a point which receives an unexpectedly dramatic emphasis later in the play when the shocked ambassador, Lodovico, watches him abuse his wife in public:

> Is this the noble Moor, whom our full senate
> Call all in all sufficient? This the noble nature,
> Whom passion could not shake? Whose solid virtue
> The shot of accident, nor dart of chance,
> Could neither graze nor pierce. (4.1.286-90)

These words reflect the character of Othello, whom people think to be noble, solid, and strong, and who is never affected by passion or chance. The words create a kind of irony because they are in contrast with the reality when we watch him fall a prey to passion and abuse his wife in public. People never expected Othello to act or behave in that manner, but one can say that when passion is concerned, one can go insane and utter objectionable words.

Cyprus: Its Symbolic Significance

It is in Cyprus that the standards established in the opening Act of the play are tested. The Precarious Venetians hold on the view that Cyprus reflects a psychological battle waged in and around the character of Othello himself, as Iago begins to undermine his authority and judgment. The stormy uncertainty of Desdemona's and Othello's arrival in Cyprus, and the victory over the Turkish fleet, create a suitable atmosphere for the moral uncertainties to come. The tension in maintained since Cyprus is in a state of military readiness, in need of defence and demanding alertness and judgment from its defenders.

Mulu thinks that what makes Othello 'survive the Venetian society' (Multu 2013, 137) after his marriage, is that his being a professional and skilled warrior. This is seen when the Duke spares Othello of any penalty when he eloped with Desdemona. The fact behind this behavior is that 'they need Othello for the current situation of Cyprus' (Multu 2013, 137). Therefore, Othello's skills appealed to him and defended him when accused by others.

The first major weakness in the Venetian defense (which is, of course, the prologue to the exposure of a more serious weakness) occurs when the drunken Cassio forgets himself and thus threatens the security of Cyprus. His violation of the standards of 'courtesy' and 'duty' expected of him is recognised by Othello himself, who places Cassio's indiscretion in a larger, more prophetic context: 'Are we turn'd Turks' (2.3.168). This disturbance not only threatens the safety of the town, but it also challenges Othello's own self-control: 'Now by heaven / My blood begins my safer guides to rule' (2.3.249-50). This precarious psychological balance, reflecting as it does, the equilibrium which was maintained in Venice, is exactly what Iago intends to upset. Thus, what is respectable in Venice loses its respectability in Cyprus; the virtuous Desdemona is transformed into a common Venetian woman who, according to Iago, habitually deceives her husband.

Cassio's loss of self-control, directly attributable to the drink thrust upon him by Iago, has an important parallel in Othello's relinquishment of his 'safer guides', as he falls prey to a feeling of suspicion which has its origin in the same source, i.e. Iago. The issues which the brawl raises reappear, in a slightly different guise at the end of the play, at the point where the now fallen Othello fights with himself to regain his self-control. According to Drakakis 'The psychological conflict which he acts out at the end of the play is reflected in the conflict between Venice and Cyprus, the Venetian and the Turk, civilization and barbarity, which is central to the action and meaning of the play' (Drakakis 1980, 31).

Towards the end of the drama, Othello 'stabs himself to death with a dagger after killing his mistress in a crime of passion and honor' (Mahfouz 2012, 159). This heinous act is considered a sin, for no religion on earth allows an individual to take away his/her soul, but in Othello's case, this act might have been done as a kind of relief when life becomes unbearable or hard to live. Again, it is in Cyprus that Othello ends his whole life, which suggests that this setting best suits his violent and brutal act, and any other place would not serve as a good setting for a man of an extraordinary character to end his life.

Conclusion

As has been seen above, one can conclude that, as a romantic tragedy, Othello violates the classical rules for dramatic construction, but that cannot be considered a fault on the part of the dramatist, for he did it intentionally for the sake of realism. The study also shows how setting, character and theme are all related and are influenced and influence each other. Although the play deals with a domestic theme which is the married life of its hero and heroine and the jealousy the husband experiences, the play is different from domestic tragedies in the sense that Shakespeare was capable of imparting universality to his play by making it deal with the external affairs of Venice and Cyprus, which are used symbolically. Venice symbolises civilized behaviour, law and order, while the reverse is symbolised by Cyprus. The action of the play is divided between Venice and Cyprus, and that these two locations affect characters' behaviour and actions. And this shift of scene doesn't cause any violation of the unity of atmosphere because the tumult and bustle of Act I, is carried over to scene I of Act II, which takes place in Cyprus. Moreover the marriage of Desdemona takes place in Venice, but it is tested with such horrible consequences in Cyprus.

    Shakespeare seems to have selected these two cities because they are suitable for Othello's character and personality, and they are fit to explore the themes of heroism, domesticity and jealousy. Venice, as setting, creates the sense of discrimination and suggests the theme of race, while Cyprus, the less civilized, suggests the atmosphere of mystery and barbaric behaviour. The psychological conflict which Othello acts out at the end of the play is reflected in the conflict between the two places, Venice and Cyprus, the Venetian and the Turk, civilization and barbarity, which is central to the action and meaning of the play.

Reference Sources

- Adade-Yeboah, A. and A. S. Amankwaah. 2012. 'The Tragic Hero of the Post-Classical Renaissance'. *Studies in Literature and Language,* 5(3): 119-123.
- Butcher, S.H. trans. 1907. *The Poetics of Aristotle* (PROJECT GUTENBERG E-TEXT # 1974). (4th ed.). London: Macmillan.
- Bradley, A.C. 1905. *Shakespearean Tragedy: Lectures on Hamlet, Othello, King Lear, Macbeth.* 2nd ed. London: Macmillan.
- Brooke, S.A. 2013. *Ten More Plays of Shakespeare.* London: Forgotten Books. (Original work published 1932, London: Constable, 172-173).
- Campbell, L.B. 1930. *Shakespeare's Tragic Heroes: Slaves of Passion.* New York: Cambridge University Press.
- Christofides, R. M. 2008) 'Shakespeare and Equivocation Language and the Doom in Hamlet, Othello, Macbeth, and King Hear'. PhD diss. Cardiff University.
- Djundjung, J.M. 2002. 'Iago and the Ambiguity of His Motives in Shakespeare's Othello'. Jurusan Sastra Inggris, Fakultas Sastra, Universitas Kristen Petra, 4(1), 1-7.
- Drakakis, J. 1980. *Notes on Shakespeare's Othello* (York Notes): Longman.
- Elroy, B. Mc. 1973. *Shakespeare's Mature Tragedies: Othello: his visage in his mind.* (Pp.1-57). Princeton University Press.
- Greenblatt, S. 1988. *Shakespearean Negotiations: The Circulation of Social Energy in Renaissance England.* Oakland: University of California Press.
- Hazlitt, W. 1818. Characters of Shakespeare's Plays (2nd ed.). London: Taylor and Hessey.
- Herford, C.H. 1920. ed. *The Warwick Shakespeare Othello: The Moor of Venice,* London: Blackie and Son Limited.
- Holloway, J. 2005. *The Story of the Night: Studies in Shakespeare's Major Tragedies.* New York: Routledge.
- Johnson, S. 1765. *Mr. Johnson's Preface to his Edition of Shakespeare's Plays.* Ed. I. Lancashire 2005. (online edition published by RPO Editors, Department of English, and University of Toronto Press as Samuel Johnson (1709-1784): Preface to his Edition of Shakespeare's Plays (1765) London: J. and R. Tonson and others. OCLC 10834559.
- Kale, R.M. 2015. 'Study of Iago's role with reference to his use of the Techniques of Manipulation in the 'Othello". In *Indian Streams Research Journal,* 4 (12).
- Knight. G.W. 1972. *The Wheel of Fire, Interpretations of Shakespearian Tragedy.* London: Methuen & Co.

- Kitishat, A.R. and M.A. Alzu'bi. 2013. 'The presentation of the
- Arabic character in Shakespeare's Othello'. *Research on Humanities and Social Sciences*, 3 (19), 41-46.
- Mahfouz, S.M. 2012. 'It is my life: A Psychoanalytical and an Existentialist Study of People of Suicidal Tendencies in Modern and Contemporary American Suicide Drama.' In *Studies in Literature and Language*, 4 (1), 158-171
- Mutlu, K. 2013. 'Racism in Othello.' *Journal of History Culture and Art Research*, 2 (2), 134-141. doi: 10.7596/taksad.v2i2.243
- Ragland, F. 1888. *Shakespeare Examinations.* Ed. W.Taylor Thom, M. A. Boston: Ginn and Co. Shakespeare Online. http://www.shakespeare-online.com/plays/othello/examqo/othellobest.html Accessed January 2016.
- Rahmani A. and M. Khodamoradpour. 2015. 'Ideological puppets: a Lacanian-Althusserian analysis of women in Shakespeare's tragedies'. In *European Journal of English Language and Literature Studies*, 3 (1), 20-28.
- Rose, M. St. n. d. 'Race and Patriarchy in Othello.' In *College of the Bahamas Research Journal.* Volume XI: 25-33.
- Ruma, M. B. 2014. 'Race, Citizenship and Social Order in
- William Shakespeare's Othello.' *International Journal of Applied Linguistics & English Literature*, 3 (2): 34-38.
- Schlegel, A.W. 1965. *Lectures on Dramatic Art and Literature.* Trans. John Black. New York: AMS Press INC.
- Shakespeare, W. 1604. (1670 Ed.). *Othello.* Harmondsworth: Penguin Books Ltd.
- Shane, R., L. Kupis and A. Liang. 2015. *An Integrated Approach for the Study of Symbolically Inspired Literature. Studies in Literature and Language*, 11(2), 1-14. doi: 10.3968/7375
- Skiba et al. 2004. *Othello: the Moor of Venice / by William Shakespeare; with related readings.* (The EMC masterpiece series access editions). ISBN 0-8219-2956-9. THE EMC MASTERPIECE SERIES, Access Editions, EMC/Paradigm Publishing St. Paul, Minnesota.
- Taylor, Ml. 2001. *Shakespeare's Criticism in the Twentieth Century.* Oxford: Oxford University Press.
- Traub, V.J. 1990. 'Desire and anxiety: The circulation of sexuality in Shakespearean drama'. PhD diss. Available from Proquest. Paper AAI9022752. http://scholarworks.umass.edu/dissertations/AAI9022752 Accessed January 2016.
- Wakefield, G. 1968. *Othello (W. Shakespeare)* (Notes on English literature). Lincoln: Blackwell.

Desdemona's Appetite
Robert Appelbaum (Malmö University, Sweden)

THE IDEA FOR this essay came from a discovery I made when I first began researching food practices in the early modern period. I was looking at Shakespeare's references to eating and drinking, and I found that Shakespeare sometimes used the word appetite as a trope for love (Appelbaum 2006, 224-35). But when he did that, he had a consistent idea in mind. Appetite is different from love; and love experienced as if it were an appetite is not love at all but rather something less impressive.

Here is an example, from Twelfth Night, Orsino speaking.

> There is no woman's sides
> Can bide the beating of so strong a passion
> As love doth give my heart; no woman's heart
> So big, to hold so much. They lack retention.
> Alas, their love may be called appetite,
> No motion of the liver, but the palate,
> That suffer surfeit, cloyment and revolt.
> But mine is all as hungry as the sea,
> And can digest as much (2.4.91-99).

Now we may well think that what Orsino is saying is foolish, dishonest, and misogynist. But the comparison is a regularly devised trope, which is consistent across most of Shakespeare's oeuvre. Love is big. The appetite is small. Love is a big, endless, unsatisfiable passion. The appetite is easily satisfied. It can lead to cloying and revulsion. And so when someone experiences a love that can lead to surfeit, cloying and revulsion, when love in other words is fickle, it is not really love; it is something akin to our appetite for food and drink.

A more elaborate development of the trope appears in Othello. It has Iago speaking to Rodrigo about Desdemona.

> Her eye must be fed, and what delight shall she have to look on the devil? When the blood is made dull with the act of sport, there should be, again to inflame it and to give satiety a fresh appetite, loveliness in favour, sympathy in years, manners and beauties; all which the Moor is defective in. Now, for want of these required conveniences, her delicate tenderness will find itself abused, begin to heave the gorge, disrelish and abhor the Moor. Very nature will instruct her in it and compel her to some second choice (2.1.220-27).

Iago claims that Desdemona was attracted to Othello because, as Othello himself had said, she loved the stories he told. But that was an impermanent attraction. And soon enough, or even now, Desdemona's appetite for Othello will have been sated, and even turn toward revulsion. Nature will therefore drive her on to a new lover, and revive her appetite for sex.

The appetite in Shakespeare is a normal, natural and cyclical function. But it is subject to vicissitudes. It can be fresh, keen or leaden, foul, bestial, riotous, or controlling. It can be confounded, dry, sharp or sick. It can even act against the interests of the body that hosts it. That is what Shakespeare refers to in Sonnet 147:

> My love is as a fever, longing still
> For that which longer nurseth the disease,
> Feeding on that which doth preserve the ill,
> The uncertain sickly appetite to please (lines 1-4).

The appetite that desires a food that is bad for the body is a desire that keeps wanting more of the bad food. The perception behind this trope is, I think, the burning of a fire: the fire in some sense wants more of the fuel that is stoking it, another log for example, and so if it gets more fuel it gets all the hotter. Starve a fever, goes the old saying, because giving it food means giving it fuel to burn all the hotter with. But what should one do if one is in love, and one's love wants a kind of food? And what should one do if one's love is bad for you, a disease, caused by eating bad food?

The study of food and food practices has many dimensions. One of the dimensions is material culture itself. How, in any given case, is food grown, processed, distributed, cooked and served? How is it eaten? What meanings are attached to different foodstuffs, and different kinds of meals? How are different foodstuffs and preparations coordinated or divided? Those are the questions common to the ethnological study of the foodway, the material culture of food in a given time and place.

But along with the study of material culture, literature provides us with a glimpse not so much into the objective facts of food but its subjective dimension. In a recent article I have called this material subjectivity (Appelbaum 2014). Material subjectivity is in general the active, constitutive relationship between individuals and things, between the I who senses, perceives, experiences and reflects and the things it senses, perceives, experiences and reflects upon. This is the domain, in part, of what in psychoanalysis is called object relations. But since we are also talking about the objects of a specific time and place – Shakespeare's England, for example, or such imaginative projections of Shakespeare's England as Desdemona's Cyprus – material subjectivity is also the domain of the specific resources that the individual can draw upon, in other words object relations with a view to a specific finite set of objects and the customs through which the objects may be approached.

We can never have direct access to another material subjectivity. I may perhaps be able to recreate an heirloom orange and an heirloom grass raised lamb, and prepare a dish of roasted lamb in bitter orange sauce as specified by a fourteenth century cookbook. I can come fairly close to recreating the objects of another material culture, even if that culture has long since passed away. But I cannot recreate the subjective experience. There are so many variables. There are so many rules and regulations, cultural memories and ideologies separating us from the material subjectivity of another time and place. I cannot, in other words, sense another material subjectivity, even though a basic component or material subjectivity is sense itself.

Certainly there are universals to rely on. Hunger and thirst, the basic flavours of sweet, sour, salty and bitter – and I will return to sweet and sour a little later – the basic textures of grain and oil, of flesh, leaves, fruits and legumes. We are not investigating the habits of another species, on another planet. But the subjectivity in the full sense that goes along with these things is inaccessible. We can only make guesses about it, try to delimit and interpret it and create a plausible model for it. We speculate – and we find through sources with as a deep a relation to material subjectivity and Shakespeare, that speculation is part of material subjectivity too.

A sign of this speculative quality of material subjectivity, as well as the difficulty of understanding the subjectivities of another time and place, is the proximity in Shakespeare between appetite and love. Shakespeare is not unique in this. The establishing of an affinity, a contiguity and a hierarchical stature for appetite and sexual desire or love – I will keep the ambiguity between desire and love open for now – is announced early in the works of Plato and developed at length in *The Republic* (196, especially 437b – 438e, 679-81). Aristotle went so far as to identify the one and the other, placing them both in the domain of what he called the nutritive soul. 'The nutritive soul', he writes in On the Soul, 'is found along with all the others and is the most primitive and widely distributed power of soul, being indeed that one in virtue of which all are said to have life. The acts in which it manifests itself are reproduction and the use of food' (Aristotle 1941, 2.4, 561). Whatever these impulses are, traditionally they belong together both as physical contiguities and as similar or identical functions. But in his poetic language and dramatic action Shakespeare not only repeats the old coupling of the two ideas, he also challenges them. He highlights a quandary in the human condition, the idea that we need to feel self-sufficient, and yet we also need to need. We have ourselves, but we must also have others, other materials, other bodies, other responses to our needs, other persons, other minds. Appetite is a word that Shakespeare uses not only to characterise a universal instinct, but also to register a large range of emotions and ideas that adhere to our seeing ourselves with such an instinct, which extends from innocent pleasure to self-disgust, from affection to hatred.

Let me make an even bigger claim about Shakespeare's use of the idea of appetite. Of all his contemporaries in England, he is the only poet and dramatist to use the idea of appetite in this way. Spenser has a clinical and moralistic interest in appetite. Sydney avoids the idea – it only occurs in his love sonnets twice, and then in innocuous contexts, although his sonnets do include the memorable line, 'Desire still cries, Give me some food' (Sonnet 71). Donne does not use it. Ben Jonson at most thinks it funny and liberating. Middleton is capable of repeating commonplaces about appetite, but does nothing speculative with it. It is Shakespeare who speculates, and who argues that appetite is itself a speculation. Appetite is a reaching out from the self to the world and its objects which is also a self-reflection.

The example from The Taming of the Shrew is well known (see e.g. Detmer 1997). Petruchio's abuse of Katherine includes starving her; it is one of his techniques of discipline. Well, we are all indignant about it. Finally, Petruchio lets her eat. But then he goes through a similarly cruel routine about the clothes she likes. And when she shows a preference for a certain cap, Petruchio answers, 'It is a paltry cap, / A custard-coffin, a bauble, a silken pie. / I love thee well, in that thou lik'st it not' (4.3.79-81). Now I want to ask this question: why, moments after denying Katherine food, does Petruchio compare a hat to a custard tart and a pie? And I want to answer that there is a very deep reason for this, indicating Shakespeare's underlying notion – or rather, his underlying problematic – about appetite, consumption and desire. We catch a glimpse of this toward the end of the play. We seem to be at the brink of an easy happy ending as Petruchio, Kate, Lucentio, Bianca, Hortensio and the Widow sit down for the banquet course at a wedding (see Meads 2001 and Thong 2010). But listen to the language:

> Lucentio: Feast with the best, and welcome to my house:
> My banquet is to close our stomachs up,
> After our great good cheer. Pray you, sit down;
> For now we sit to chat as well as eat.
>
> Petruchio: Nothing but sit and sit, and eat and eat (5.2.7-12).

This is peculiar language. Petruchio seems to grumble, or else to jokingly belittle the occasion, as if staring at this sequel to a feast, a dessert course, is staring into an abyss of boredom. Eating and drinking seems to contiguous not only with making love, but with revulsion at our creatureliness.

This has nothing to do with whether the partygoers are eating beef or pork, custard or pie, or here the candied fruits and compotes that comprised a 'banquet'; it has to do with something more fundamental, a sense of life, and a sense of its hollowness when all is said and done. 'What is a man', asks Hamlet, ' / If his chief good and market of his time / Be but to sleep and feed? a beast, no more' (4.4.9[23-5]).

In Shakespeare's work, the idea of the appetite has a kind of double life. On the one hand, it signifies the specific desire for food and drink, and the specific experience of accommodating oneself to it. And hence it has a lot of metaphorical and analogical value. But on the other hand, the appetite signifies a category of human existence. And hence it has a lot of theoretical value. In this second respect it is what

Aristotle called the appetitive function, the process through which the embodied soul places demands on the world outside of itself. No soul can live in isolation. The soul is in need. Its neediness is its appetite, and so far as it is drawn in sensory delight, in passion and in ambition to other things, other persons, other experiences, it is expressing what Aristotle calls appetite.

Shakespeare is amazed at this aspect of human nature. Human beings are in need. Human beings are designed to take in the world, and make something out of it. And although a reflection on this fact may lead one, as it does both Aristotle and Spenser, to think about self-regulation, about moderation and the means toward attaining it, it leads Shakespeare to think about immoderation, dissatisfaction, beastliness and boredom, as well as to the quality of the lives of the people who experience these feelings.

I wish to digress a moment and say a little bit about the relation I see between Shakespeare, Plato and Aristotle. Much of Shakespeare's thought is balanced between the two extremes of Platonism and Aristotelianism, not as developed philosophies but as ways of thinking, of formulating and solving problems. Had Shakespeare ever read either? My guess is probably not, apart from maybe Aristotle's Politics, although there have been scholars who claim more forcefully otherwise one way or the other (Crosbie 2007; Elton 1997; Kaytor 2012; Parker 1993). But certainly Shakespeare had read Spenser and others and had had conversations with others who had read both Plato and Aristotle. And more to the point, the Renaissance view of the body and the soul was balanced between Platonism and Aristotelianism. Aristotle ruled the roost when it came to medicine, although usually refracted through the lens of Galenism, and thereby combined with still another Greek tradition, originating with Empedocles (Albala 2001; Appelbaum 2006). Plato ruled the roost when it came to the concept of love, although that concept too could be refracted through Galenism, not to mention Christian theology and Petrarchanism, as well as through a fourth Greek tradition, the materialism originating with Democritus. When

Shakespeare has his characters or his lyrical 'I' talk about the body, the appetite, the soul and love, he draws upon those two tendencies of Aristotelianism and Platonism, with the added elements of Galenism and Democritean materialism. And then, of course, he adds something uniquely his own.

The most extreme version of what is uniquely Shakespeare's probably comes during the famous speech on degree, made by Ulysses in *Troilus and Cressida*.

> Take but degree away, untune that string,
> And, hark! what discord follows. Each thing meets
> In mere oppugnancy. The bounded waters
> Should lift their bosoms higher than the shores,
> And make a sop of all this solid globe;
> Strength should be lord of imbecility,
> And the rude son should strike his father dead.
> Force should be right – or rather, right and wrong
> Between whose endless jar justice resides,
> Should lose their names, and so should justice too.
> Then every thing includes itself in power,
> Power into will, will into appetite;
> And appetite, an universal wolf,
> So doubly seconded with will and power,
> Must make perforce a universal prey,
> And last eat up himself (1.3.109-24).

Ulysses argues that a respect for degree, for hierarchical differences, can serve as the principle for moderating natural impulses, and that without that respect chaos inevitably ensues. A lot of people have commented on this passage, but let us think about it in terms of the idea of appetite. There is no analogy between appetite and love here, although there are undertones of an analogy between appetite and lust, since this universal wolf is derived from will and the will, in Shakespeare, often signifies lust. If there is no respect for degree, Ulysses argues, then there is no impediment to the tendency of all things to clash together and absorb one another. Seas will rise above their borders and awash the earth, make a sop of it, literally a piece of wet bread. There will be no difference between right and wrong except as force makes it so. There will be no law at all except power, no law for power except the will, and no law for will except the appetite. In this vision of the world, everything wants to eat everything else, and the only thing that prevents everything from doing this is respect for degree, in other words respect for a certain form of difference. Appetite here is the neediness of everything to master, absorb and assimilate everything. It is a universal wolf. And, as we have seen in other examples, appetite is an immoderate power which ultimately leads to its own conclusion. It eats itself up.

Of course, we are not supposed to agree with Ulysses. We are supposed to listen to what he says and think about his motives for saying it. We may wish to take exception to his conflation of the natural and the human, or his mistaking the natural order of the chain of being, or what today we call the food chain, with the human orders of hierarchy and respect. But we may also want to think along with Ulysses about what it is that keeps up order in the human and natural worlds. We may want to think about what it is that keeps us from attacking and eating one another indiscriminately. There is a similar concern, answered with a different form of philosophy, in the words of Othello himself. 'Perdition catch my soul!' says Othello, after parting with Desdemona, 'But I do love thee! and when I love thee not, Chaos is come again' (3.3.91-2). Othello's statement is an allusion to Empedocles and the doctrine that the universe is born out of chaos, and made orderly out of love. Empedocles's doctrine is tricky, however, for the love that makes order is matched by a principle of strife that makes everything opposed to everything else and separate, and yet love is also a principle of attraction and assimilation (Parry 2012). Strife and love together both counteract chaos and imitate it. What holds things together is what holds things apart, and vice versa. And it is still not clear why we don't assault and absorb one another apart from the fine 'double' balance (as Empedocles puts it) between the two.

In Shakespeare, who is not a philosopher but a poet who makes other people speak snippets of philosophy and figures of speech that depend upon philosophical ideas, we find registered not just suppositions about the body, the soul and their needs, but fears about what happens to the body and the soul when they get their deepest wishes. Those fears may be implicit in Plato and Aristotle, but they become explicit sources of dramatic conflict and destiny in Shakespeare. Let me stress, again, though, that the appetite for food and the desire for love are supposed to be two very different sorts of need for Shakespeare, and so lead to different kinds of outcomes. The universal wolf, as in Troilus and Cressida, left to itself, will eat itself up. It will annihilate itself by bringing itself to an end. Appetite, in other words, is finite, even when it becomes its own object. But the excessive love that Othello talks about leads not to annihilation but chaos. It leads to the dissolution of everything in everything else – a chaos in which everything still exists, but nothing exists as itself.

Let us recall Orsino's tortured, self-defensive remarks about appetite and love.

> There is no woman's sides
> Can bide the beating of so strong a passion
> As love doth give my heart; no woman's heart
> So big, to hold so much; they lack retention
> Alas, their love may be call'd appetite,
> No motion of the liver, but the palate,
> That suffer surfeit, cloyment and revolt;
> But mine is all as hungry as the sea,
> And can digest as much.

Orsino betrays himself in this speech. In the end he too can only express the idea of love in terms of the idea of taking something in and therefore of digesting it. But love for Orsino is a taking in to be compared with the taking in of the sea. We may be reminded of a speech by Antipholous of Syracuse at the beginning of *The Comedy of Errors:*

> I to the world am like a drop of water
> That in the ocean seeks another drop,
> Who, falling there to find his fellow forth,
> Unseen, inquisitive, confounds himself:
> So I, to find a mother and a brother,
> In quest of them, unhappy, lose myself (1.2.35-40).

The sea is a chaos, everything gets lost in it. The problem of love, as we see in the outcome of Othello, is not only that without it there is nothing but chaos, but that with it there may be chaos too.

Meanwhile, there is the finite world of the appetite. And one of the great spokesmen for the idea of appetite and what to do about it is Iago. Let us look again at the speech by Iago I cited at the beginning:

> Her eye must be fed, and what delight shall she have to look on the devil? When the blood is made dull with the act of sport, there should be, again to inflame it and to give satiety a fresh appetite, loveliness in favour, sympathy in years, manners and beauties; all which the Moor is defective in. Now, for want of these required conveniences, her delicate tenderness will find itself abused, begin to heave the gorge, disrelish and abhor the Moor. Very nature will instruct her in it and compel her to some second choice.

Iago imagines Desdemona as a sexual being, but he imagines her sexuality as a form of appetite. And that means that it is on the one hand finite and on the other hand promiscuous. It is finite because it satiates and makes the blood dull; it leads to promiscuity because what once excites the appetite later comes to repel it. Satiation, which brings along with it fatigue, is appetite achieved. Desire for variety is the mechanism through which appetite may be aroused again, but that leads toward gustatory promiscuity. Think of it this way, if you are in love and make love, and find yourself exhausted in the act, the next time you are aroused to make love again will probably be with the same person. For your love is like an ocean. It cannot be satiated. But if you are hungry and eat, and find yourself exhausted in the act, the next time you are aroused to eat again you will probably want something different. Yesterday was lamb; tomorrow I want fish. In fact, in the eyes of many characters in Shakespeare, if you are given the same food to eat over and over again, you are going to get sick of it. Literally it will make you sick. Lamb again. I am sick of it. In fact, it disgusts me.

That is how Iago thinks of Desdemona's appetite for Othello. There was a novelty that attracted her to him. But once she is satiated with him she will want something else. In fact, if she wants to enjoy sex again, she will have to have something else. For Othello was too unusual. He is defective, and if his defectiveness at first attracted her, her 'very nature', as Iago puts it, will eventually be repelled by it. I ate that! I made love to that man! No, it cannot be, for it is not just the orifices of the body that need to be stimulated in the act of love, but the eye and the mind. It is not only that after lamb you need to have fish; you need to have a serving of fish that is suitable to you, that looks good and smells good and that appeals to your sense of taste.

A paradox that ensues is that Iago at once imagines the subject as someone who is in charge of his or her own pleasures and as someone who is nevertheless subject to whims beyond his or her control. The smart person is someone who knows how to manage the appetites that arouse him, even the appetite that the person he is speaking to, Rodrigo, calls love:

Our bodies are our gardens, to the which our wills are gardeners: so that if we will plant nettles, or sow lettuce, set hyssop and weed up thyme, supply it with one gender of herbs, or distract it with many, either to have it sterile with idleness, or manured with industry, why, the power and corrigible authority of this lies in our wills. If the balance of our lives had not one scale of reason to poise another of sensuality, the blood and baseness of our natures would conduct us to most preposterous conclusions: but we have reason to cool our raging motions, our carnal stings, our unbitted lusts, whereof I take this that you call love to be a sect or scion (1.3.317-37).

There is something almost Freudian here: what Iago calls the will is something like what Freud calls the ego, and our raging motions are like the id. Notice that when Iago refers to sensuality and lust, he says that if we allowed them free range, if we left them 'unbitted', the results would be 'preposterous', meaning out of order, perverse, contrary to reason or nature. Our id-like sensuality too may lead to either self-consumption or chaos, for the id, as Freud said, cannot understand the word no. But Iago imagines that we can treat our bodies like gardens, that we can make them serve our reason and our will, even if in doing so we are mainly satisfying our sensual appetites. Love, of course, is just an outgrowth of the sexual appetite we call lust. It is nothing in itself. Love, Iago goes on to say, 'is merely a lust of the blood and a permission of the will'.

So on the one hand, we are in control of ourselves if we use our reason and, among other things, undertake the practice of delayed gratification. On the other hand, we are our motions, and it is our motions that reason is designed to serve. Neither here nor anywhere else do we need to take Iago at his word, of course. When Iago says 'I am not what I am' (1.1.65) he lets us know that he is not worried about contradicting himself. The problem is that on many occasions Iago seems so sensible. He even sees here that it could be useful to convince

Rodrigo of any idea about love that Iago does not believe, or rather that Iago believes no more than any other idea. Love is merely lust, Iago says. That's why it is like appetite.

But we also hear Iago say something very different in another context.

> That Cassio loves [Desdemona], I do well believe it.
> That she loves him, 'tis apt and of great credit.
> The Moor – howbeit that I endure him not –
> Is of a constant, loving, noble nature,
> And I dare think he'll prove to Desdemona
> A most dear husband. Now, I do love her too,
> Not out of absolute lust – though peradventure
> I stand accountant for as great a sin ... (2.3.273-80)

Here we find Iago using the word love several times, and apparently thinking of it as something that is apart from, or capable of being separate from lust. Love is considered in light of constancy, friendship, loyalty and generosity, what Aristotle calls *philia*, and also, when crossed, in terms of things like sin and revenge. This is the speech where Iago reiterates the idea that 'I do suspect the lusty Moor / Hath leap'd into my seat', and says that he would be willing to have sex with Desdemona in order to get even with Othello: in fact, he says that he would 'diet' his revenge, that is feed it as if it were a fever that needed more stoking, by thinking about wanting to have sex with Desdemona.

Iago is not always a Freudian *avant la lettre*, then; he is not even always cynical about love. But when he is cynical about love – when in other words it suits his purpose to be cynical about love – he compares love to an appetite, and so argues about the inevitability of inconstancy.

He is not the only person in the play to make this point, it is important to add. There is at least one other, Emilia. It is in her speech to Desdemona.

> Let husbands know
> Their wives have sense like them. They see, and smell,
> And have their palates both for sweet and sour,
> As husbands have. What is it that they do
> When they change us for others? Is it sport?
> I think it is. And doth affection breed it?
> I think it doth. Is't frailty that thus errs?
> It is so too. And have not we affections,
> Desires for sport, and frailty, as men have?
> Then let them use us well, else let them know,
> The ills we do, their ills instruct us so (5.1.91-101).

Unlike Iago, Emilia does not throw away morality when she argues in favour of satisfying lust. She knows it is a sign of frailty, and a condition of 'sport', a word which may have negative connotations, and which in any case may lead to an 'ill'. But 'affection' is an appetitive emotion; and there it is, a palate both for sweet and sour. This is the only use of the expression in Shakespeare, for whom, unless the context is ironic, sweet is always good and sour is always bad and no one ever desires a sour thing. Emilia does not develop the correlative idea that appetites get cloyed or dulled, but at least implies that appetites are changeable. Her reference to both sweet and sour is the best evidence we have that Iago is right, and that she has actually slept with Othello. In any case, it alerts us to the idea that we do not only incline toward the obvious in our tastes and loves: sometimes we are inclined toward unobvious objects of desire.

And it leads back to the other correlative idea that appetites are not reliable, that appetites can be addressed to the bad as well as the good and that individuals can even be drawn into an excessive appetite for things, people or experiences which are bad for them. And so we come to a final problem that haunts the work of Shakespeare in this vein. Love is something that must be reliable. In contrast to appetite, love cannot, must not be fickle. There is a constant demand in

Shakespeare's works for a kind of love that is not a scion of lust. And yet love is a transaction between two people, and the reliability of the other is frequently a worry, and even one's own reliability can be a problem. After all, even if we love, we have appetites. Even if we love, we live in a transient world and our emotional states and loyalties are transitory. Hence there are moments in Shakespeare when the appetite / love distinction gets turned on its head, and people end up desperately longing for a love as hungry as an appetite. The most plaintive and moving case of this probably comes in Sonnet 56.

> Sweet love, renew thy force; be it not said
> Thy edge should blunter be than appetite,
> Which but today by feeding is allayed,
> To-morrow sharpened in his former might.
> So, love, be thou; although today thou fill
> Thy hungry eyes even till they wink with fullness,
> Tomorrow see again, and do not kill
> The spirit of love with a perpetual dullness.
> Let this sad int'rim like the ocean be
> Which parts the shore, where two contracted new
> Come daily to the banks, that, when they see
> Return of love, more blest may be the view;
> Or call it winter, which being full of care
> Makes summer's welcome thrice more wished, more rare.

This is apparently a communication with the young man of the early sonnets – and the same young man who was told in Sonnet 55 that 'Not marble, nor the gilded monuments / Of princes, shall outlive' the 'powerful rhyme' being written in his honour. Sonnet 55 is all about permanence. Sonnet 56, one of the most sexually direct of the sonnets apparently addressed to the young man, is all about the fear of impermanence. The speaker pleads, Do not allow your desire for me to be blunted by an impending period of separation. Be as sharp as an appetite in renewing a need which has earlier been satisfied to repletion. At the same time he pleads to himself, and to the power of love, to do the same. Renew thy force. Tomorrow see again. Because of the ambiguity of the language, we are alerted to a double danger. Tomorrow see again. I am in love and I am in love with you – therefore, please, be reliable and continue to love me too. But also, I am in love, but I fear that my own love is unreliable, I fear that it will lose its force, that it will fail to see the object of its adoration.

We are apparently in the same territory in this poem as the Tragedy of Othello. We must love, a character like Othello insists. But how can we love what is after all another person, and how can we love when we too are other persons?

> O curse of marriage,
> That we can call these delicate creatures ours,
> And not their appetites! (3.3.272-74)

This sounds terribly possessive, and patriarchal, but it is also realistic. There is something in the other that I cannot control. There is something in the other person that exceeds the limits of the economy of love. And this limit-breaker is precisely something that makes my beloved available to others. And so the jealous Othello continues:

> I had rather be a toad,
> And live upon the vapour of a dungeon,
> Than keep a corner in the thing I love
> For others' uses (3.3.274-77).

Note that Othello does not seem to fear that he will lose Desdemona's love. He is afraid that her appetite will cause her to give something to another man, her sensuality and passion, that ought to be his alone. If Othello is afraid of a failure of love, he is afraid of it for his own sake.

Like the speaker of Sonnet 56, he is afraid of the force of love, that it will fail him and bring chaos upon him.

And what about Desdemona? She does not seem to understand any of this. Desdemona would seem to be at peace with her love for Othello, and at peace with love itself. For Desdemona, love is bounteous. It is perhaps even truly Platonic, not in the sense that it is sexless, for it isn't, but in the sense that it is a form of devotion. It is unconditional.

Material subjectivity hardly even seems to enter the picture. For everyone else, Desdemona is a creature of appetites. And her appetite must be for variety. It must be for sour as well as sweet. It must also be finite, easily exhausted, and only by effort renewed. But Desdemona just doesn't see this. Her language is devoid of references to food and drink or to the idea of the appetite in general. We know that she is a sexually active being, but when she sees her sexuality she does not see an appetite. This amounts to a negation of the principle of material subjectivity. I have said that this principle is speculative in the sense that when the subject sees herself she will see a principle of what Aristotle calls the appetitive soul. I am what I desire. That is Iago's point; that is Othello's point. I am what I desire, meaning that I construct myself as an ego in order to accommodate myself to what I would like to have. But when Iago sees the I which is desire, he sees an appetite that is like an appetite for food, which needs constantly to be satisfied and constantly to be changed and renewed. And when Othello sees the I which is desire, he sees the chaos that comes when desire ends. But Desdemona sees only her unconditional and unlimited fidelity to Othello, an eros that is also a *philia* and an *agape*.

I have called this paper 'Desdemona's Appetite', but in the end we probably have to say Desdemona represents an effort to transcend appetite and live for love and in love alone. Everyone else wants to be in control of Desdemona's appetite. But Desdemona's response is to declare that, whatever may be the case when she eats and drinks, when she experiences love, appetite has nothing to do with it at all.

In sum, then, with reference to Othello and other texts, I believe I have begun to sketch out some of the main contours of Shakespeare's thought about appetite, love and subjectivity. These are thoughts that come from within the context of a society that was familiar with both hedonism and asceticism, and with both reductive and transcendent notions of the human body and its needs. It was a society affected both by Hellenic thought and by often Hellenized Christian doctrine. It was not, yet, a consumer society. But it was capable both of thinking about delayed gratification as a means towards rationally abetted consumption and of imagining that love between two people could be harmed by the need for pleasure. Shakespeare's characters by and large express both a demand to have their appetites fulfilled and a fear of what might happen if they were. Material subjectivity in Shakespeare's world turns out to be a dangerous territory of the body and the soul. But Desdemona's appetite is different. It has no dangers because it is entirely subordinated to love. That is a very romantic idea, surely; but it is also one of the things that leads to her being killed by her husband.

Reference Sources

- Albala, K. 2002. *Eating right in the Renaissance.* Berkeley: University of California Press.
- Appelbaum, R. 2006. *Aguecheek's beef, Belch's hiccup, and other gastronomic interjections: literature, culture and food among the early moderns.* Chicago: University of Chicago Press.
- _____. 2014. 'Judith dines alone, from the Bible to Du Bartas'. *Modern Philology* 111.4: 683-710.
- Aristotle. 1941. *The basic works of Aristotle.* Ed. R. McKeon. New York: Random House.
- Cefalu, 2013. 'The burdens of mind reading in Shakespeare's Othello: A Cognitive and Psychoanalytic Approach to Iago's Theory of Mind'. *Shakespeare Quarterly* 64: 265-294.
- Charney, M. 1999. *Shakespeare on love and lust.* New York: Columbia University Press.

- Crosbie, C. 2007. 'Fixing moderation: Titus Andronicus and the Aristotelian determination of value'. *Shakespeare Quarterly* 58(2): 147-173.
- Detmer, E. 1997. 'Civilizing subordination: Domestic violence and The Taming of the Shrew'. *Shakespeare Quarterly* 48.3: 273-294.
- Elton, W. R. 1997. 'Aristotle's Nicomachean Ethics and Shakespeare's Troilus and Cressida'. *Journal of the History of Ideas* 58(2): 331-337
- Girard, R. 1985. 'The politics of desire in Troilus and Cressida'. In *Shakespeare and the question of theory.* Ed. Parker and G. Hartman. 188-209. New York: Methuen
- Grady, H. 1996. *Shakespeare's universal wolf: studies in early modern reification.* Oxford: Clarendon.
- Kaytor, D. 2012. 'Shakespeare's political philosophy: A debt to Plato in Timon Of Athens'. *Philosophy and Literature* 36 (1): 136-152.
- Meads, C. 2001. *Banquets set forth: banqueting in English Renaissance drama.* Manchester: Manchester University Press.
- Parker, B. 1993. "A thing unfirm': Plato's Republic and Shakespeare's Julius Caesar'. *Shakespeare Quarterly* 44 (1): 30-43.
- Parry, R., 2012. 'Empedocles'. *The Stanford Encyclopedia of Philosophy* (Fall 2012 Edition). Ed. E.N. Zalta http://plato.stanford.edu/archives/fall2012/entries/empedocles (8/18/14).
- Plato. 1961. *Collected Dialogues.* Ed. E. Hamilton and H. Cairns. Princeton: Princeton University Press.
- Saunders, B. 2004. 'Iago's clyster: purgation, anality, and the civilizing process'. *Shakespeare Quarterly* 55.2 : 148-176.
- Shakespeare, W. 2008. *The Norton Shakespeare.* Ed. S. Greenblatt. New York: Norton.
- Sydney, 1995. *Astrophel and Stella.* Ed. A.B. Grosart and R.S. Bear. http://pages.uoregon.edu/rbear/stella.html (8/18/2014).
- Thong, R. 2010. 'Performance of the banquet course in early modern drama.' in *Renaissance Food from Rabelais to Shakespeare: culinary readings and culinary histories.* Ed. Joan Fitzpatrick. 107-26. Farnham, Surrey: Ashgate.

Omkara: Moor of Meerut: Reconfiguring the Sacred and Profane of Othello

Natasha Cooper (University of Durham, UK)

Introduction

THIS PAPER PROCEEDS from the standpoint that the functioning of Shakespearean tragedy can be read as being built of the religious traditions of the time in which it is produced in performance. Notably, there was a marked secularisation in Elizabethan and Jacobean drama, of which Shakespeare is regarded as largely representative. There is then, most naturally, an ease of adaptation that marks the Shakespearean tradition, which sees such drama re-born in literary and artistic avenues of various generations – a view that has been long established by critics such as Jonathan Dollimore, whose popular text on tragic convention *Radical Tragedy*, both observes and predicts for the future that: 'every age interprets [and indeed will continue to interpret] Shakespeare for itself'. In re-interpretation of its plot and narrative conventions, Shakespearean drama moves from the stage into other narrative forms, and through this shift it has emigrated from the land of its birth, and in travelling the world has become a welcome refugee in world literature, forming a part of a pan-cultural literary corpus. Thus exists the Russian opera *Lady Macbeth of the Mtensk District* (1934), the American Gil Junger's cinematic *10 Things I Hate About You* (1999), and the English Jeremy Trafford's novel *Ophelia* (2001). Similarly, Tim Supple's 2006 dramatic production of *A Midsummer Night's Dream* –

performed in both the UK and India – contains a multilingual dialogue, scripted in a mixture of English and six other Indian languages, performed for audiences who curiously, required no translation.

The Indian Bollywood film industry has been one emergent outlet for such re-workings, a convention that has its roots in the social-history of British colonisation and its after effects. In his text *On Heroes and Hero Worship*, Thomas Carlyle famously demands of his fellow countrymen: 'Consider now if they asked us, Will you give-up your Indian Empire or your Shakespeare'. Carlyle rhetorically presents his own answer: 'Indian Empire or no Indian Empire; we cannot do without Shakespeare! Indian Empire will go, at any rate, some day; but this Shakespeare does not go, he lasts forever with us'. Carlyle's foretelling of the fall of Empire was indeed true, as historical events in the mid-1900s proved. However his declaration of the intrinsic value of Shakespeare to that of the British identity, while undoubtedly true, has also left its mark on the now dissolved empire, made possible in the literary and cinematic art produced in the wake of the modern world's dissolution of imperialism. The importing of Shakespeare is not a new or revolutionary idea in India, a country that saw over a hundred years of British Raj. There exists a trend for re-writing narratives in India – that perhaps exists in all once-colonised nations – possibly developed out of the necessity of staging a revolt and asserting a national identity through its literature. This trend has continued in the modern and contemporary age, with its emphasis on new literary and artistic forms, bringing such re-writings into the cinematic genre of narrative. Shakespeare is arguably today an influencer of Bollywood cinema, the Hindi language film industry based out of the city of Bombay. Dollimore's provision of a theoretical response to the possible Indianisation of Shakespeare, explicates adaptation techniques through which the British Bard impacts the Indian masses, gaining popularity with films such as *Angoor* (1982; *The Comedy of Errors)*, *Qayamat se Qayamat Tak* (1988; *Romeo and Juliet)* and *10ML Love* (2010; *A Midsummer Night's*

Dream); and through which his influence has sparked a series of film adaptations, allowing the sun to rise on a literary and cinematic empire that acclimates and adjusts the dramatic plot to its own purposes. While the language does indeed change — literal translations from Shakespearean English to modern Hindi are rare — Shakespearean drama is still thematically able to lend itself to the formulaic assumptions that underlie the plot of the average Bollywood film: hero, heroine, villain; confusion, jealousy, love-triangles, resolution. There is an innate similarity between Bollywood cinema and Shakespearean drama, where veteran Bollywood actor, Naseeruddin Shah, while observing the Indian fondness for traditional adaptations of Shakespeare, speaks of 'how deeply we [Indians] worship Shakespeare in India. More than they do in England!' Yet Shah observes a parallel between Shakespeare and Bollywood, stating: 'Hindi cinema has borrowed so heavily from Shakespeare that if you do a Shakespeare play today it will look like a Hindi film .... There isn't a cliché in Hindi cinema that's not borrowed from Shakespeare!'

The Sacred and the Profane

The relationship between tragedy and religion, concepts that might generally be deemed as theoretically inequitable, stems from a similar origin, where the earliest Greek tragedies were cultish and ritualistic. René Girard observes violence – that element which so often characterises the tragic – as a 'ritualised' part of society. Assuredly then, tragic art, which includes Shakespearean drama and its adaptations, stems from some basis within the theological tradition (even if the focus is generally secular). However, it is through the sacrificial element that is intimated in the etymological idea of the *tragoidia* – the sacrificial goat – re-formed and iconised in theological figures (such as that of Christ the redeemer dying for man's sins), that theorists of religion and literature have observed a commonality between tragedy and religion, where, as Girard continues to write: 'A single principle is at work in primitive religion and classical tragedy'. There is then a violent aspect to sacrifice, which might translate to a sense of violence in religious belief, analogous to that in tragedy. Terry Eagleton's more recent forward (2004) to Dollimore's text observes the continuation of the theological element within tragedy, even in the modern, secularising age, as key in the maintenance of religious or elevated impulses, articulated in the hero's summons to his tragic quest: Macbeth summoned and instigated by the 'weird sisters' and his wife; 'Honourable' Brutus by Cassius.

Omkara: Moor of Meerut

Thus, returning to the concept of Shakespearean adaptation, specifically Shakespeares on the Indian stage, possibly one of the first Bollywood adaptations to draw critical attention to its construction as one borrowed from Shakespearean plot was director Vishal Bhardwaj's film *Omkara* (2006), a re-working of Shakespeare's *Othello*. Within the film, the religious principles that affect tragic art are transferred from religious concepts to cinematic elements. Here, Hinduism, India's most widely recognised religious philosophy, is superimposed on Shakespearean convention. While *Omkara*, alongside Bhardwaj's other Shakespearean-inspired films *Maqbool* (2003; *Macbeth*) and *Haider* (2014; *Hamlet*) form his own intertextual universe; here images of love and religiosity are contrasted with those of violence and bloodshed, in an adapted montage of Shakespearean – and indeed generic Bollywood – themes. There are, however, variations on the original: in presenting a mix of passion and violent imagery, drawn from the darker underbelly of Indian society, where killings, mafia lords, and honour crimes predominate, Bhardwaj's cinematic imagery juxtapositions love and violence, where tender moments are often accompanied by images of guns. In *Maqbool*, the characters Maqbool and Nimmi often intersperse violent moments within their tender caresses, replacing loving fingers with arms. Later, the blood that will not wash from Lady Macbeth's palms appears on Nimmi's hands, where it merges into the wedding-ceremonial painted-on henna, providing a direct contrast between and the linking of religious festivity and joy with murder; and so Bhardwaj blends contradictory elements where love and religion subsist in even the violent aspects of existence. In *Omkara* similarly, an early song in flashback reveals the potentially romantic event of Omkara and Dolly's first meeting, yet this is shot with the implication of the tragic plot that will characterise their relationship and the film to follow: she opens the door to him and his blood, resultant of a bullet wound, stains her clothes, marking her in both future ownership and love, and prefiguring her fate as sacrificial victim, where the traditional Hindu bride is marked by her husband's application of red vermillion powder, sindoor, upon her forehead.

While violent acts might be carried out offstage in *Othello*, in *Omkara*, these acts are offered up to the audience for their viewing pleasure, possibly in the hope of effecting a classical catharsis – pity for sacrificial victims and fear that they might encounter such tragedy in their own religious rites – or conceivably to satisfy the histrionic element that is demanded by Bollywood convention. Shakespeare confronts issues that are ones of concern even in the contemporary Indian scenario: the issue of choice versus that of traditional arranged marriage and the consequences of that choice, issues of inter-racial (or inter-caste) love, and the consequences of honorific conduct. However, a recognition of the religious element within *Omkara* – the link between the theological and the tragic – perhaps requires the viewing of the film through an Indianised lens, more specifically through the concept of the Indian wedding and its ceremonial after effects, a much-celebrated and ritualised part of a highly ritualistic society, through which the film's sacred and profane elements are best recognised. Othello and Desdemona's own love is here, in this paper, read through the traditional and modern contexts of Indian society's courtship rituals, which are framed by a religious, sacred tradition, the violation of which contains its profane element. It is perhaps essential to note that within the Indian scenario, while legislation – much like the importation of

Shakespeare and an English education – was generally formulated by colonial and foreign powers, legalities were also largely shaped and interpreted through a theological (generally Hindu) lens, where laws are often formed of codified religious convention. Colonial powers in India largely refrained from conversion but continued to operate a system of exclusion and otherness in relation to the colonised majority. While representations of Othello popularly depict him as of a differing race to the rest of the play's protagonists and supposed audience, in their introduction to Shakespeare's *Othello*, Jonathan Bate and Eric Rasmussen are quick to note the religious connotations behind *Othello's* Moorish moniker, where: 'The primary usage of the term 'Moor' in early modern English was as a religious, not a racial identification' (2007, 2082). *Othello, Moor of Venice*, unrecognisable to both a Christian English and a Catholic Italian context is from a strange land. Yet he speaks the language of the mainstream and of Shakespeare's audience, and in doing so is able to address them while retaining his religious otherness. Bate and Rasmussen's comment lends itself similarly to the thematically religious element of *Omkara*, where violence, not race, is the primary thematic subject. At its root, *Omkara*, like *Othello*, is a story of violence: namely the violence of Othello's strangling of Desdemona, the violence that words might instigate, the violence of defending one's honour, and above all the violence that exists even in religious elements, where the sacrificed *tragoidia*, Desdemona, becomes the focal point of violent and instigated action. Bhardwaj transposes the Christian elements of Shakespeare's drama to that of a home-grown Indian context, from Bhardwaj's own home province of Uttar Pradesh, so that the Moor of Meerut emerges from the narrative of the Moor of Venice. In deliberately setting this film within India but outside of the Bollywood conventionalism of Bombay, the city of familiarity that in his other films he has paid homage to, where in *Maqbool* the Duncan figure declares: 'Mumbai is my beloved', in *Omkara*, Bhardwaj creates from the outset striking similarities between Shakespeare's narrative and his own. The explicit nature of the adaptation is contained within naming and characterisation, where each character in the film shares the same sound of their first name as with their doppelgänger in the original drama: Omkara Shukla – Othello, Dolly Mishra – Desdemona, Ishwar Tyagi – Iago, Indu Tyagi – Emilia, Keshav 'Firagi' Upadhyaya – Cassio. There is a re-iteration of Shakespearean dialogue in translation:

> Iago: I lay with Cassio lately
> And, being troubled with a raging tooth,
> I could not sleep. There are a kind of men
> So loose of soul that in their sleeps will mutter
>   Their affairs: one of this kind is Cassio.
> In sleep I heard him say, 'Sweet Desdemona,
> Let us be wary, let us hide our loves.'

Ishwar imitates these words in *Omkara* (in translation):

> When I stayed at Kesu's house, I heard him mutter in his sleep: 'Dolly, if our love has to live, we'll have to hide it from the entire world.'

Elsewhere, upon her elopement, Dolly's father dismisses her, warning Omkara: 'Joh apne baap ko tagh sakti hain, woh kisi ki sagi nahin ho sakti,' ('She who can dupe her own father will never be anyone's to claim'). These lines echo Shakespeare: 'Look to her, Moor, if thou hast eyes to see. She has deceived her father and may thee'.

However, this instigation in Bhardwaj – as in Shakespeare – demands greater evidence. Where later in the drama, Othello requests 'ocular proof' of Desdemona's infidelity, Omkara in a parallel episode says to an instigating Ishwar: 'When you see your dreams you see it alone.… When I look in Dolly's eyes, your entire Ramayana [a major Hindu religious epic] sounds false'. However, the film's final song shatters Omkara's belief in his ability to see Dolly's virtue, and reminds of the demand of greater evidence than what might be seen in 'ocular proof' where: 'Naina thag lenge, nainaa thag lenge / Nainaon kee mat maniyo, nainon kee mat suniyo re,' ('Eyes will cheat you; / Do not listen to them; do not see with them').

Developed from this Shakespeare-formed structure, the film delves into its religious element. Referring to the naming of characters, the critic Lalita Hogan's essay on the film notes: 'Bhardwaj's *Omkara* focuses on the Hindu tradition and uses many of its symbols, colours and iconography, one of which is his transcription of Shakespearean names to Hindu names that orient the viewer into regional and caste identities of the characters.' The Hindu sacred reverberates throughout the film, beginning with Omkara's name which contains within it the sacred sound that denotes the soul and cosmic knowledge: 'om'; which in its connection to the soul relates to a Christian psychology that begins with passion (including violent passion) as an act of the body inspired by the impassioned soul, where Thomas Dixon's treatise on emotive theory arising from Renaissance passions suggests that, 'it had been the soul and not the body that was active .... Treatments of the passions, affections and emotions that were authentic representatives of this Christian tradition insisted on the activity of the soul.' This impassioned soul finding its human form in *Omkara*. The observance of passion was key to the Renaissance – a shared ingredient in Shakespearean and Bollywood formulations. Thus, in naming, Bhardwaj begins to write a Hindu-influenced narrative that parallels Shakespeare's. In order to re-iterate Shakespearean implications and through this draw attention to Othello's reputation as a Moor, Bhardwaj re-produces the Hindu caste system, a religiously instituted hierarchical scheme of racial distinction through which occupation was denoted in ancient India. The character Omkara, as Bhardwaj re-creates him, is of a lower caste than that of the rest of the film's characters. While religious casteism and discrimination was outlawed by modern India's constitution, Bhardwaj relies on the pervasive lingering of such discriminatory, religious institutionalising in the subconscious of modern Indian society. Omkara, a mixed-caste who lacks the racial purity of his peers remains on the fringes of acceptance of his society while simultaneously excluded from it. While the majority of the characters in the film are given surnames of the highest-ranked holy Brahmin ('priestly') – caste: Shukla, Mishra, Tyagi, Upadhaya – Omkara is fathered by a Brahmin, with a lower caste, kanjri ('prostitute') mother, and in his mixed parentage becomes Shakespeare's Moorish hero who in being of Venice, would have evoked a sense of recognisable sophistication to a European Renaissance audience, yet who in being a Moor would have simultaneously presented himself as a figure of the unknown. As 'valiant Moor' Othello is appointed Governor of Cyprus, lauded for his valour yet retaining his Moorish moniker. On the one hand Othello is a much-needed general, while on the other hand he is destined to remain an outsider. Though he is a Moor, a suggestion that Shakespearean critics have long-since read as carrying within it suggestions of otherness and Islamic undertones, he is paradoxically also often read as a Christian. In response to a drunken brawl in Cyprus he exclaims: 'Are we turned Turks' – including himself in the society which regards him as foreign, and allying himself with the Christian:

> Othello: Are we turned Turks, and to ourselves do that
> Which heaven hath forbid the Ottomites?
> For Christian shame, put by this barborous brawl!

Bate and Rasmussen assume such Christian language as indicative of Othello's possible Christian conversion. The same can be applied to Omkara, accepted yet in sudden moments excluded – the film dialogue exclaims: 'I had forgotten that you are a half-caste.'

Yet, even as he presents the sacred caste system, Bhardwaj destabilises it. Brahmins of the ancient Hindu Vedic age did not customarily bear arms, contrasting with the violence they carry out in *Omkara*. The caste system as reproduced by Bhardwaj contains a fluidity, where while traditionally it was only the Kshatriyas ('warrior caste') who might engage in violence, Omkara as a lower caste engages in the same violence with great success. While modern India's demolishing of the caste system and independent India's focus on non-violence laid down the weapons of the warrior caste, reforming contemporary Hinduism, this is both subverted and lost in Bhardwaj's narrative which harks back to more ancient religious customs. In ancient India, where occupation was dictated by a hereditary caste system, most briefly summarised as Brahmins (priests), Kshatriyas (warriors), Vaishyas (merchants), and Shudhras (untouchables), and where the institutionalising of these castes functioned out of religious conservatism, there was little chance for mobility. Here in the film, weapons are taken up, regardless of caste. Still, Bhardwaj reiterates caste identities by providing pseudo-religious shots of certain characters' yajnopavitas ('sacred threads') strung across their chests, and not worn by lower castes. In one episode Omkara, dismissing the Hindu notion of salvation says to Ishwar: 'There is no salvation either for you, or me.' Here, he perhaps refers not only to the sins they have carried out in their lifetimes, but their transgression of the religious-inspired caste system. Hindu philosophy dictates that there can be no moksha ('salvation') without dharma ('duty'), and it is only through the attainment of moksha that the hero lives on, from which he escapes the cycle of saṃsāra (reincarnation). In violating the caste regulated system of work, there is then a violation of religiously prescribed duty.

Yet even in lifting up the arms which belong to the warrior caste, and consequently performing their duty, Omkara cannot change his religiously-bequeathed caste status, further emphasised in his racial colouring. Omkara's darker complexion does not lend itself to the Brahmin and Kshatriya myths of lighter skin. In numerous productions of Shakespeare, Othello is represented as having darker features. Bhardwaj incorporates this within an Indian society where skin colour remains – perhaps resulting from a still-existing colonial mentality – a marker of beauty and class (and indeed caste). The film highlights racial issues by giving Omkara swarthier features than the rest of the characters. Hogan similarly notes that, 'we see that parity with the white and black difference between Iago and Othello is established in terms of caste and sub-caste hierarchies.' Hogan's essay on *Omkara* establishes that while race is not the primary focus of the film, the issue of colour is mythologised within the Hindu context. The character Indu's exuberant and friendly exclamation upon seeing Dolly, for instance, collocates religious casteism with skin colour, by comparing the pure Brahmin Dolly with the white flute of the exceedingly dark blue-black Hindu god Krishna: '… like milk in a pot of coal … like a sandal shining in the darkest night … like a magic flute in the hand of the dark lord.'

The idea of the 'dark lord' and his flute reproduce for an Indian audience the idea of the Hindu flautist god, Krishna. In Hindu iconography Krishna, is often accompanied by his consort Radha, whom mythology dictates as being married to someone else. In insinuating that at one level Omkara is a re-formed Krishna and that Dolly is a version of Radha, Bhardwaj forms an interesting commentary on the marriage tradition. Radha's inability to truly marry Krishna is rooted in the inappropriateness of her as a legalised wife in that she is otherwise committed to someone else, and that in being mortal she is a different caste, of sorts, when contrasted with Krishna's immortality. The Manusmriti, laws attributed to the Hindu sage Manu, which were a commentary on the social conduct and laws of ancient India's Vedic Age (1500 – 500 BC), dictates that for marriage, '[Wives] of equal caste are recommended.' While caste is of occupational importance, it is – as illustrated in Omkara's half-caste status – of supreme importance within marital arrangements, translated on screen to Dolly's father's rejection of their marriage. The wedding ceremony in Indian cinema is generally supplemented by a range of emotion: song and dance sequences and melodramatic monologues articulating feelings of joy and sadness. In the actual religious wedding, the bride and groom are elevated to the positions of mythically divine gods and goddesses for the day. The Indian cinema viewer's expectation of joy and sorrow are heightened in the film through the marriage spectacle, where the action both begins and ends with the prospect of a modern Indian wedding, still a sacred covenant – yet in the first instance, this wedding is interrupted in its most recognised form for an abduction to take its place, and in the second instance reaches a gruesome finality, where death is interspersed with the beginnings of a new wedded life. *Omkara* thus contains within it three prospective weddings: Dolly and Rajan's (Roderigo's) formal ceremony, which is interrupted by Omkara's abduction (which in itself is the second ceremony), and the third ceremony, which is the formal wedding of Dolly and Omkara. It is the second and third ceremonies that are of particular importance, in their forms as elopement and traditional ritualisation. The space between the weddings is filled with plots and politically instigated murders.

In *Othello*, Brabantio's suspicion of Othello is resultant of Desdemona's elopement (the second wedding), which is against the courtly code and so against her father's instruction and the values of accepted feminine behaviour: 'A maiden never bold, / Of spirit so still and quiet that her motion / Blush'd at herself.' The courtly code of behaviour was paramount to the construction of appropriate Renaissance behaviour, considered natural to the human condition, and emphasised in 'the rules of nature' (1.3.112), that Brabantio accuses Desdemona of violating. Geoffrey Bullough's text speaks of *Othello* as a 'tragedy of Honour ... based on the notion of marital honour', where the drama follows the expected conventions of the time. It is Othello's 'honours and [his] valiant parts' that Desdemona falls in love with. Desdemona's elopement is of concern in the dishonour it has brought upon her family. In Renaissance society the dangers of elopement were in its effects on masculine power and influence, where Cristina Malcolmson's essay on Jacobean drama notes that, 'a daughter's chastity preserves the father's right to determine who his allies will be, since it is through sexual intercourse with the daughter that a husband gains access to a larger intercourse with the father's family or city.' In eloping with Othello, Desdemona denies her father the opportunity to decide his allies, bereaving him of his fatherly duty. In *Omkara*, there is a similar episode of elopement. The Manusmriti notes that: 'The gift of daughters among Brahmanas [Brahmins] is most approved.' The legacy of marriage within India as a personal law rather than a legal sacrament is paralleled in Omkara's abduction of Dolly, which harks back to a Vedic system of marriage, where a marriage by abduction, also known as the daemonic or rakshasa marriage, was a valid marital ceremony for the Kshatriya caste, as outlined in the Manusmriti, where the abductor appeared in his chariot, announced his lineage and intentions, and then captured the woman he wanted to abduct. In her essay on Indian women, Sona Khan reports that in India, 'cultural, customary and religion-based laws are ancient, and their mandate flows either from their respective religious scriptures or traditions or customs which the community acquires in due course.' While legally tolerated in ancient India, the marriage by abduction was generally regarded to be an unwelcome system of marriage, as opposed to the more welcome traditional courting ceremony. In the Hindu epic the Mahābhārata, the hero Arjun abducts the heroine Subhadra, whom he later marries. Subhadra, much like Dolly, is a willing victim. In the film's title song, Omkara is introduced in the song sequence as 'sabse bade ladiya re,' the 'greatest warrior', paralleling Hindu myth's Arjuna and highlighting the connection between the film and the Vedic text. That Dolly's abduction is a willing one, is key to the transposing of plot from the Shakespearean to the Bhardwajian: within Renaissance society rape, which often constitutes a part of abduction, was as Deborah Burks has observed, a capital offence in its being a 'social threat to women ... [in] the distress it causes her family and peers.' Victims were often married to their rapists to prevent the embarrassment of the raped woman's family. In conjunction with this, Shakespearean literature abstains from glorifying rape, and so Bhardwaj in a similar vein must soften Dolly's abduction. The vehicle for this softening is his reverting to the Hindu systems of marriage and the comparison of the abductor with a mythologised and venerated hero.

Formal introduction, however, remained the most preferred legal variation of the marriage ceremony. Later in the film, Omkara's introduction to Dolly's father legalises the marriage in another aspect by formally introducing the groom to the father-in-law to be, and in seeking his blessings, attempts to render an unwelcome marriage ceremony, a welcome one. The Manusmriti notes that 'a prudent man should not marry (a maiden) who has no brother, nor one whose father is not known'. Introductions in a sense are born of an ancient legal requirement. Then as the abduction itself was a form of marriage in the Vedic age, the formal wedding ceremony at the end of the film is mere religious conventionalism, injected into the narrative to placate the morality of modern India, and also to provide for the spectacle that trademarks the Bollywood film industry.

The marker of a Hindu wedding and of such a married woman is her mangalasutra, a necklace given by the bridegroom to his wife by wearing which, as Khan notes, the wife 'ensures the welfare of her husband and his longevity. A married woman wears it as long as her husband is alive or as long as she remains married to him'. While the religious magalasutra might provide a simple replacement of Desdemona's secular and familiar handkerchief, Bhardwaj dismisses both by replacing them with an even more elaborate item in the kamarbandh, a richly ornate belt that functions as a piece of jewellery. The kamarbandh functions at two levels. Firstly, in being given by Omkara to Dolly as a consolidation of their marriage, it replaces the traditional Hindu mangalasutra, secularising and modernising the traditional. The wearing of the kamarbadh removes the mangalsutra from the neck and puts viewer focus around the waist, both contrasting and linking disparate images of prostitution and fidelity by drawing attention to Dolly's sensuality (the kamarbadh having belonged to Omkara's prostitute mother) as well as recalling a kind of chastity belt, given as a wedding present. Secondly, the ornate nature of the kamarbandh is perhaps better suited to the Bollywood genre with its emphasis on spectacle, an emphasis which was also prevalent in the Shakespearean tradition where ornate, elaborate dialogue was preferred to the prosaic, redeeming otherwise fallen characters whose potentiality for evil was blurred in poetic language.

While there is no formal wedding ceremony in *Othello*, Shakespeare speaks of the interrupted wedding in Cyprus and notes the marriage bed as the scene of infidelity rather than the chastity it ought to symbolise, which in being so inverted becomes the ultimate scene of crime of murder. Noting this marraige bed, Iago instigates: 'Do it not with poison, strangle her in her bed, even the bed she hath contaminated'. In Omkara the marriage bed – here a cot-like sleeping-swing upon which Dolly lies – becomes the scene of her murder, its 'tragic loading'. Iago's instigation of Omkara results in his killing of Dolly, which when transported to the Indian context becomes an honour-crime, where he must kill his cheating wife to protect his izzat, his honour. The film negates the myths of Hindu immortality on the wedding day, killing its bride and groom, god and goddess, and clashing the vibrancy of celebration with the realities of death. The religiosity of the wedding ceremony ends with the realities of tragedy, providing jarring images in Bhardwaj's horrific re-packaging of the Shakespearean macabre: the corpse of the joyous bride, bedecked with flowers and henna swings ominously above her dead bridegroom, her red 'sari' – a celebratory wedding dress in the Hindu tradition – echoing the redness of his blood that had stained her clothes on their first meeting. Beneath, Omkara lies in a white kurta, the colour of funeral-wear. Red recalls Hinduism's colour of love and marriage, both in dress and sindoor markings; white remains the colour of death.

Omkara must die because he has killed Dolly, an honour killing which is revealed to be an act of unjustified violence, resulting from a misguided passion that haunts his soul. The killing of an innocent wife, as in *Othello*, was perhaps against the courtly virtues of the Renaissance where while Bullough notes that while in Mediterranean (possibly

Moorish) climates a cuckolded husband might avenge himself on his wife and her lover, this was less acceptable in English society. Jean Klene's essay on *Othello* notes: 'The man of honour was also obliged to maintain the fidelity of his wife, or at least the appearance of it, as his most valuable property'. Thus, the man of honour might avenge himself on his wife's lover but must restrain himself from killing his wife. Desdemona's conversation with Emilia is similarly, a moral debate on honourable female behaviour, and on women's 'sense', where women's morality is dependent on men's honour, and so: 'Then let them [men] use us [women] well: else let them know, / The ills we do, their ills instruct us so'. For Desdemona, it is a betrayal of honour for a wife to cheat on her husband, not simply a betrayal of love: 'That there be women do abuse their husbands / In such gross kind?' The drama of Othello killing Desdemona exposes this courtly code of honour: he admits himself to have been an ardent lover, if not a wise one, having loved 'not wisely, but too well'. While previously in the drama he remains unaffected by insinuations against his honorific conduct, claiming himself to be 'one not easily jealous', dismissing those who speak ill of him ('Let him do his spite'), and asserting his own goodness ('My parts, my title and my perfect soul / Shall manifest me rightly'); here he admits himself unable to see beyond a courtly code which blurs his vision and the 'ocular proof' that he has previously demanded of Iago.

Similarly, Baldesar Castiglione's discourse on Renaissance court life, *The Courtier*, while dictating the behaviour expected of men according to courtly virtues, also notes the role of women where in courtly manners, 'women as well as men have constantly given proof of their worth'. Women of the Renaissance, existing within the male described code of honour are compelled to adjust their expectations within it. Comparably, the ancient Hindu religious text, the Rigveda, describes the state of femininity within a patriarchal society, dictating the primary duty of the female as that of marriage and the bearing of children, a convention that continues to be embedded in the Indian mind-set, where Geetha Ramanathan's essay observes of the modern scenario: 'In India, despite feminist protest and struggle, femininity is maternity ... Maternity becomes the pre-condition of the foreclosure of the female's sexuality and autonomy'. However, any child that Omkara and Dolly might produce would continue to be regarded as half-caste, alien and outside the normative religious system, and so to end the re-incarnatory cycle of saṃsāra, Omkara must kill any possibility of his future progeny. While the sound that denotes Omkara's naming, 'om', might, in representing the soul that in Hindu doctrine is in a state of perpetual re-incarnation, suggest Omkara's own perpetual re-creation, Omkara shows no desire for life nor living through his future progeny, any possibility of which he kills with the murder of the wife who will bear them. Marriage was a legal, social, and religious duty, which neither Omkara nor Dolly are able to fulfil. The Mahābhārata observes motherhood as an all-encompassing duty: 'She is a wife who is handy in the house, she is a wife who bears children, she is a wife whose life is her husband'. While scenes in the film show Dolly attempting to be a helpful partner to Omkara, devoted to keeping his house, she is denied motherhood in her death. She is thus unable to fulfil de Beauvoir's much-cited 'physiological destiny' as a result of her murder as ritualised tragoidia. It is her life that till the end remains empty, signifying nothing.

Ultimately the film wonders: *Who is the victor?* Certainly, it cannot be its now dead lover-protagonists. Bhardwaj heightens his viewer's sensory cathartic experience. While Iago refrains from speaking at the end of *Othello*, proclaiming: 'From this time forth I never will speak word'; in Omkara, Ishwar's wife Indu (who is also Omkara's sister), kills him by slitting his throat, literally cutting off his ability to speak. Indu does what Shakespeare's Emilia cannot. In killing Ishwar she avenges her brother and sister-in-law's deaths and restores a sense of honour to her family, the izzat that Omkara cannot protect.

While Indian, the Cassio-character Keshav (Kesu) is often referred to as 'firangi', a term which, much like Othello's moniker

'Moor', implies a foreigner. Unlike in the cases of Omkara and Ishwar, there are no instances where he is seen wearing his sacred thread. He appears less focused on ritualisation, indulging in alcohol and more focused on the lighter aspects of being. Keshav forms the strand of modernity that links the Vedic connotations in the film with the contemporary Indian. His English is perhaps the best of any characters, the rest of whom continue to speak in the region's Khariboli-Hindi dialect. In one episode he plays the guitar while attempting to teach Dolly a popular Stevie Wonder song, drawing attention to his engagement with Western popular culture. Yet, like the firangi Shakespeare, whose works continue to exist within Indian language systems and contexts, he too continues to survive, in fact becoming, despite (or perhaps because of) his foreigner insinuations, the inheritor of Omkara's legacy. In a religious turn, Keshav's name is one of the many names of the Hindu god Vishnu, the god of preservation. Keshav thus enters the Hindu holy trinity, the trimūrti, that features a triumvirate of sovereign Hindu gods: Brahma – Shiva – Vishnu, represented in the film as Ishwar – Omkara – Kesu. Omkara, in his murdering and marriage avatar, is perhaps most representative of the god Shiva, the destroyer, while Ishwar is re-formed as the supreme god Brahma the creator. While Ishwar's name translated into English, literally produces the name of 'God', this is a god whose schematic narratives build a narrative of destruction rather than creation. Yet it is the preserver god incarnate Keshav who survives.

Continuing to view the film's characters as representative of divinities, Indu, in previous moments as critic Mike Hidenberg observes, might be compared with the goddess Parvati, wife of Shiva, where in mortal form as Indu she is a nurturing figure who minds her son, loves her husband, and counsels Dolly. The Manusmriti notes: 'She must always be cheerful, clever in (the management of her) household affairs'; while 'a husband must be constantly worshipped as a god by a faithful wife' – this is Indu, an earthier, happier version of Dolly's ethereal beauty, whose marriage provides a more practical instance of a relationship than that of Dolly's and Omkara's in the scenes that reproduce her as friend, wife and mother. However, it is not in Indu's earthy human-ness that her prominence lies, but in her relation to religious avatars. In religious re-production she becomes the hero, her kohl-lined eyes mimicking those of goddesses in Hindu art. Indu, whose name in Sanskrit denotes the moon, is at the end eclipsed in her anger, and thus the ever-smiling, ever-playful Indu transforms, rejecting her associations with the goddess Parvati and in doing so takes on the metaphorical mantle of the darker goddess Kali, destroyer of evil. In Indu's killing of Ishwar the imagery of Kali slaying Brahma, shows the creator god killed by the destroyer of evil, conflicting images of creation and destruction, where creation itself must be slain to be born. Yet, the new world, as in the society predicted at the close of Shakespeare's Hamlet, has yet to be formed. The death of the creator god in Ishwar signifies the end of any further narrative, indeed it is his instigation that causes much of the narrative, and with his death the narrative ceases to exist.

However, the crux of Bhardwaj's narrative is that, as in Shakespeare's drama, it is not a mythologised anecdote of divine figures and narrative strategies, but one that provides a view into the rawness of basic human passions – love, anger, jealousy, betrayal, innocence. Omkara's murder of Dolly is an honour killing, performed by a man experiencing a very real jealousy. Vishnu as Keshav is a surviving but humanised figure, stripped of godly connotations. Indu's pain is that of a wife mourning for the husband she kills, not of an unmoving goddess. Her final scene shows her crying out with heart-wrenchingly emotional pain for the husband she murders, whose loss she mourns in spite of the tragic plot that demanded his death. The inability for salvation, Omkara's previously spoken words to Ishwar, is in the sins they carry out: Desdemona's / Dolly's murder, lies, and instigations. The god's revenge for this is Omkara's anagnorisis, his moment of recognition of his own manipulation and so his suicide, followed by Indu as Kali's killing of Ishwar. Yet killing a husband is equally sinful, and so Indu must end her own life. She stands before a well, and this is the last view of her that Bhardwaj allows his audience. The audience remains aware however, that this act will leave her son an orphan, inheritor of this destroyed and still to be rebuilt world, in a twist that is perhaps more Shakespearean tragic than it is Bollywood convention.

Encompassing the human emotion of the film is the Hindu social and complicated pantheistic element. The god Vishnu (here Keshav) is mythologically accepted as a re-incarnated form of Krishna, 'the dark lord' as Indu describes him at the start, Omkara himself, playing his white flute that he will later destroy – and so the out-caste becomes the foreigner, Moor. So too, the Shakespearean protagonist, like a humanised and mythologised divine figure might continue to survive so that he might be intextextually re-created in other narratives of the modern and ancient world, in various protagonists who are mirrored in generations of protagonists to come. Of its primary characters, only Keshav, representative of modern India, survives the film, and so modern India, influenced by a Western, Shakespearean ethos is ultimately the only victor in the story of a religious India. The Indian Empire might have 'gone' as Carlyle foretold to be replaced by the modern subcontinent, but in its going it left a legacy of the Shakespearean tradition for future generations, assuming the essence of Britishness in drama but translating it to a localised Indian scenario, and thus with it conjoining the ethnic with the external, the Vedic sacred with the tragic profane.

Reference Sources

- Bate, J. and Rasmussen, E. 2007. 'The Tragedy of Othello, The Moor of Venice –Introduction'. In *The RSC Shakespeare: William Shakespeare: Complete Works.* Basingstoke: Macmillan.
- Bullough, G. 1973. *Narrative and Dramatic Sources of Shakespeare: Major Tragedies: Hamlet. Othello. King Lear. Macbeth.* London: Routledge..
- Burks, D.G. 1995. "I'll Want My Will Else': The Changeling and Women's Complicity with their Rapists'. *ELH* 62, no. 4 (2016): 759-90.

- Carlyle, T. 1841 *On Heroes, Hero-Worship, and the Heroic in History.* Ed. H.D. Gray. NY: Longmans.
- Castiglione, B. 1528. *The Courtier.* Trans. G. Bull. London: Penguin, 1967.
- De Beauvoir, S. 1949. *The Second Sex.* Translated by H.M. Parshley. London: Vintage-Random, 1953.
- Dixon, Thomas. 2003. *From Passions to Emotions: The Creation of a Secular Psychological Category.* Cambridge: Cambridge UP.
- Dollimore, J. 1984. *Radical Tragedy: Religion, Ideology and Power in the Drama of Shakespeare and his Contemporaries.* Basingstoke: Palgrave-Macmillan.
- Eagleton, T. 1984. 'Forward.' In *Radical Tragedy: Religion, Ideology and Power in the Drama of Shakespeare and his Contemporaries.* x-xiii. Basingstoke: Palgrave-Macmillan.
- Girard, R. 1972. *Violence and the Sacred.* Trans. Gregory. Baltimore: John Hopkins UP.
- *Haider.* Directed by Vishal Bhardwaj. VB Pictures, 2014. DVD
- Heidenberg, M. 2004. 'No Country for Young Women: Empowering Emilia in Vishal Bhardwaj's 'Omkara". In *Bollywood Shakespeares (Reproducing Shakespeare).* Ed. C. Dionne and Kapadia, 87-106. NY: Palgrave Macmillan.
- Hogan, L. 2010. 'The Sacred and the Profane in Omkara: Vishal Bhardwaj's Hindi Adaptation of Othello.' *Image and Narrative* 11, no. 2: 49-61
- Junger, G. dir. *10 Things I Hate About You.* Touchstone Pictures, 1999. DVD.
- Khan, S. 'Inheritance of Indian Women: A Perspective'. *India International Centre Quarterly* 27, no. 2: 139-54 (2000).
- Klene, J. 'Othello: 'A Fixed Figure for the Time of Scorn''. *Shakespeare Quarterly* 26, no. 2 (1975): 39-150.
- Malcolmson, Cristina. ''As Tame as the Ladies': Politics and Gender in 'The Changeling''. *English Literary Renaissance* 20, no. 2 (1990): 320-39.
- *Manusmriti: The Laws of Manu.* 1500 BC. Trans. G. Buhler.
- *Maqbool.* Directed by Vishal Bhardwaj. Kaleidescope Entertainment, 2003. DVD.
- *A Midsummer Night's Dream.* Directed by Tim Supple. British Council, 2006.
- Naseeruddin S. and S. Naseeruddin. 2016. 'Most Hindi Movies are Silly'. By Shiva Kumar Thekkepat. *Friday.* January 31, 2014. Accessed September 29, 2016.
- *Omkara.* Directed by Vishal Bhardwaj. Shemaroo Entertainment, 2006. DVD.
- Rajagopalachari, C. 1951. *Mahābhārata.* Bombay: Bharatiya Vidya Bhavan.

- Ramananthan, G. 1993. 'Sexual Violence / Textual Violence: Desai's 'Fire on the Mountain' and Shirazi's 'Javady Alley'.' *Modern Fiction Studies* 39, no. 1: 17-35.
- Shakespeare, W. 1622. 'The Tragedy of Othello, The Moor of Venice'. In *The RSC Shakespeare: William Shakespeare: Complete Works.* Ed. J. Bate and E. Rasmussen. Basingstoke: Macmillan, 2007.
- *Lady Macbeth of the Mtsensk District.* Directed by Dimitri Shostakovich. Leningrad Maly Operny, St. Petersburg. 1934.
- Trafford, J. 2001. *Ophelia.* Thirsk: House of Stratus.
- Vyāsa, V. 1975. *The Mahābhārata.* Trans. J.A.B Buitenen. Book 1. Chicago: University of Chicago Press.
- Wilkins, W. J. 1972. *Hindu Mythology: Vedic and Puranic.* Delhi: Delhi Bookstore.

Nine Plates, Two Adventūs and One True Cross

Richard Maguire (University of East Anglia, UK)

JERUSALEM IS WIDELY accepted as the pre-eminent locus sanctus of the religion enfranchised by Constantine and Licinius in 313. Emperors invested in Christendom's emblematic capital, but were otherwise entirely absent from it. According to the early seventh-century court poet, George of Pisidia, 'No emperor of the Christians, in human memory, had come to Jerusalem' until the Emperor Heraclius (r.610-641) returned a relic of the True Cross to the Holy Sepulchre in 630 (Kaegi 2003, 206; Drijvers 2002, 178; Spain 1977, 302; Kiilerich 2001, 172). From 612 to 628, according to Kaegi, Heraclius was 'criss-crossing parts of Anatolia and the Tauros and the Amanos ranges' as part of his long expedition against the Sasanian Persians.[14] Emperors, so mobile in pursuit of military victory, appear to have been averse to visiting the metropolis which instantiated the faith they principally embodied? Do the so-called David Plates from the Second Cyprus treasure shed light on this peculiar anomaly and, conversely, how might Heraclius' Jerusalem adventus impact on our reading of the plates.

---

[14] For the preference 'expedition' over 'campaign' see George of Pisidia's narrative, *Expeditio Persica*, trans. Pertusi 1959: 84-136, composed shortly after the end of the Byzantine-Persian war in 628.

Nine Plates

On the 12th February 1902 two quarrymen, excavating in the vicinity of the twin towns of Karavàs-Lapithos on the north coast of Cyprus, discovered a hoard - the so-called Second Cyprus Treasure - amongst which were nine repoussé silver plates decorated with episodes from the life of David as told in I Samuel 16-18.[15] Evidence for a connection between the David Plates and Heraclius is material and iconographic. I will deal with the dating and place of manufacture first, and then questions of narrative and display, before, finally, discussing the relationship between Constantinople, Jerusalem and the plates.

On the evidence of the control stamps on the reverse of the plates, Cruikshank Dodd proposed a date of 613-629/630, that is, to the reign Heraclius and more specifically, to the war against the Sasanians begun under Heraclius' predecessor Phocas (r.602-610), in 602 and concluded, under Heraclius, in 628.

Heraclius's bust marks the underside of six of the plates, of which two have an additional bust.[16] This is an imperial imprimatur of a sort given that, as Grierson has pointed out, unauthorised representations of the emperor's head rendered the perpetrator liable to 'a charge of sacrilege, which carried with it the unpleasant penalty of being burnt live' (Grierson 1955, 59 n.15).[17] Any analogy with coins,

---

15 Biblical references are from the Douai-Rheims bible.

16 Cruikshank Dodd 1961: Battle of David and Goliath: 178-9 No 58 figs. a. and b; David's Marriage to Michal: 180-1 No.59 figs. a. and b; Introduction of David to Saul: 182-183 No.60 figs. a. and b; David Trying on Saul's Armour: 184-5 No.61 figs. a. and b; Anointing of David: 186-7 No.62 figs. a. and b; David Slaying Lion: 188-89 No 63 figs. a. and b; David and Soldier: 190-91 No 64 figs. a. and b; David Summoned to Samuel: 192-93 No 65 figs. a. and b; David Slaying Bear: 194-195 No. 66 figs. a and b.

17 MacCormack 1972: 747 argues that '[v]iolation of the imperial image was *lèse majesté*', while the image itself was 'treated with the same reverence and decorum as the emperor'. Leader 2000, 407-27 has argued against the Plates as 'vehicles of imperial representation'.

however, should be treated with caution. On coins '[t]he reverse bore an evident connection with the obverse', which may not have been the case with the Plates where control stamps assayed the silver independently of their iconography' (Wallace-Hadrill 1981, 299, 315). Moreover, 'the propaganda of coinage was aimed at a wide social range,' and the David Plates were clearly elite artefacts (Wallace-Hadrill 1981, 299).

Cruikshank Dodd argues that the silver was assayed in Constantinople: 'The presence of five imperial stamps…indicates that they were applied by an especially designated group of officials, of whom there were five at one time; and, further, that these officials represented imperial authority in the capital itself, rather than elsewhere,' a hypothesis supported by two contemporary accounts (Cruikshank Dodd 1961, 23 and 27). A Vita of the Cypriot, John the Almoner refers to 'silver of the best quality with five stamps' and another of Theodore of Sykeon, referenced a silver vessel, the quality of which was 'proved by the five-fold stamp upon it' (Cruickshank Dodd 1961, 26 for Theodore of Sykeon, 118).

Others, however, urge caution: Rodley points out that 'Although…[stamps] are usually taken to indicate Constantinopolitan manufacture…imperial stamps were applied to the products of state silver factories in several parts of the empire'.[18] In respect of coins, too, Grierson, argued, 'that even in the east CONOB does not necessarily imply the mint of Constantinople. It has long been recognised that it was used by Ravenna, Rome, and Carthage as well as by Constantinople, mints to which, because its scarcity, silver was restricted (Grierson 1955, 65; Cruickshank Dodd 1961, 31). Moreover, because the Plates were double sheeted to conceal the embossments it cannot be assumed that they were assayed and received their decor at the same time, or even in the same place.

---

[18] Rodley 1994: 99. C.f. Noga-Banai 2002: 226: 'stamps alone do not assure the place of origin'.

Following Cruikshank Dodds, Wander, too, argued that the plates were Constantinopolitan (Wander 1973, 102). Leader was more circumspect, allowing only that 'they were very probably made in Constantinople…' (Leader 2000, 421). Certainly, no authority has promoted Cyprus. In 1907, Dalton dismissed that possibility, arguing for Antioch, given that Syria was noted for its silversmiths (Dalton 1907, 355). The case for Antioch over Constantinople lacks consensus; hence as a working hypothesis we might accept Cruickshank Dodds' principal conclusions: that the plates were assayed c.613-629/30 in Constantinople where they also received their décor.

The background to the décor of the plates is God's instruction to Samuel to go to Jesse from amongst whose sons God sought to replace Saul, who '…the Lord hath rejected…from being king over Israel'.[19] When all the sons were found wanting, Samuel asked Jesse if he had another son to which Jesse replied that his youngest, David, was guarding the sheep. David was summoned and anointed by Samuel. Both episodes appear on the plates – but not unproblematically. David is shown with a halo at the Summoning and without a halo at the Anointing. As an initiatory rite, anointing might begin the narrative, were it not that God had already chosen David, which the halo of the Summoning might signify. The order of the plates is problematic in other respects too. Some draw on more than one verse from I Samuel 16-18 and, on another plate, the subject is disputed. Hence, the following sequence is no more than provisional (Figure 1). Small plate: the summoning of David (1 Sam. 16:11/17-19) (Figure 2). Intermediate plate: Samuel Anointing David (1 Sam. 16:13, for the main scene, 16:2-3 for the exergue). Jesse may be the figure behind David and the framing figures may be two of David's brothers. The sword probably refers to the sacrificial heifer of 1 Samuel 16:2-3, as well as prefiguring David's slaying of the lion, the bear and, ultimately, Goliath (Figure 3).

---

[19] 1 Sam. 15:26. Saul had offended God by sparing Agag, the Amalekite invader of Israel.

Intermediate plate: David before Saul (1 Sam. 16:21) (Figure 4).[20] Small plate: identified by the Metropolitan Museum as David conversing with his brother, Eliab (1 Sam 17:28-29), and by Dalton, Cruikshank Dodd, Wander, Spain Alexander and Leader as David conversing with a soldier. Van Grunsven-Eygenraam's identification of this tableau as the first meeting of David and Goliath is more plausible, providing consistency, focus and narrative impetus (Van Grunsven-Eygenraam 1973, 158-174). 1 Samuel 17 has two encounters between David and Goliath: verses 23 and 41-49. In each encounter the sun is assigned to David and the moon to Goliath. Moreover, the difference in height between the two is suggested by the upwards glance of David and a forward-leaning Goliath who, attired with helmet, chain mail, greaves and buckler, is comparable with the similarly attired Goliath in the upper and central registers of the Large Plate where the dramatis personae are not in doubt (Figures 5 & 6).Small plates: David Slaying the Lion and Slaying the Bear (1 Sam. 17:34-7). David recalls this double slaughter as recommendation to Saul that he would have both courage and God's protection in the battle with Goliath. George of Pisidia describes Heraclius as charming 'all the beasts first with weapons, next with words'. (Whitby 1998: 252)[21] Although neither Plate is overtly 'imperial', Henry Maguire cites 'a common convention of imperial art…[in which] the emperor's foes could be compared to wild beasts' (Maguire 1988, 93) (Figure 7). Intermediate plate: The Arming of David (1 Sam. 17:38) (Figure 8). The large plate: The Battle of David and Goliath. Lunette (1 Sam.17:41-47); main scene (1 Sam.

---

[20] Van Grunsven-Eygenraam 1973: 163 identifies the bodyguards framing the composition as wearing the Persian costume worn at court in the early Byzantine period. According to Kenfield 2009: 56 the framing figures on the Missorium of Theodosius, with remarkably similar hairstyles to the David Plates, identify them as German, the ethnic group from which praetorian units were predominantly drawn.

[21] Both compositions are reminiscent of a mithraic *tauroctony*.

17:48-50) exergue (1 Sam.17:51) (Figure 9).[22] Intermediate plate: The Marriage of David and Michal (1 Sam. 18:27, exergue 1 Sam. 17:25).

One of the most remarkable qualities of the plates is that they tell a story. For Weitzmann '[t]he distribution of narrative scenes over a series of individual plates is…without parallel in the history of Byzantine silverwork' (Weitzmann 1977, 99). If telling a story was primary the plates would surely have been displayed in a manner which accorded with that intention. In the Metropolitan Museum Journal for 1973, Wander published a layout - an alternation of the small and intermediate plates around the largest - making the scarcely credible claim that it took the form of a Chrismon (Figure 10) (Wander 1973, 95, Fig.10). The principal objection to Wander's layout is its preference for symmetry over story, despite his claim that 'the narrative unfolds in a clockwise direction in near perfect chronological order' (Wander 1973, 95). His layout is also undermined because, as Ratcliffe and Evans have demonstrated, the feet of the plates lack holes for suspension. (Ratcliffe and Evans 2012: 17 n.12)[23] Trilling suggests that '…the Goliath plate, by virtue of its size, must have occupied the position of greatest importance, presumably the centre. The ceremonial plates are smaller…and it is reasonable to assume that they originally flanked or surrounded it.' (Trilling 1978: 262)[24] However, if a symmetrical and linear arrangement makes most narrative sense, we are faced with a dilemma. Arranged according to the narrative of 1 Samuel, the largest plate, far from being central, is the penultimate

---

[22] The lunette may represent the second meeting of David and Goliath immediately before the Battle which took place between the towns of Sokoh and Azekah.

[23] C.f. the symmetrical arrangement of the girdle of coins and medallions of Maurice (r.582-602) also from the second Cyprus Treasure: Grierson 1955: 55-70: Weitzmann 1979, 72.

[24] Wander's alternating, concentric layout might just as readily, but with no greater relevance, be contrued as a Seal of Melchisedek: see the Justinian, Theodora and Abel and Melchisedek mosaics at S.Vitale, Ravenna

plate of a series ending with the Marriage of David and Michal (Ratliff and Evans 2012, 17). Reinstating its centrality would require the completion of the series, ISISSSILI (I=intermediate; S=small; L=large), with a further four small plates and two additional intermediate plates. Has the complementarity of four small plates with rural settings and four intermediate plates with regal settings engendered a false sense of completeness (Brown 1942, 389-399).

Certainly, the circumstances surrounding the discovery of the plates might give pause for thought. The authorities were not immediately informed. According to van Grunsven-Eygenraam, the quarrymen gave part of the Treasure to their daughters and the remainder to the head of the village, who rewarded one quarryman with 'seven donums of land and six hours of water from the old spring of Karavas' while the other was supplied with the means to acquire 'a good husband for his daughter' (Entwhistle 2003, 226-267). Once the authorities heard of the finds they 'confiscated what was still to be found of the treasure'. According to Entwhistle when '[v]arious houses were raided…part of the treasure was apprehended; most was not' (Entwhistle 2003, 227). In 1904 Dalton, in Cyprus to examine the three plates now in Nicosia, lamented that 'As to the part of the treasure which was illegally sold and smuggled out of the island, there is naturally less precise information' (Entwhistle 2003, 227, 288). Three years later he wrote, 'We have a considerable number of scenes from the career of the Israelite hero, though there are omissions…which suggest that the series is even yet incomplete'. (Dalton 1907: 355)[25] Entwhistle summed up the state of play: '[i]t is clear…both from the later published accounts of the treasure and from the archival material, that the treasure was undoubtedly larger than that realised in print by Dalton' (Entwhistle 2003, 229). He concludes: 'it is quite clear that the composition of the treasure as published by Dalton [in 1906] and the Stylianous [in 1969]…was much larger than previously thought', while

---

[25] 'the finders…pleaded that all these objects were family heirlooms'.

adding that, '[t]here is no evidence...that there were any more silver plates devoted to the David cycle' (Entwhistle 2003, 229-230).

For Spain Alexander the Plates are concerned with the legitimacy of David's kingship (Spain Alexander 1977, 217). Leader largely agrees: '[t]he plates represent his youthful preparation for his subsequent role as king of Israel' (Leader 2000, 423). That being the case, ending with The Marriage raises some difficult questions: was an intention to continue the series never carried to completion; was the treasure divided into lots; do some plates await discovery etc.? The hand of Michal is not David's reward for defeating Goliath, but an opportunity for Saul to conspire against David, coercing him into further confrontation with the enemy, by demanding a dowry of 'a hundred foreskins of the Philistines'(1 Sam 18:25). David's progress towards kingship, announced with such promise in the Summoning and Anointing, comes to a sudden halt. His accession as king of Judah (2 Sam. 2:7) and Israel (2 Sam. 5:2-4) lies some way in the future and is, furthermore, predicated on the decapitation of Saul (1 Sam. 31.9). Not only do the plates lack the climax of an enthronement which the early plates promise, closing the chronology with The Marriage is contrary to God's will because the discredited Saul continues to rule.

It has been argued that the Plates are about David and not Heraclius given the absence of crucial imperial signatures, including an imperial diadem. In David before Saul and The Marriage, Saul wears an undecorated band, similar, for example, to the coinage of Antiochus III (223-187 BC), sometime ruler of Cyprus. This may have been intentional archaising, identifying Saul as the old king. The new king, David, lacks a diadem because the narrative closes before his enthronement, a lacuna noted by Dalton in 1907 (Dalton 1907, 361). Nevertheless, the points at which the biographies of David and Heraclius correlate are striking. As usurpers for whom military victory was key in legitimising their kingship, both exemplify the trope of armies embodied as individuals, wars conceived as single combat, enemies identified as infidels, and victory exemplified by decapitation.²⁶ Moreover, the audience for silverware of this distinction was unlikely to have taken either narrative or dramatis personae at face value: Late Antique elites were accustomed to employing interpretative strategies in elucidating levels of meaning (Dunbabin 2014, 234; Leader 2000, 424). Against the background of the current war, a partisan audience would have little difficulty identifying Heraclius with David, Byzantines with Israelites and Philistines with Sasanid Persians. It would, then, have been but a short step to identify an imperial court with a royal one. In all four intermediate plates, the arch of an arcuated lintel honours the principal figure (Dalton 1906, 5). According to Dalton, in the two plates in which Saul presides - David before Saul and The Marriage - he 'wears royal costume and has a nimbus like other kings…in Early Christian and Byzantine art' (Dalton 1906, 5). For the only time in the series, in The Marriage, David wears a tablion, the lozenge-shaped segmentum of a court dignitary, notably worn by Justinian and his court officials at SanVitale in Ravenna (547). (Wander 1973, 94)²⁷ The identification of Emperors with biblical kings has a precedent in the markedly Justinianic David, consistent with the Justinian of San Vitale, who appears in the axial medallion in the apse at Sinai and in the Sinope Gospels, both from the mid-sixth century (Sinope Gospels, Paris, Bibliothèque Nationale, MS gr.1286; Leader 2000: 417-18; Forsyth and Weitzmann, 1973, Pl.CXIX).

Much of the evidence for early-seventh century Davidic kingship comes from the literary circle surrounding Sergius, patriarch of Constantinople. In the late stages of the expedition against Persia,

---

26 The panegyric tone of the plates precludes references to David's 'adulterous' marriage to Bathsheba, which was 'displeasing to the Lord' (2 Sam.11.27), and its possible corollary, Heraclius marriage to his niece Martina, described by Nikephorus 'as an unlawful deed, one that is forbidden by Roman custom'. Nikephorus 11 in Mango 1990: 53, 179.

27 Wander sees anointing and arming as 'associated in the Byzantine world with the conference of kingship – coronation and consecration'.

George of Pisidia records Heraclius addressing his troops as '...the ones about whom David divinely spoke out, saying 'blessed is he who strikes down the sons of Persia...' (Kaegi 2003, 114). In a sermon delivered in 627, close to the conclusion of the war, Theodore Synkellos identified Heraclius as 'our basileus' like '...David...[M]ay the Lord crown him with victories, just as with David' (Shahîd 1972, 309-10 n.65). At the end of the expedition, in 629, Heraclius accepted the Davidic epithet, abandoning autocrator (αὐτοκράτωρ) for basileus (βασιλεύς), a title redolent of Old Testament kingship (Humphreys 2015, 31; Shahîd, 1972, 302).

Episodes from Heraclius' rise to power can be mapped onto the Cyprus Plates with little difficulty. Cruikshank Dodd's terminus post quem – 613 – might be identified with Heraclius' landing in Constantinople in 610, possibly via Cyprus, to overthrow the tyrant Phocas (Mitchell 2007, 411: against, see Kaegi 2003, 46 n.75 and 47). David's kingship was preceded by two beheadings, of Goliath and Saul. On 5th October 610 Heraclius was 'crowned by the patriarch Sergius' and the same day saw the decapitation of Phocas (Theophanes in Mango and Scott 1997, 428).[28] Heraclius may have performed the rite of trachelismos, trampling on the neck of the vanquished in a symbolic decapitation, prior to the actual beheading. However, the seventh-century Chronicon Paschale describes how Phocas was brought before Heraclius: 'And his right arm was removed at the shoulder, as well as his head...His head was put on a pole, and thus it too was paraded around' (Chronicon Paschale 610 in Whitby and Whitby 1989, 153).

Cruikshank Dodd's terminus ante quem – 629/30 – offers some particularly close parallels. The middle-aged Heraclius in the final phase of the Persian expedition was clearly not the teenager who

---

[28] McCormick 1986: 70. C.f. 1 Samuel 17:50-1: 'And as David had no sword He ran and stood over the Philistine': for 'standing over' we might read 'trampling'.

confronted Goliath.²⁹ Nevertheless, according to Nikephorus' Short History, on December 12th 627 Heraclius, challenged to single combat by the Sasanian general Razates, 'sliced off with his sword the shoulder of Razates; and when the latter had fallen down, the emperor... straightaway cut off his head.³⁰ The encounter occurred at Ancient Nineveh, close to the River Zab, perhaps personified by the river God in the lunette of the Large Plate who may also be a reference to the Elan brook from which David chose the stones that felled Goliath. In the central register of the Large Plate, the combat of David and Goliath, the defining act of Israelite-Philistine war, is about to begin. Reacting to the outcome of an encounter still in its preliminary stages, the Israelites on the left might be understood as the advancing Byzantines 'filled with ardor' with, on the right, the Philistines, representing the 'utterly defeated' Persians fleeing after the humiliation of Razates (Nikephorus 14 in Mango 1990, 61).

If the plates were issued to celebrate Heraclius's victory over the Persians they would have coincided with the 'very years' (628-30) which, according to Spain Alexander, 'witnessed the culmination of the association between Heraclius and David, an association based on the imperial cult, but [which] intensified as a result of the Persian war' (Spain Alexander 1977, 236). There is, however, one stumbling block to a full identification of Heraclius with the David of the plates. After the war Heraclius made two adventūs associated with the restitution of the True Cross, for which the plates offer no corollary. Yet the Book of Samuel provides us with a parallel so pertinent, that the absence of the episode from the plates is, at the very least, surprising

---

29   According to I Samuel 17.33, 'And Saul said to David...thou art but a boy'.
30   Nikephorus 14 in Mango 1990: 61, 182. Gibbon 1994: v.4, 587 has 'a Persian of gigantic size was slain...by the hand of the emperor himself'.

Two Adventūs and One True Cross

In 614 the Persians took Jerusalem, they 'broke down the churches of Christ,' and 'the portion of the salvific wood that the pious Empress [Helena] had left there...[they] carried off' (Borghammer 2009, 181-183). Heraclius celebrated the recovery and restitution of the Cross in two strikingly different adventūs, one into Constantinople and the unprecedented adventus into Jerusalem. More than any of his predecessors, Heraclius defines the character of these two 'capitals': the adventus of 629 attesting to the continuity of Constantinople as the pre-eminent nikopolis of the imperial cult and the adventus of 630 attesting to Jerusalem as the Theopolis of the cult of 'Jesus the Christ, the son of David' (Matthew 1:1).

Despite an account of c.636, in which 'the Holy Cross had been taken out of the temple of ...[the Persian King] by Heraclius,' there is no evidence that the Byzantine-Persian war was a proto-crusade (Borghammer 2009, 189). Had it been, Heraclius might have pressed on to the Persian capital, Ctesiphon, to which the Cross had been removed, rather than returning to Armenia (Shahîd 1972, 309-10 n.65; Chronicon Paschale 628 in Whitby and Whitby 1989, 187-88). Heraclius' goal had been the recovery of Mesopotamia, Syria, Palestine and Cilicia. Once the status quo ante bellum had been restored, the Emperor wrote to the Persian king on 6th January 628: 'I do not willingly burn Persia...Let us now throw down our arms and embrace peace' (Keagi 2003, 172; cf Theophanes in Mango and Scott 1997, 453). The Cross relic seems to have reappeared as a footnote to the peace negotiations.[31] However, once in his possession, Heraclius was keen to exploit its political potential, returning to a form of urban ceremonial which by the seventh century was already old fashioned,

---

[31] Drijvers 2002: 177, suggests that, in 628 Heraclius agreed a peace treaty with the Persians the terms of which included the handing over of the Cross relic. Spain Alexander 1977: 233.

and, moreover, returning to it twice in seven months (MacCormack 1972, 735).

Drijvers argues that 'In spite of the wealth of sources, it is hard, if not impossible, to reconstruct from them the historical 'reality' about the restoration of the Cross; the available material is contradictory and fact and fiction are not always easily distinguishable…' (Drijvers 2002, 177-8; Theophanes in Mango and Scott 1997, 458 n.3).

Most authorities date the Jerusalem adventus after Constantinople; thus Theophanes dates Constantinople to 626/7: 'Now the emperor, having defeated Persia in the course of six years, made peace in the seventh and returned with great joy to Constantinople' (Theophanes in Mango and Scott 1997, 457). From Constantinople, in 627/8, 'setting forth from the Imperial City in the early spring, the Emperor proceeded to Jerusalem, taking with him the venerable and life-giving Cross so as to offer thanks to God' (Theohanes in Mango and Scott 1997, 458).] That chronology is confirmed in the Sermo de exaltatione sanctae crucis of c.630-6, a document particularly close to the events it described (Borghammer 2009, 187).

The year 629 is more widely accepted for the Constantinople adventus. The date, September 14th, was rich in Jerusalemite references as the anniversary of the discovery of the Cross c.328, the dedication of the Holy Sepulchre in 335 and the feast of the Encaenia, the Veneration of the Cross. The adventus probably began at the Hebdomon, the maritime suburb on the Sea of Marmara where emperors were traditionally legitimated. Theophanes describes the customary excursion from the city by a population 'holding olive branches and lights', and led by their patriarch, from whence 'they entered the city dancing with joy' (MacCormack 1972, 751; Theophanes, Chronicle 6119 in Mango and Scott, 1997, 457). Despite its Jerusalemite accents, this adventus was suffused with imperial, and particularly Constantinian and Theodosian references. Indeed the presence of an emperor in urban ceremonial had been a Theodosian innovation (Jacobs 2012, 145). Kitzinger observed that the Cyprus

Plates were 'a conscious and somewhat studied effort to imitate – and vie with – work of the Theodosian period', not the least of which was the Missorium of Theodosius (Figure 11). (Kitzinger 1976: 6/162.)[32]

The Golden Gate, originally a freestanding triumphal arch now incorporated into the Theodosian walls, was rarely opened for anything less than imperial victory (Bardhill 1999, 696). Crowning the Gate, Theodosius stood in a quadriga drawn by four elephants with, on either side, Nike and Tyche.[33] The inscription on the outer face of the arch ran: 'Theodosius adorned these gates after the fall of a tyrant', probably the usurper Magnus Maximus, executed in the presence of Theodosius in 388. The Golden Gate, then, stood as an unequivocal claim that Constantinople was the imperial city.

In an extraordinary act of mimesis, Heraclius entered Constantinople in a quadriga also drawn by four elephants. By the end of the fourth century emperors in quadrigae were so rare that Heraclius was clearly affirming his credentials as the legitimate successor of the dynasties of Constantine and Theodosius, a claim reinforced by stations at a succession of fora each accented by imperial stylites. The Sigma Forum, dominated by an honorific column of Theodosius II, served as the forecourt for the Helenianae Palace, associated with the True Cross through the relic with which Theodosius had endowed it. (Maguire 1995: 59)[34] Here, Heraclius probably abandoned his military dress for garments appropriate to the imperial office. The procession then passed

---

[32] The senate conferred on Heraclius the title the 'new Theodosius'; Whitby 2002: 157; Kaegi 2003: 192.

[33] 'Four' may be an exemplary number. For four elephants see Nicephorus description of the adventus in MacCormack 1972: 75. Bryan Ward-Perkins (pers comm) cautions that Theodosius would hardly been visible behind the elephants on top the Golden Gate, and, at ground level, it is similarly doubtful that four elephants could have passed through the Gate's central arch.

[34] At the Coronation of Leo I (r.457-474), recalled in the *Book of Ceremonies*, the emperor changed from military to imperial costume: Dagron, 2003, 62.

through the Golden Gate in the Constantinian walls and through the fora of Arcadius, Theodosius and Constantine. Heraclius may also have stopped at the Forum Bovis, in the centre of which was a huge bronze bull's head into which, according to Gibbon, 'the mangled trunk [of Phocas] was cast into the flames'. (Gibbon 1994: v.4 568)[35]

Heraclius' final station would have been Justinian's remodelled Augustaeon, the square joining the imperial palace to Ayia Sofia where, as the conclusion to this adventus, the Cross relic was raised over the altar. The Augustaeon was dominated by a 70m-high column surmounted by an equestrian Justinian with which Heraclius must have felt a particular affinity: Procopius describes Justinian as 'directing his course...against the Persians...[holding] a globe...which...signifies that the whole earth and the sea are subject to him...a cross stands upon the globe which he carries, the emblem by which alone he obtained both his empire and his victory in war' (Procopius 1.ii.5-12 in Dewing 1954, 35). The cross served as the sign under which Constantine, Justinian and now Heraclius triumphed, but Nike rather than Christ sanctioned this thoroughly imperial adventus, such that spectators at the events on that September day could have been in no doubt about the continuity of the emperor cult and Constantinople as its nikopolis. For an adventus imbued with the sacrality of the Cross, we must look elsewhere – to Jerusalem on the 21st March 630.

Heraclius' second adventus opened with a similar signature to the first – a congregational acclamation outside the walls by the 'monks...with the citizens of Jerusalem and Modestus (their acting patriarch), carrying incense'.[36] In Jerusalem, too, the city was entered through a Golden Gate. But from the moment Heraclius reached the Gate the tone of this adventus changed radically.

---

[35] The head was usually reserved for burning miscreants whose last cries caused the bull to bellow.

[36] Eutychius of Alexandria in MacCormack 1972: 750: MacCormack places the Jerusalem *adventus* before Constantinople.

The Golden Gate in Jerusalem opened onto the Temple platform where Christ had made His adventus on a donkey, through which He passed on the way to His crucifixion and through which He would appear at the Second Coming. The almost contemporary Reversio Sanctae Crucis of the mid-630s, describes how, '...when the Emperor...sitting on the Royal horse decorated with imperial ornaments wanted to enter...the stones of the gate suddenly descended...making a solid wall. As they were wondering in astonishment they...saw the sign of the Cross in the sky...An angel of the Lord took it in his hands, stood above the gate and said. 'When the king of the heavens...entered through this gate...he did not appear in purple or in a shining diadem...but sitting on the back of a humble donkey he left his servants a paradigm of humility....' Then the Emperor rejoiced in the Lord...and having removed the tokens of imperial rank he proceeded without shoes, girded only with a linen belt, took the Cross of the Lord in his hands and hastened forward, face covered with tears and eyes raised to the sky, making his way to the gate'. (Borghammer 2009, 187)[37] The Reversio continues, '[a]s soon as he approached with humility the hard stones sensed the celestial command, and raising itself...the gate gave free access to those who were going in...[Heraclius] restored the precious part of the Tree that he had brought with him to its proper place.' (Borghammer 2009, 187).

One of the signifiers of transformation in Late Antiquity was change of attire – a preliminary in both adventūs. Furthermore, both involved mimesis: a Constantinian/Theodosian Heraclius in Constantinople and a Davidic/Christomimetic Heraclius in Jerusalem. Both adventūs emphasise Golden Gates, while their goals, respectively Ayia Sofia and the Holy Sepulchre, are more peremptorily referenced. In the Constantinople adventus the Cross was not only supplementary, it elided with a tropaion (τρόπαιον), the victory trophy in the form of

---

[37] The angel is not the successor of the Constantinopolitan Nike and Tyche so much as their equivalent and contemporary.

tree trunks set crosswise, on which the armour and weapons of the vanquished were hung. Stripped of the imperial paraphernalia which dominated in Constantinople, the Jerusalem adventus was a dressed-down, demilitarised affair. An exemplary Theodosius now gave way to an exemplary David.[38] Heraclius was more closely identified with David than any of his predecessors and no city was more Davidic than Jerusalem. Breaking imperial precedent in which '[n]o emperor of the Christians, in human memory, had come to Jerusalem', Heraclius was the new David, restoring to 'the city of David', the relics of the Cross, the New Testament pendant to 'the ark of the Lord [that] was come into the city of David' (2 Sam. 6:16: see also 2 Sam. 5:7; 5:9; 6:10).

If the plates predate the return of the Cross in 628, the absence of any reference to David's recovery of the Ark would be understandable. However, if we accept Cruikshank Dodds' later date of 629/30, the plates may well have celebrated both the end of the war and the recovery of the Cross. The rather inexplicable and inconclusive concentration of the plates on the early life of David might well, and with much greater narrative purpose, have been extended to an Old Testament and particularly telling corollary for the recovery and restitution of the Cross in David's recovery and restitution of the Ark: 1 Samuel 4:11 describes how 'the ark of God was taken' by the Philistine's and 2 Samuel 6: 2-17 tells of David's recovery and restitution of the Ark to Jerusalem, and at 2 Samuel 6:14, how 'David danced with all his might before the Lord' echoing the first Heraclian adventus at which the population 'entered the city dancing with joy'. The case for a more extended David narrative is that, as we have seen, ending with the Marriage leaves Saul as king, David as pretender, and

---

[38] Ambrose used an exemplary David to illustrate how Theodosius was *unlike* David. A letter of 390, censuring Theodosius for massacre of 7000 at Thessalonike, contained no less than nine Davidic examples upon which the emperor might model his behavior. Ambrose *Letter* LI 7-10. 1881, pp.324-329.

God's plan to replace the former with the latter entirely unfulfilled. The battle of David and Goliath may have been pivotal but with the sole exception of the Marriage, the episodes it portends are entirely unreferenced and unresolved. If one of the principle absentees is any reference to David's coronation, surely another, given a date of 629/30, would have been David's restitution of the Ark to Jerusalem.

Coda

Why were the David Plates concealed on Cyprus? The island was known as a refuge for iconodules, and it is possible that plates with a biblical décor were remitted there for safe keeping (Auzépy 1997, 219-20; Theophanes Chronicle 6262 in Mango and Scott 1997, 614). Alternatively, Syria, famous for its silverware, fell to the Arabs in 634, initiating a westward surge of refugees, some perhaps with high status silver to protect (Theophanes Chronicle 6305 in Mango and Scott 1997, 683).

There was a shortage of silver throughout the period covered by Cruickshank Dodd's dates. In 615 Heraclius had introduced the silver hexagram, principally to pay the military, with the result, according to Cruikshank Dodd, that 'all procurable silver would have been used for coinage rather than silver vessels' (Cruickshank Dodd 1961, 33). The situation was no better at the end of the war. Patriarch Sergius, having funded Heraclius' Persian expedition from the sale of church plate, needed the loan repaid. Despite their narrative there is no evidence that the David Plates had a liturgical function and if churches had given what they could, secular silver would have been vulnerable to appropriation to replenish Constantinople's ecclesiastical silver. The Plates are sometimes introduced as evidence for the increasing influence of Constantinople in Late Antique Cyprus, but if to conceal is also to decontexualise - to cover one's tracks - Cyprus may have been no more than a refuge at the eastern margins of an increasingly vulnerable empire.

Reference Sources

- Ambrose of Milan. 1881. *Letters*. London, Oxford and Cambridge: James Parker.
- Auzépy, M.-F. 1997. *La Vie d'Étienne le Jeune par Étienne le Diacre*. Aldershot: Variorum.
- Bardill, J. 1999. 'The Golden Gate in Constantinople: A Triumphal Arch of Theodsius I'. In *American Journal of Archaeology* 103 (4): 671-96.
- Borghammer, S. 2009. 'Heraclius Learns Humility: Two Early Latin Accounts Composed for the Celebration of Exultatio Crucis.' In *Millenium: Jahrbuch zu Kultur und Geschichte des Erst-Everymanen Jahrtausends*, ed. Wolfram Brandes, 145-201. Berlin: Verlag Walter de Gruyter.
- Brown, D.F. 1942. 'The arcuated lintel and its symbolic interpretation in Late Antiquity,' *American Journal of Archaeology* 46 (3): 389-399.
- *Chronicon Paschale 284-628*. 1989. Trans. Michael and Mary Whitby. Liverpool: Liverpool University Press.
- Cruikshank Dodd, E. 1961. *Byzantine Silver Stamps*. Washington DC: Dumbarton Oaks Research Library.
- Dagron, G. 2003, *Emperor and Priest: The Imperial Office in Byzantium*. Cambridge: Cambridge University Press
- Dalton, O.M. 1906 'A Second Silver Treasure from Cyprus' *Archaeologia* 60: 1-24.
- --- 1907. 'Byzantine Plate and Jewellery from Cyprus in Mr. Morgan's Collection.' *Burlington Magazine* X: 355-362.
- Dawes, E. and N. Baynes. 1948. *Three Byzantine Saints*. Oxford: Blackwell.
- de Corselas, L. and M. Parada. 2013. 'The arcuated lintel and the 'Serlian Motif'. Imperial identity, architectural and symbolic interactions in Ancient Rome.' In *SOMA 2012: Identity and Connectivity*, ed. L. Bombardieri, 479-486. Oxford: Archaeopress.
- Drijvers, J.W. 2002. 'Heraclius and the Restitutio Crucis: Notes on Symbolism and Ideology.' In *The Reign of Heraclius (610-641)*, eds. G.J. Reinink and B.H. Stolte, 175-190. Leuven: Peeters.
- Dunbabin, K. 2014. 'Mythology and Theatre in the Mosaics of the of the Graeco-Roman East.' In *Using Images in Late Antiquity*, ed. S. Birk, T. Myrup Kristensen and B.Poulson, 227-252. Oxford: Oxbow Books.
- Entwistle, C. 2003. 'Lay not up for yourselves treasure on earth': the British Museum and the second Cyprus treasure.' In *Through a Glass Brightly*, 226-235. Oxford: Oxbow Books.

- Forsyth, G.H. and K. Weitzmann. 1973. *The Monastery of Saint Catherine at Mount Sinai: The Church and Fortress of Justinian.* Ann Arbor MI: University of Michigan Press.
- George of Pisidia. 1959. 'Expeditio Persica.' In *Giorgio di Pisidia, Poemi 1. Panegirici*, ed. A. Pertusi, 84-136. Ettal: Buch-Kunstverlag.
- Gibbon, E. 1994. Decline and Fall of the Roman Empire. v.4. London: David Campbell Publishers.
- Grierson, 1955. 'The Kyrenia Girdle of Byzantine Medallions and Solidi.' *The Numismatic Chronicle and Journal of the Royal Numismatic Society* 15.45: 55-70.
- Humphreys, M.T. G. 2015. *Law, Power and Imperial Ideology in the Iconoclast Era: c.680-850.* Oxford: Oxford University Press.
- Jacobs, I. 2012 'The Creation of the Late Antique City: Constantinople and Asia Minor During the Theodosian Renaissance.' *Byzantion* 82: 113-164.
- Kaegi, W. 2003. *Heraclius, Emperor of Byzantium.* Cambridge: Cambridge University Press.
- Kenfield, J. 2009. 'Heaven's Exarchs: Observations on Early Byzantine Archangels.' In *Koine: Mediterranean Studies in Honor of R.Ross Holloway,* eds. D.B. Counts and A.S. Tuck, 54-63. Oxford: Oxbow Books.
- Kiilerich, B. 2001. 'The Image of Anicia Juliana in the Vienna Diosurides'. In *Symbolae Osloensis* 76: 169-189.
- Kitzinger, E. 1976. 'Byzantine Art in the Period between Justinian and Iconoclasm.' *The Art of Byzantium and the Medieval West*, ed. W. Eugene Kleinbauer. Bloomington IN: Indiana University Press.
- Leader, R.E. 2000. 'The David Plates Revisited: Transforming the Secular in Byzantium.' *The Art Bulletin.* 82 (3): 407-427.
- MacCormack S. 1972. 'Change and Continuity in Late Antiquity: The Ceremony of 'Adventus" *Historia: Zeitschrift fur Alte Geschichte* 21 (4) 721-52.
- Maguire, H. 1988. 'The Art of Comparing in Byzantium.' *Art Bulletin* 70 (1): 88-103.
- --- 1995. *Byzantine Court Culture from 829 to 1204.* Washington DC: Harvard University Press.
- McCormick, M. 1986. *Eternal Victory.* Cambridge: Cambridge University Press.
- Mitchell, S. 2007. *A History of the Later Roman Empire. AD 284-641.* Oxford: Wiley Blackwell.
- Nikephoros, *Patriarch of Constantinople.* 1990. Short History. Trans. C. Mango. Washington DC: Dumbarton Oaks.
- Noga-Banai, G. 2002. 'Byzantine Elite Style: The David Plates and Related Works.' *Boreas,* 25: 225-37.

- Procopius. 1954. *On Buildings.* Trans H. B. Dewing. London: William Heinemann.
- Ratcliffe, B. and H.C. Evans. 2012. *Byzantium and Islam: Age of Transition, 7th-9th Century.* New York: Metropolitan Museum of Art.
- Rodley, L. 1994. Byzantine Art and Architecture: An Introduction. Cambridge: Cambridge University Press.
- Shahîd, Ifan 1972. 'The Iranian Factor in Byzantium during the Reign of Heraclius.' *Dumbarton Oaks Papers* 26: 293-320.
- Spain Alexander, S. 1977. 'Heraclius, Byzantine Imperial Ideology, and the David Plates.' *Speculum* 52 (2): 217-237.
- Stylianou, A. and J. 1969. *The Treasures of Lambousa.* Nicosia: Zavallis Press.
- Theophanes.1997. *The Chronicle of Theophanes Confessor.* Trans. C. Mango, R. Scott and G.Greatrex. Oxford: Clarendon Press.
- Trilling, J. 1978. 'Myth and Metaphor in the Byzantine Court. A Literary Approach to the David Plates.' *Byzantion* 48. 249-263.
- van Grunsven-Eygenraam, M. 1973. 'Heraclius and the David Plates.' *Bulletin antieke Beschaving.* 48: 158-174.
- Wallace-Hadrill, A. 1981. 'The Emperor and his Virtues.' *Historia* 30: 298-323.
- Wander, S.H. 1973. 'The Cyprus Plates: The Story of David and Goliath.' *Metropolitan Museum Journal* 8: 89-104.
- Weitzmann, K. 1970. 'Prolegomena to a Study of the Cyprus Plates.' *Metropolitan Museum Journal* 3: 97-111
- --- 1979 *Age of Spirituality.* Princeton NJ: Princeton University Press.
- Whitby, M. 2002. 'George of Pisidia's Presentation of the Emperor Heraclius and his Campaigns: variety and Development.' In *The Reign of Heraclius (610-641),* eds. G.J. Reinink and B.H. Stolte. Leuven: Peeters.
- Whitby, M. 1988. *The Emperor Maurice and his Historian. Theophylact Simocatta on Persian and Balkan Warfare.* Oxford: Clarendon Press.

Illustrations

Fig. 1 Summoning of David (Author, courtesy of the Department of Antiquities, Cyprus)

Fig. 2 Samuel Anointing David (OASC www.metmuseum.org)

Fig. 3 David Before Saul (OASC. www.metmuseum.org)

Fig. 4 First Meeting of David and Goliath
(OASC. www.metmuseum.org)

Fig. 5 David Slaying the Lion
(OASC. www.metmuseum.org)

Fig. 6 David Slaying the Bear
(Author, courtesy of the Department of Antiquities, Cyprus)

Fig. 7 Arming of David
(OASC. www.metmuseum.org)

Fig. 8 Battle of David and Goliath
(OASC. www.metmuseum.org)

Fig. 9 Marriage of David and Michal
(Author, courtesy of the Department of Antiquities, Cyprus)

Fig. 10 Wander's arrangement of the Plates
(after Wander, courtesy of the Department of Antiquities, Cyprus/
OASC. www.metmuseum.org)

Fig. 11 Missorium of Theodosius: replica
(Author)

Tea-trays and longing: mapping Giorgione's *Sleeping Venus* onto Cyprus

Michael Paraskos (Imperial College London, UK)

AS A CHILD, in the summers, my parents would take my bothers, sister and myself out of school in England early, before the start of the official summer holidays, and we would travel to Cyprus. 'Going home', we would call it, or sometimes with a more melodramatic flourish, 'returning to the homeland', although we children were all born in England, and were only really Cypriots in our own minds. Once in Cyprus, my father, the painter Stass Paraskos, would set up the famous annual summer camp he ran for artists, the Cyprus Summer School, and we would spend the hot months of the καλοκαίρι playing on the beach, swimming, eating σουβλάκι, and listening to discussions on art in the decidedly bohemian company of artists from all over the world — the likes of Terry Frost, Mali Morris, Dennis Creffield, Euan Uglow and numerous others.

As the summer drew to a close, and we faced the unhappy prospect of returning to England, being young children we were invariably drawn to the tourist tat shops, with their cheap and tacky souvenirs, usually mass-produced in Hong Kong or Taiwan, in search of tangible signifiers of our obsessive desire to be Cypriot, physical things to take back to with us to what was our real home in Britain. On these souvenirs would usually be printed things like a scene of *Petra tou Romiou*, the alleged birthplace of the goddess Aphrodite, or the view of some monastery on the Kyrenia mountains we had never seen, or a map of Cyprus, emblazoned with hand-drawn images such as Aphrodite floating off the coastline, a dubious representation of Kolossi Castle near Limassol, or Venetian galleons, sometimes alongside a giant fish, lurking near Famagusta. This map was printed on almost every conceivable object a tourist could buy, from post cards, to boxes of the local sweet λουκούμια, to oversized pencils, to tee-shirts, to tea-towels, and plastic trays. (Figs. 1, 2, 3) Even at the time it was notable to me, how the maps focussed so much on the medieval and renaissance periods in Cyprus, with their sailing ships and heraldic crests. Yet alongside that medieval world they still showed Aphrodite, or Venus, the pagan goddess of love. In modern Cyprus at least, the ancient and medieval co-existed, at least in the fantasy space of the tourist souvenir artefact.

A few years later, as I set out on another journey, this time to become the eminent art historian you see before you now, a trace memory of those tea-towels and cheap trays, and the maps printed on them, returned to me in an unexpected place. Sitting in a darkened classroom at Canterbury College of Technology, starting my studies as a part-time student of art history, my tutor John Millest projected an image of a painting onto the classroom wall. It was a beautiful painting, unknown to me at the time, but strangely familiar. It was Giorgione's *The Sleeping Venus.* (Fig. 4) Alongside the Aphrodite of Milos, Giorgione's Venus has been one of the ur-sources for representing Aphrodite-Venus for centuries, a fact the kind and gentle Mr Millest explained, starting with Titian's reworking of it into *The Venus of Urbino,* moving on to Velázquez's creation of the *Rokeby Venus,* and on into Manet's *Olympia* and modernist reinterpretations by Picasso, Matisse and Tom Wesselmann.

All of this was very interesting, of course, and necessary knowledge to get a student through a university-entrance examination. But what really struck me when I first saw the image of that Giorgione painting was its resemblance, in my mind at least, to those tourist souvenir maps of Cyprus I coveted as a child. I know this will seem a strange claim — one which divides those I suggest it to into those who see it and those who don't. In my defence I would say that the human mind is a creative daemon that throws up some surprising connotations. For me, one of those was, and still is, the juxtaposition of Giorgione's painting and a 1970s tourist map of Cyprus.

Consequently, in the context of the claim by Othello's Island to be a conference open to speculative ideas, I am presumptuous enough to speculate on why I find it so difficult to get this connection out of my mind. From this a curious possibility has emerged, for which I offer nothing except circumstantial evidence, and sometimes oblique visual affinities — an art historical method too often neglected even by art historians and possibly alien to academics engaged in document-rich areas of study. That possibility is that, at some level, the Giorgione and the souvenir maps are analogous objects, not simply for the connotations they evoked in my adolescent mind, but in their functions.

I am tempted to suggest that the easiest of these two claims to deal with is the visual form of the tourist souvenir maps being analogous to Giorgione's Venus. Except, if it is so easy, I wonder why the connection has never been made before. Perhaps the idea that the form of the Giorgione painting is not unlike a map of Cyprus carries more weight if we think of Giorgione's representation in terms of psychological *proximity*, using an understanding of the word proximity from Gestalt theory. (Kubovy, 2000:41) If we move our eye from map (fig. 1), to map (fig. 2), to map (fig. 3), and then finally to Giorgione's *Sleeping Venus* (fig. 4), I believe a certain kind of formal connection is established visually. I call this a kind of *psychological* proximity simply because as I sat in the darkened classroom of my art history class in Canterbury some thirty-odd years ago, Mr Millest did not show any of the Cyprus maps. He showed *The Sleeping Venus* followed by Giorgione's later artist-followers, so that they became its actual proximity images. It was only in my mind that the various iterations of the Cyprus tourist maps came into additional play — thus, memory of map (fig. 1), to memory of map (fig. 2), to memory of map (fig. 3), to photographic reproduction of Giorgione's *Sleeping Venus* (fig. 4). The formal elements of the Giorgione allow this in terms of the body of his representation of Venus looking not unlike the island of Cyprus, even if this might lead us to make some prurient associations. Venus resembles the island of Cyprus in the way her legs stretch out like the island's peninsula panhandle region, called Karpasia, her voluptuous body evokes the main expanse of the island, and the sharp angle of her right arm the Akamas peninsula. In this mapping schema, the breasts of Giorgione's Venus occupy the space of the Troodhos mountains, and more intriguingly still, her naval is set in the location of the Lusignan and Venetian capital of Cyprus, Nicosia.

This kind of visual blazon, bringing map or landscape and female body together, is not unusual in the context of Renaissance Europe. As Mariann Sanders Regan has shown in relation to the poet Petrarch, a poetic correlation between womens' bodies and the landscape was a very early feature of Italian Renaissance artistic life. (Sanders Regan, 1982:195). In English Renaissance poetry this trope took particular hold, as shown by Thomas Carew's 'The Complement':

> I do not love thee for those mountains
> Hill'd with snow, whence milky fountains
> (Sugar'd sweets, as syrup'd berries),
> Must one day run through pipes of cherries :
> O how much those breasts do move me!
> Yet for them I do not love thee.

As we see here, the correlation of breasts with mountains is made explicit by Carew, and in a more Cypriot context the same trope is used by Shakespeare in his poem 'Venus and Adonis'. There Venus tells her lover that he should be like a deer, free to wander around her body-landscape:

> I'll be a park, and thou shalt be my deer;
> Feed where thou wilt, on mountain or in dale:

> Graze on my lips; and if those hills be dry,
> Stray lower, where the pleasant fountains lie. (250-255)

In this case Venus likens her own breasts to mountains, and the cleavage between them to a valley or dale, and she invites Adonis not only to kiss the lips of her mouth, as if he is a deer grazing, but to engage in cunnilingus, as though her genitalia are a walled Elizabethan garden, complete with 'pleasant fountains'. In the Giorgione painting, as in the Shakespeare poem, the goddess's genitals are not referenced obliquely, or hidden, but are emphasised by the goddess's left hand. Indeed, it has been suggested that far from hiding her genitalia, as though Giorgione's painting is a chaste image, the goddess is engaged in an act of masturbation, paralleling the invitation from Shakespeare's Venus for Adonis to 'graze' on her genitalia. (Paoletti and Radke, 2005:466; Tinagli, 1997:124; Kieran and McIver Lopes, 2007:30)

Although this correlation between landscape, female body and sex in the painting and poetry of the period can elicit some agreement amongst academic authorities, the possibility that *The Sleeping Venus* shows a Cyprus landscape, and that Venus herself is Cyprus, is unacknowledged. A more standard understanding is that we are looking at an 'Arcadian landscape' (Brown et al, 2006:22), possibly influenced by literary evocations of Arcadia at the time, prevalent in the cultural circles in which Giorgione moved. (Ruff, 2015:35) John T. Paoletti and Gary M. Radke are more specific in identifying a locale for the landscape, linking the body of Venus to Venice and its allegorical personification as *Venetia*. In this the landscape is Venice (or at least the Veneto) and Venus becomes Venetia. (Paoletti and Radke, 2005:466) Although there is some reason to accept the setting of the painting as a fantasy rendering of Arcadia, the idea Venus is Venetia is less convincing given the coexistent representation of Venetia and Venus as separate allegorical entities on the Loggetta in St Marks Square, with the latter very definitely representing Cyprus.

We will return to the Loggetta later in this paper, but at this point it is worth noting that one of the very few writers on *The Sleeping Venus* to make any connection between the painting and Cyprus is Allan Ruff, who acknowledges Giorgione moved in the circles associated with Katerina Cornaro, the deposed Queen of Cyprus, who took up residence in Asolo in the Veneto in 1489. Yet, even with Ruff, the connection to Cyprus is blunted as he seems to link Venus more to the island of Kythira, than her mythological birthplace on Cyprus. (Ruff, 2015:35) An art historian with a suspicious mind might be tempted to think there is a conspiracy against mentioning Cyprus, let alone suggesting it has any significant impact on Venice. At the very least, art historians writing on Venice seem to have a kind of *kyprophobia* in their thinking. In that context, no wonder it took a tacky souvenir tea-tray to introduce the possibility of a connection into my adolescent mind.

* * *

After I went away to university, to study English Literature and History of Art, I didn't visit Canterbury very often, but when I did, I would sometimes call in on my old art history tutor, Mr Millest, to let him know how I was doing. He always seemed pleased to see me. But one day, I visited the old technical college and could not find him. His office was empty, and a new name was written on the door. I stopped at the reception desk by the main entrance and asked the woman there whether Mr Millest was around. The woman apologised. She was sorry to tell me Mr Millest had died from cancer. It had been some time earlier. I was shocked. I had no idea he was ill. I stepped outside, found a secluded spot and cried. What seemed like a rare place of comfort had been ripped from my map.

* * *

If the appearance of Giorgione's *The Sleeping Venus* suggests a resemblance to a 1970s souvenir map of Cyprus, perhaps we can continue our speculation to consider it as a kind of souvenir of Cyprus, acting for sections of the Lusignan and Venetian nobility of Cyprus, partially expelled from the island by the exiling of the royal court of Queen Katarina Cornaro by the new Venetian overlords of the island in 1489, much as the tourist maps on tee-shirts and tea trays did for me in the 1970s. Of course there is a difference in that I was not expelled from Cyprus and am not a refugee from the island. I am a second generation émigré, but still I wonder if those exiles from Cyprus in 1489, and perhaps even more so the refugees who fled following the Ottoman takeover of the island in 1571, also felt they had experienced a kind of expulsion and a consequent longing for a lost Arcadia or Eden. I wonder too if this left them feeling restless, alienated and ill-at-ease in their exile, much as we did in racist Britain in the 1970s. Like us too, perhaps this led them to latch on to tangible images of Cyprus, physical objects signifying it as a somewhere else, a somewhere better, they wanted to call home. (Ritivoi, 2002:131) This phenomenon has been explored by social geographers such as Tom Brocket, quoting an interview in his research on second-generation Palestinians in the United States, his interviewee, called Nadia, stated:

> When you are in America, you feel like you want to go back – you want to be in Palestine, connect to Palestine – like you can't relate to everybody, but when you are in Palestine you also can't relate to everybody. So you are stuck in this weird space in-between. (Brocket, 2018)

I remember the feelings Nadia describes from my own experience in England in the 1970s and 1980s, but did the Lusignans and Venetians in the court of Queen Katerina Cornaro feel the same in their exile from Cyprus in 1489?

On the face of it, the Venetian aspect of this sense of loss might seem counter-intuitive. Queen Katerina Cornaro was not Cypriot by birth, but by marriage, and only arrived in Cyprus in 1472, having married the Lusignan king of the island, James II, by proxy in 1468. Moreover, the death of James II, also in 1472, and the subsequent death of their son, James III, left Katerina sole monarch of Cyprus in 1474. For the following 15 years Katerina managed to keep Cyprus nominally independent from the Turks to the north, the Mamluks to the south and east, and the Venetian state to the west, until 1489 when she was forced to abdicate in favour of Venice and depart the island. Yet, according to the contemporary Cypriot historian George Voustronios, the Queen's departure was a mournful affair, suggesting a coercive exile.

> [T]he queen exited from Nicosia in order to go to Famagusta, to leave [the island]. And when she went on horseback wearing a black silken cloak, with all the ladies and the knights in her company [...] Her eyes, moreover did not cease to shed tears throughout the procession. The people likewise shed many tears. (Voustronios, 2005:174)

If this coercive exile fuelled a mournful atmosphere at the Queen's new residence at Asolo in the Veneto, granted to her by the Venetian state, where Katerina was permitted to establish a proxy Cypriot court and retain the title of Queen of Cyprus, perhaps paintings like *The Sleeping Venus* should be viewed as the physical mementos of exile, loss and longing.

As Charles Hope has noted, in the Venetian context the decades around 1500 were significant in the development of classical pagan subject matter, with images of Venus appearing quite suddenly in the repertoire of Venetian artists. Most notable of these was the artist Giorgione and specifically his *Sleeping Venus*. (Hope 1994:52) Given the proximity of the dates, it is hard not to think there is a connection between the increasingly frequent depiction of Venus in Venetian art and the events in Cyprus, particularly given Giorgione's known visits to Asolo and his work for the Cornaro family. (King 1991:236) Most art historians accept *The Sleeping Venus* was commissioned by Girolamo Marcello, circa 1507. Marcello was a Venetian patrician with close family ties to the Cornaros, but this origin for the painting is by no means proven. (Joannides 2007:41) Consequently the best we can say is that it was commissioned by a member of the Venetian nobility, and probably someone with close social, political and possibly familial connections to the Cornaros. In this scenario, it is not unreasonable to surmise that Giorgione's Venus is not simply the Venus of Cyprus, but is in a sense Cyprus.

As I warned earlier this kind of reasoning might appear circumstantial. However, we do know that the use of Venus as a female personification of Cyprus was already established in Venetian art by this date. For example, she appears in the Doge's palace in the ornate carving of a fireplace commissioned by Doge Agostino Barbarigo in 1492. In this Cyprus is represented very clearly as Venus, coming under the suzerainty of Venice, represented as the lion of St Mark. (Cocke 2004:424) This use of Venus continued later too, on the Loggetta del Sansovino in St Mark's Square, designed by Jacopo Sansovino between 1538 and 1546, on which there are three carved relief panels by Danese Cattaneo, Gerolamo Lombardo and Tiziano Minio. (Fig. 5) These represent Venice in the centre, Crete on the left and Cyprus on the right. In each case a classical mythological figure is used to represent the territories, with Venice depicted as Venezia or Justice; Crete as Jupiter; and Cyprus as Venus (Lorenzetti, 149).[1] It is significant that the location of these panels is in the heart the Venetian Republic itself. Inevitably the allegorical representation of Venezia is in the centre, but with Crete and Cyprus placed prominently alongside her,

---

[1] It is not hard to deduce the Venus of the Loggetta is the probable source for the Venus in some of the 1970s tourist maps. (Fig. 3).

the symbolic significance seems clear — Crete and Cyprus were seen by the Venetians as integral parts of Venice, and not simply adjuncts to it.

Barbarigo's fireplace and Loggetta reliefs show Cyprus as Venus in clear, even propagandistic, terms, something that cannot be said of Giorgione's *Sleeping Venus*. From this I would suggest the Venus of Giorgione is a more personal, and therefore nostalgic, evocation of the lost Kingdom of Cyprus. The not infrequent comment made of Giorgione's paintings — and specifically *The Sleeping Venus* — that it evokes a dream-like quality (Roskill, 1989:98) might also be significant here, as the evocation of Cyprus, and its possible topographical rendering, is as if remembered in a dream, as though the kingdom is not lost, but only sleeping, and is visualised not in its actuality but in reverie. Presumably Giorgione never saw the Cypriot landscape himself, but as a regular visitor to a court filled with exiles from Cyprus perhaps nostalgic descriptions of the island permeated the discussions he overheard. Certainly the buildings in *The Sleeping Venus* do not indicate that Venus is located in a straightforwardly classical world. Indeed, modern estate buildings dominate the centre right of the painting, while the strongest classical elements are pushed further back in the pictorial space. This suggests Venus sleeps in some kind of post-classical world, but one in which the classical past remains present and redolent, as it did and still does in Cyprus. One might be hesitant in claiming this is a straightforward image of Cyprus, as it is clearly not a Cypriot landscape in its colouring and the essentials of its forms: but neither are the various elements entirely Italian. (Paolettii 2005:466) But to anyone who has visited Cyprus there is surely something reminiscent in the painting of the experience of driving from Caterina's summer palace at Potamia in the south-east of the island, across the broad, flat and fertile plain of Mesorea towards the distant Troodhos mountains, with the very strong presence of the Kyrenia mountains to one's right (or north), on which is set the classical massing of castles of St Hilarion, Kantara and Buffavento. In this setting of the land in the form of Venus herself, and the landscape with potentially mappable features, we seem again to find ourselves perilously close to something that was intended to operate much as the souvenir tourist maps did for we second-generation émigrés from Cyprus in the 1970s, who longed to be in the Cyprus of our own dreams.

* * *

In his study of second generation Palestinian exiles in the United States, Tom Brocket quotes a man named Samer who recalled attending a wedding in Palestine where he was introduced as 'the American'. According to Samer the description 'stung.' (Brocket, 2018) I know the feel of that sting in my own relationship to Cyprus. Eventually it happened so often it led me to throw away all my souvenirs of childhood visits to the island, and to describe myself very firmly when asked as being English, not Greek and not even Cypriot, whatever the passport I hold. For me Cyprus became the island of loss and lost hope. It became the island of hate.

And yet, Aphrodite set this template herself when she found her lover, Adonis, dead in a Cyprian vale, gored to death by a jealous pig. The island of love taught us both how to hate. Yet still in my mind, this is the island on which I spent the hot summer months playing on the beach, eating kebabs, and listening to people from all over the world talk about art. This is the island where my father taught me how to swim, at the Birthplace of Venus no less, in the same foamy water from which Aphrodite was said to be born. It was an unlikely place to learn to swim. The sea is rough there. It would be a better place to learn to drown, but I learned to swim.

On my desk *at home* in London I have a black pyramidal stone, flat at its base, like a paperweight, taken from the beach that day at *Petra tou Romiou*. (Fig. 6) It is my own aniconic image of the goddess, or perhaps part of the goddess. When I am ill-at-ease I sometimes clasp it in the palm of my hand and I feel a moment of comfort. The comfort of the goddess. The top of the stone is being slowly polished by this handling. Or rather, its top is being rapidly polished by this handling. This stone is the last of my souvenir objects from Cyprus. The last to which I feel any personal connection.

* * *

As a postlude to this speculative paper, and in light of discussion at Othello's Island, it is perhaps necessary to address the issue that the landscape in *The Sleeping Venus* might not be by the hand of Giorgione at all, but by Titian. If this is the case, then surely any indication that Giorgione is moving in the circles of the exiled court of the Kingdom of Cyprus in Asolo is irrelevant, and by implication, the idea he is evoking a lost landscape remembered by members of that court is rendered invalid.

Although the jury is still out on who painted what particular parts of *The Sleeping Venus*, I do not intend to attempt to argue the landscape is really by Giorgione. Rather I would like to amplify the presence of Cyprus in Venetian artistic circles during the Renaissance so that it also encompasses Titian. I believe we gain a sense of this by looking at another painting, this time Titian's *The Flaying of Marsyas* (circa 1570–1576) (fig. 7), which there is good reason to believe is an allegorical rendering of contemporary events in Venetian Cyprus, (Sohm, 2007:97) albeit this time in the public sphere rather than the hypothesised private sphere of *The Sleeping Venus*.

In 1570 Ottoman Turkish forces landed on Cyprus and quickly took control of most of the towns and countryside, including the capital Nicosia. By the autumn of 1570 only the city of Famagusta resisted and was besieged by land and sea. The siege lasted almost a year, but by the middle of 1571 it was clear the Venetians and their allies in the city could no longer hold out. As a consequence the Venetian commander, Marcantonio Bragadin, negotiated a surrender with the Turks that would see the Christian defenders of the city guaranteed safe passage from Cyprus to Venice. Despite this, shortly after the Venetians surrendered, the Turks reneged on their agreement, killing or enslaving most of the Venetian forces. Bragadin was tortured and publicly humiliated, before being tied to a column, still to be seen outside Famagusta Cathedral, and skinned alive. As Mark Hudson has noted, the murder of Bragadin, 'haunted the Venetian imagination for decades.' (Hudson 2009:263) Arguably it haunted the imagination of Shakespeare too, as thirty years later he turned the failed Venetian defence of Cyprus under Bragadin into a 'what if' history tale by making the Venetians victorious under the leadership of Othello.

In real life the slow and ritualistic nature of the execution of Bragadin by the Turks may have been particularly resonant to the Venetians. Bragadin had his ears and nose cut off and witnessed up to three-hundred of his comrades executed, their decapitated heads piled high in the square between Famagusta's Venetian palace and cathedral. Over the course of the subsequent fortnight, as his wounds festered, Bragadin was paraded daily around the city walls of Famagusta, reputedly being forced to carry large rocks, in what was surely a parody of the Passion of Christ, but also perhaps a mockery of the regular civic parades and pageants carried out by the Venetians in St Mark's Square in Venice, designed to reinforce a sense of the city's strength and mission. (Sethre 2009:83) It was after all this that Bragadin was tied to a column in front of Famagusta Cathedral, at the time being ransacked of its Christian paraphernalia and converted into a mosque, to be flayed. After his death Bragadin was further humiliated by being decapitated, his body quartered and his skin stuffed with straw and sent to the Turkish sultan in Constantinople as a victory gift.[2] (Sethre 2003:64) Even by the standards of the time this was a brutal death.

---

[2] It is significant that the Venetians were so enraged by this treatment of Bragadin that almost a decade later, in 1580, a Venetian sailor named Girolamo Polidori risked his life to steal the skin of Bragadin from the Ottoman arsenal in Constantinople and return it to Venice. This was itself a kind of re-enactment of the stealing of the body of the patron saint of Venice, St Mark from Alexandria in AD 828. Bragadin's remains were eventually interred in the Basilica di San Giovanni e Paolo in Venice.

It is in this context that the hypothesis has been raised that Titian's *The Flaying of Marsyas* is not simply as a neutral illustration of one of the classical myths being rediscovered by a Renaissance elite, but a response to the loss of Cyprus. (Freedberg 1984:56) We know that Cyprus mattered to Venice, appearing in the heart of the ritualistic space of St Mark's Square on the Loggetta, and contrary to partisan assumptions that Venetian rule over Cyprus was marks by little more than abuse and plunder, (Boatswain 2011:91; Maric 2009:29; Jennings 1993:297-310; Yilmaz 2005:74; Papadakis 2008:7;13) Venetian families were encouraged to settle on the island, and its economy and population actually expanded. (Arbel 1998:353; Grivaud 2009:75)

If Titian's *The Flaying of Marsyas* is a physical manifestation of the Venetian shock at the brutal loss of Cyprus in 1571 then I would argue that it is not unreasonable to surmise that even under the hand of Titian *The Sleeping Venus* remains a self-conscious evocation of Cyprus.

Reference Sources

- Arbel, B. 1998 'The Roots of Poverty and Sources of Richness in Venetian Cyprus' in Chryssa A. Maltezou ed. *Πλούσιοι καί Φτωχοί στην Κοινωνία της Ελληνολατινικής Ανατολής – Ricchi e poveri nella società dell'Oriente Grecolatino*. Venice: Istituto Ellenico
- Barry, F. 2010 'Disiecta Membra' in Maguire, H, and Nelson, R eds., *San Marco, Byzantium, and the Myths of Venice*. Cambridge, USA: Harvard University Press
- Boatswain, T. 2011. *A Traveller's History of Cyprus*. London: Bookhaus.
- Brocket, T. 2018 'From "in-betweenness" to "positioned belongings": second-generation Palestinian-Americans negotiate the tensions of assimilation and transnationalism,' in *Ethnic and Racial Studies*, December 2018
- Brown, D. et al 2006, *Bellini, Giorgione, Titian, and the Renaissance of Venetian Painting* New Haven: Yale University Press
- Cheney, L. 2013 'Caterina Cornaro Queen of Cyprus' in Barrett-Graves, D, ed., *The Emblematic Queen: Extra-Literary Representations of Early Modern Queenship*. London: Palgrave.

- Cocke, R. 2004 'Doge Agostino Barbarigo and the Image of Cyprus' in *Zeitschrift für Kunstgeschichte* 67. Bd., H. 3
- Doody, M. 2009 *Tropic of Venice*. Philadelphia: University of Pennsylvania Press
- Enlart, C. 1899 *L'Architecture gothique et de la Renaissance en Chypre*. Paris: Leroux
- Freedberg, S. 1984 'Titian and Marsyas', in *FMR*, no. 4
- French, D. 2015. *Fighting EOKA: The British Counter-Insurgency Campaign on Cyprus, 1955-1959*. Oxford: Oxford University Press.
- Grivaud, G. 2009 'Villages désertés à Chypre fin XIIe- fin XIXe siècle: bilan et questions' in John Bintliff Hanna Stöger eds., *Medieval and Post-Medieval Greece: The Corfu Papers*. Oxford: Archaeopress.
- Gunnis, R. 1936 *Historic Cyprus*. London: Methuen
- Hale, S. 2012 *Titian: His Life*. London: HarperPress.
- Christopher Hitchens. 1997 *Hostage to History: Cyprus from the Ottomans to Kissinger*. London: Verso.
- Hope, C. 1994 'Classsical Antiquity and Venetian Renaissance Subject Matter', in Francis Ames-Lewis ed., *New Interpretations of Venetian Renaissance Painting*. London: Birkbeck, 1994.
- Howard, D. 1991 'Venice and Islam in the Middle Ages: Some Observations on the Question of Architectural Influence' in *Architectural History*, vol. 34
- Howard, D. 2000, *Venice and the East*. New Haven: Yale University Press.
- Holly H. 2009 'Body of Empire: Caterina Corner in Venetian History and Iconography' in *Early Modern Women: An Interdisciplinary Journal*, vol. 4
- Imhaus, B. 2000. 'La minorité chypriote de Venise du XVIe siècle au début du XVIIe siècle', in Jean Pouilloux ed., *Chypre et la Méditerranée orientale. Formations identitaires : perspectives historiques et enjeux contemporains*. Lyon : Maison de l'Orient et de la Méditerranée.
- Jacoby, D. 2004, 'Silk Economics and Cross-Cultural Artistic Interaction: Byzantium, the Muslim World, and the Christian West' in *Dumbarton Oaks Papers*, vol. 58.
- Jeffrey, G. 1918 *A Description of the Historic Monuments of Cyprus*. Nicosia: Government of Cyprus, 1918.
- Jeffrey, G. 1926 *Cyprus Under an English King in the Twelfth Century* Nicosia: Archer, 1926.
- Jennings, R. 1993 *Christians and Muslims in Ottoman Cyprus and the Mediterranean World, 1571-1640*. New York: New York University Press.
- Joannides, and Dunkerton, J. 2007 'A Boy with a Bird in the National Gallery: Two Responses to a Titian Question' in *The National Gallery Technical Bulletin*, vol. 28.

- Lorenzetti, G. 2007 *Venice and Its Lagoon*, Edizioni Erredici, Padova.
- Keshishian, K. 1972 *Everybody's Guide to Romantic Cyprus* Nicosia: Keshishian Publications.
- Kieran, M. and McIver Lopes, D 2007, *Knowing Art: Essays in Aesthetics and Epistemology*, Dordrecht: Springer
- Kubovy, M. and Gephstein, S. 2000 'Gestalt: From Phenomena to Laws' in Boyer K.L., Sarkar S. (eds) *Perceptual Organization for Artificial Vision Systems*. The Kluwer International Series in Engineering and Computer Science, vol 546. Springer, Boston, MA
- Leichtentritt, H. 1906 'Was lehren uns die Bildwerke des 14.-17. Jahrhunderts über die Instrumentalmusik ihrer Zeit?', in *Sammelbände der Internationalen Musikgesellschaft*. 7. Jahrg., H. 3
- Levith, M. 2007 *Shakespeare's Cues and Prompts: Intertextuality and Sources*. London: Bloomsbury Academic.
- Malik, R. 2009 *From Venice to Byzantium and Back: Relations between Venetians and Greeks, 1200-1600*, PhD thesis, Wesleyan University, Middletown, Connecticut
- Maric, V. 2009 *Lonely Planet Guide to Cyprus*. Footscray: Lonely Planet
- Martin, L. 2001, *The Art and Archaeology of Venetian Ships and Boats*. College Station: Texas A&M University Press.
- Morgan, T. 2010 *Sweet and Bitter Island: A History of the British in Cyprus*. London: IB Taurus.
- Muir, E. 1986 *Civic Ritual in Renaissance Venice*. Princeton: Princeton University Press.
- Nicol, D. 1988 *Byzantium and Venice: A Study in Diplomatic and Cultural Relations*. Cambridge: Cambridge University Press.
- Ousterhout, R. 2001 'Review Article: In Pursuit of the Exotic Orient' in *The Journal of Aesthetic Education*, vol. 35, no. 4.
- Paolettii, J, and Radke, G. 2005. *Art in Renaissance Italy*. London: Lawrence King.
- Papoulia, E. 2015 'Gregory XIII 1572-85: The Idea of Union', paper delivered at Othello's Island: The Annual Conference of Medieval and Renaissance Studies, Centre for Visual Arts and Research, Nicosia, Cyprus, 22 March 2015.
- Paraskos, M. 1999 'The Influence of Cyprus on European Art', in *The Cyprus Mail* newspaper, 12 September 1999.
- Philippou, S. 2013, 'Europe' Turned Local - The Local Turned European? Münster: Lit Verlag.

- Ritivoi, A. D. 2002 *Yesterday's Self: Nostalgia and the Immigrant Identity* Lanham: Rowman & Littlefield
- Romano, D. 1993 'Aspects of Patronage in Fifteenth- and Sixteenth-Century Venice' in *Renaissance Quarterly*, vol. 46, no. 4.
- Rosand, D. 2005 *The Myth of Venice*. Chapel Hill: University of North Carolina Press.
- Roskill, M.W. 1989. *What is Art History?* Amhurst: University of Massachusetts Press
- Ruff, A.R. 2015 *Arcadian Visions: Pastoral Influences on Poetry, Painting, and the Design of Landscape* Oxford: Windgather
- Sanders Regan, M. 1982, *Love Words: The Self and the Text in Medieval and Renaissance Poetry* Ithaca, Cornell University Press
- Sethre, J. 2009 'The Souls of Venice' in du Toit, H ed., *Pageants and Processions: Images and Idiom as Spectacle*. Cambridge: Cambridge Scholars Press
- Sohm, P. 2007 *The Artist Grows Old: The Ageing of Art and Artists in Italy, 1500–1800*, New Haven: Yale University Press
- Spencer, T. 1952 'Turks and Trojans in the Renaissance', in *The Modern Language Review*, vol. 47, no. 3 July
- Tinagli, P. 1997 *Women in Italian Renaissance Art: Gender, representation, identity*, Manchester: Manchester University Press
- Tortora, P, and Johnson, I. 2013 *The Fairchild Books Dictionary of Textiles*. London: Fairchild Books, 2013.
- Varella, S, Language. 2005 *Contact and the Lexicon in the History of Cypriot Greek*. Bern: Peter Lang.
- Voustronios, G. 2005 *A Narrative of the Chronicle of Cyprus, 1456-1489*, translated and edited by Nicholas Coureas and Hans A. Pohlsander, Nicosia: Cyprus Research Centre
- Yilmaz, M. 2005 'The Cyprus Conflict and the Question of Identity' in *Uluslararasr Hukuk ve Politika*, vol. 1 no. 4.

Illustrations

Fig. 1 Cyprus tourist map tray from 1970s

Fig. 2 Version of the tourist map that appeared
on postcards (as shown), tee-shirts and boxes of local sweets

Fig. 3 Another version of the tourist map

Fig. 4 Giorgione (with Titian), *The Sleeping Venus*, c.1510
(Gemäldegalerie Alte Meister, Dresden)

Fig. 5 Cyprus Panel from the Loggetta, St Mark's Square, Venice
(Photo by Wolfgang Moroder)

Fig. 6 Pyramidal rock taken from *Petra tou Romiou* (the Birthplace of
Aphrodite-Venus), Cyprus. Approx. 75mm high.

Fig. 7 Titian, The Flaying of Marsyas, circa 1570-1576
(Archdiocesan Museum Kroměříž, Archbishopric Castle
Kroměříž, Kroměříž)

The Old English Translation of the Orosius's *History Against Pagans* as a Homiletic Text

Zoya Metlitskaya (Lomonosov Moscow State University, Russia)

THE OLD ENGLISH translation of the *History Against Pagans* by Paul Orosius (below Old English Orosius), belongs to the group of the so called 'Aefredian translations' – the translations of Latin patristic texts into Old English, produced, presumably, at the end of the ninth century. It is commonly believed that these translations were created by command of and under the supervision of King Alfred the Great; they include, along with Orosius's work, translations of *Pastoral Care* and *Dialogues* by Gregory the Great, *The Ecclesiastical History of English People* by the Venerable Bede, *Consolation of Philosophy* by Boethius, *Soliloquies* by St Augustine, as well as prose translation of Psalms 1-50. All these texts extant in the manuscripts dated to 10th-11th century.

A legendary tradition states that the translator was King Alfred himself, and the efforts to confirm or reject this legend kept scholars busy until the 1990s. In the twentieth century almost all studies of 'Alfredian translations' were focused on an analysis of their syntax and vocabulary to find similarities and variations between the styles and usages of the translators of different texts, in order to address the unresolvable problem of their authorship.

The Old English translation of Orosius's *History* was not an exclusion. The text had been published twice by the Early English Texts Society (Sweet 1883, Bately 1980); the admirable second edition prepared by Janet Bately in 1980 contains detailed commentaries, which provide the reader with sophisticated comparison of The Old English translation and Latin original. Very little may be added to Janet Bately's analysis of translator's tackling of the original text, his additions and omissions and their possible sources and it is her work that I am greatly indebted to.

The previous Old English Orosius scholarship addressed, as a rule, traditional linguistic matters, in particular similarities and differences between the Old English Orosius and the Anglo-Saxon Chronicle. Also great attention has been paid to the geographical preface and its most interesting fragment – the story of voyages of Ohthere and Wulfsan.

Meanwhile the rest (and greater) part of the text was to a large degree neglected in recent scholarship: the reason for that neglect may lay in widely held opinion that Orosius's translator did not really have the skills or intelligence of the person(s), which contributed to the Old English translations of Boethius and Augustine. Such a negative assessment was argued by Michael Godden (Godden 2011). Godden asserted that the Anglo-Saxon translator (as well as Orosius himself) was not attempting 'to write straight history', but 'making his own contribution to a long series of imaginative 'reshaping' of history' (Godden, 2011, 319). However Godden's main aim was to discuss the translator's strategy in using his sources and he was not very keen on conceptions on which the 'reshaping' was based.

Meanwhile it seems that the question of aims and intentions which underlay the Old English Orosius and the presumed audience of the text no less deserved to be posed and investigated. An appropriate way to begin the discussion of the Old English translation of Orosius's work is to put forward the question: why Orosius? (One could ask also: why Boethius? And with even more reason: why 'Soliloques'? But it is not our concern now).

Paul Orosius wrote his book as a piece of polemic against pagan critics of Christianity claiming that the present misfortunes of

Roman Empire and, in particular the siege of Rome by Alarich in AD 410, were due to the Romans forsaking of the old gods. The main aim of Orosius's polemic was to demonstrate that the past times, which his opponents were lamenting for, were in fact much worse than the present, and did not deserve any good feelings. To prove this idea Orosius tried to present pre-Christian history as the endless sequence of troubles, evils and misfortunes, either due to human crimes or God's punishment. After Christ's incarnation, he supposed, the prayers of the faithful might temper the deserved penalties of the world and the just judgment of God. To put this in Orosius's own words, his main polemical thesis was that in past times, 'those things also which are regarded as evils by men, of whatever kind they are, were more severe without doubts.' (Deferrary 1964, 232).

According to well-established scholarly opinion, Orosius's work was chosen for translation because it was a patristic text giving a Christian view of history and so it provided the translator with the opportunity to present his readers/listeners with a narrative of world history from a specifically Christian point of view. As Janet Bately stated:

> This view... was modified by the translator, but nonetheless forcefully expressed. If dates are treated highhandedly by the translator, facts distorted, invented, or even flatly contradicted, this is perhaps simply because what is most important to him is the way history reveals an overall picture of God's hand in events (Bately 1986, 12).

She adds:

> [The translator's] focal point is the birth of Christ and, in spite of his primary source's concentration on evil and misery, his interpretation of history allows him to see much good in both

times and people B.C. It also enabled him to see much mercy in God's control of events after Christ's birth (Bately 1986, 18-19). Another possible answer to the question of *why Orosius?*, is that Orosius's providential conception of the transition of Empire between four great kingdoms and the suggestion that the rise of Rome to power was a Divine Plan for the preparation of the Incarnation of Christ, allowed the text to be read as a reflection on kingship and power, and to act as a piece of monarchical propaganda. For example, William Kretzschmar states that the translator may have had in mind the idea of 'translation of the Empire' from Roman emperors to Anglo-Saxon kings (Kretzschmar 1987).

In Stephan Harris view:

a general emphasis on Christian kingship and Christendom seems to be the thematic aim of the Alfredian World History... The World History omits Orosius's explanation of the historical role of Christ in the rise of Rome, instead emphasising the tangible relation between a good, Christian king and the prosperity of his people in the complex of Christendom... The Roman past in the World History may be called to testify to the power of Christendom's faithful leaders over heathens (Harris 2001, 101).

In light of these views, in this paper I want to begin with pointing out some differences between the Latin original and the Old English Orosius. It is worth beginning with the structure of the two texts. Orosius's work contains seven books. The first deals with the world's history (naturally, as it was seen in Late Antiquity) from the time of Babylon until the foundation of Rome. The second book is concerned with the period from the foundation of Rome to its ravage by the Gauls. Book three narrates the wars between the Greek city states and the Persians, as well as the conquests of Alexander the Great and the Samnite wars, ending with a description of the wars between

Alexander's heirs. Book four focuses on the Punic wars. Book five describes civil conflicts in Rome and the Jugurthine war. Book six relates the establishment of the Roman Empire - from the Gallican campaigns of Julius Caesar and his ascension to power, the Mithradatic Wars, and onto the rule of Augustus. And finally, book seven addresses the history of the Roman Empire from the birth of Christ until the death of Emperor Honorius.

The Anglo-Saxon translator of Orosius's work largely follows this pattern until the end of book four. However, books five to seven are severely abridged. The translator omits the descriptions of the civil wars in Rome and the Jugurthine war, cuts the story of Julius Caesar into two paragraphs, and the story of the Mithradatic wars, which took up originally six chapters, is related in one paragraph. Very little was kept of the story of Augustus, and book seven is reduced from Orosius's rather elaborate narrative to no more than a list of emperors with brief information on their rule.

In all of this, we might be bewildered by the Anglo-Saxon translator's omission of almost all stories by which Orosius wanted to demonstrate that the recent miseries of Roman Empire and Rome itself were due to divine anger because of earlier persecutions of Christians. Even the history of the first Christian emperor, Constantine the Great, is abbreviated to almost nothing.

Such radical changes in the structure of the narrative have made scholars wonder why the Punic Wars seemed, to the Anglo-Saxons, more significant in the context of pre-Christian World history then the campaigns of Julius Caesar, or why the wars between Athens and Sparta deserved more attention than the Mithradatic wars. The radical abridgement of the books concerned with the Christian epoch seems even stranger if we believe that the translator's aim was to narrate the world history from the Christian point of view. The odd transformation of the text is one of the reasons that some critics disapprove of the Anglo-Saxon translator's work, as mentioned previously. It was also the base of Janet Bately's belief in the translator's 'weariness' in the process of his work.

However, there may be another explanation for the structural transformations made by the Anglo-Saxon translator. Book four ends with the story of the destruction of Carthage, followed by Orosius's reflections on the significance of this event in the history of Rome. A translation into modern English from the original Latin reads:

> But, since some Romans proposed that Carthage must be destroyed for the sake of the permanent security of Rome and others, on the other hand, because of their constant anxiety for Roman courage which they always applied to themselves out of suspicion of a rival city, lest the Roman energy always exercised in war should be relaxed by freedom from anxiety and leisure into a sluggish indolence, moved that Carthage be left to itself in safety…Since this is so, why do they impute to Christian times their dullness and ruse with which they are outwardly solid but inwardly corroded? Furthermore, these men, almost six hundred years before, as their wise and cautious citizens had predicted, lost that great whetstone of their brilliance and sharpness— Carthage (Deferrary 1964, 171-172).

In the Old English this passage is paraphrased as:

> [The] Romans had before long consultation about it, whether it is more reasonable for them utterly to destroyed the city, that they ever after might have peace on that side, or they should let it stand to the end that war may again arise from thence, because they dreaded, if they did not sometimes wage war, that they would too soon become drowsy and slothful. So that, to you, Romans, it is now again made known, since the Christianity came', said Orosius, 'that ye had lost the whetstone of your elders, of your wars and of your bravery; for ye are

> now fat without and lean within; but your elders were lean without and fat within, of a strong and firm mind (Bosworth 1858, 136-137).

Both Orosius and the Anglo-Saxon translator view the end of the Punic Wars and the destruction of Carthage as the end of the heroic epoch in the history of Rome. Consequently, one of the possible reasons for the substantial abridgements to books five, six and seven is that the Anglo-Saxon translator was not really interested in the creation or history of the Roman Empire, or even its Christian political history. He was interested in the struggle of the Romans for the continued existence of their city, and their *anwald*, an Old English word meaning sphere of power.

Some additional notices may enforce this thesis. It may be said that Orosius, in his interpretation of the events of the pre-Christian past, highlights two different patterns: on the one hand there is an escalation of natural calamities and human crimes, on the other hand there is the preparation, according to the Divine Plan, of the Incarnation of Christ. Orosius describes this pre-Christian history as a succession of wars and natural disasters, which are either the inevitable result of human sins or punishment for sin. He misses no opportunity to emphasise the miserable ends of numerous great enterprises and to list the crimes committed by famous heroes. Yet, many of these stories are omitted in the Old English Orosius. Often, even if the story itself is told, the translator chooses not to interpret it in a negative way.

Orosius also tries to demonstrate, in accordance with the conception of the original sin, that in the pre-Christian world there was no need for special or personal reasons for God's punishment. Humanity as a whole merited permanent punishment. Among fifty three mentions of different calamities and supernatural phenomena contained in the first five books, only four events are explained as the result of God's wrath addressed to a particular person or people due to particular deeds. Orosius speaks more eagerly of God's providence, power or His 'secret measure'. Terrible natural phenomena are often treated, not as tokens - that is, a kind of message or warning that God sends to men - but as His tools in dealing with humanity. Three times Orosius writes explicitly about such things as thunder or that, 'there was not a sign or token, but a calamity itself'.

In books six and seven, Orosius uses all possibilities to emphasise the causal relationships between human deeds and subsequent calamities and disasters. His main task is to demonstrate that God takes care of the Church by punishing its persecutors and favouring its protectors. The punishment may be either shared or personal. It is worth noticing that Orosius continues in this part of his work to mention natural calamities without any explanation. God's wrath reveals itself more often in the form of military disasters. Accordingly, God's favour reveals itself in military victories. The Anglo-Saxon translator preserved almost all mentions of natural calamities and supernatural events in the first five books of Orosius work, omitting only five instances out of a total of fifty-three. But in some cases the Anglo-Saxon translator tries to make God's presence more personal and the punishment more addressed. He adds four new references to God's wrath, where Orosius speaks only of Divine providence. For example, Orosius, after describing a grave fate of King Xerxes I, reflects on the reversal of fortune:

> It was truly a sight for the race of men to view and bemoan, as it measured the changes of events especially by this reversal of fortune; he was content to hide in a small boat, before whom the very sea had before lain concealed and had borne as a yoke of its captivity the bridge that joined its shores; he lacked the very menial services of a single slave, to whose power, while mountains were levelled, valleys were filled, and rivers were drained, the very nature of things had yielded (Deferrary 1964, 59-60).

The Anglo-Saxon translator, on the other hand, puts it forth more explicitly, suggesting that God punishes the king for his pride:

> God so humbled the greatest pride and the greatest undertaking in so worthless a trust in self, that he, who formerly thought that no sea could keep him from covering it with his ships and with his army afterward begged for a poor man's little boat that he might save his life (Bosworth 1858, 90).

In certain passages of the Old English Orosius the order of the original narrative is changed to make connections between supernatural phenomena and historical events more clear. In books six and seven, of the fifty six references the Anglo-Saxon translator retains only sixteen. He omits all unexplained mentions of natural calamities. Moreover, in his narrative of imperial history, penalties almost always fall on particular people. He also highlights the connection between the justice of the ruler and God's help to his people. It seems that the Anglo-Saxon translator deliberately avoids the idea of shared punishment. It is perhaps even more significant that he omits almost all references to the connections between God's punishment and military affairs.

Representing the pre-Christian past as the preparation of the Incarnation of Christ, Orosius appealed not so to Biblical narration, but his own conception of 'four kingdoms', namely, Babylon, Macedonia, Carthage and Rome, already mentioned as it was predestined that Christ would be born in the empire; and if in contrast to other three 'kingdoms', Rome had not perished, it was only because his rulers accepted Christianity.

> Behold, the similar beginnings of Babylonia and Rome, the similar powers, the similar greatness, the similar times, the similar blessings, and the similar evils, yet not a similar decline or similar fall. For the one lost its power, the other retains it; the one was deprived of its king by murder, the other is secure with

its emperor unharmed. And why is this? Because in the one case the turpitude of the passions was punished in the king; in the other the very serene tranquility of the Christian religion was preserved in the king; in Babylon, without reverence for religion, furious license satisfied thirst for pleasure; in Rome, there were Christians who showed mercy, and Christians to whom mercy was shown, and Christians because of whose memory and in whose memory mercy was shown (Deferrary 1964, 47).

The Anglo-Saxon translator delivered more or less accurately, although in an abridged form, Orosius's idea of the 'four kingdoms' which received their power from God, but lost it over time. However, the whole message was somewhat different. Whereas Orosius appealed particularly to the Divine Plan and Predestination, the Old English text told more about penance and good will.

How like was the beginning that the two cities had, and how like these days were both in good and evil! But the ends of their empires were very unlike; for the Babylonians and their king lived in manifold wickedness and sensuality, without any remorse, that they would not amend till God humbled them with the greatest disgrace when he took away both their king and their dominion. But the Roman, with their Christian king serve God wherefore he gave them both their king and their empire (Bosworth 1858, 81).

As may be noticed, in contrast with Orosius striving to emphasise the sinfulness and corruption of human nature, which could not be healed or overcome in the pre-Christian world, the Anglo-Saxon translator implied the opportunity for penance and honesty in all humans, including the heathen Babylonians.

To summarise this part of my observations it may be concluded that in his dealings with the history of the pre-Christian past, the Anglo-Saxon translator was keen, not so much on the demonstration of the terrible state of the world, but on a description of the brave, if desperate, and the efforts of men to survive and act in this world.

Orosius's work contains a great many theological and polemical speculations that form rather independent parts of the text. These fragments thematically can be divided into three groups: theological reflections about the divine designs of human history; commentaries to the main narrative that reflect Orosius view of human history as a never-ceasing sequence of sufferings and evils; and polemical discussions with imaginary 'grumbling Romans', as J. Bately called them, which is to say the pagan Roman opponents of Orosius who sought to explain the sack of Rome by the Goths as revenge by the pagan gods for the widespread adoption of Christianity. The Anglo-Saxon translator retained, in a very abridged form, only three of the thirteen reflections by Orosius on the Divine plan of history and God's role as the master of the humanity. All three of these were concerned with the concept of the transition of the empire. Almost all of Orosius's speculations on human history as a series of disasters were omitted or abridged to nothing, while ten of the thirteen discussions with 'grumbling Romans' were preserved. Moreover, they are marked as Orosius own declaration ('cweþ Orosius'), even if the following text only slightly resembles the Latin original.

Janet Bately, in the introduction to her edition of the Old English Orosius, noted quite rightly that 'the sack of Rome in 410 was hardly a burning issue in ninth-century England'. Yet, one may wonder whether the Anglo-Saxon translator saw before him some equivalents in his own time to the 'grumbling Romans', effectively substitutions of the pagan opponents of Orosius. Answering this question is, in my opinion, the key to understanding the whole text, but before I give my version of it, it makes sense to look at polemical monologues more closely.

Orosius himself in his pieces of polemic castigated his opponents with three theses. First: the present troubles and miseries are lighter than those of ancient times because there is always the possibility to negotiate peace and, arguably, the ways of the world were more merciful in the present time due to God's mercy. Second: his opponents hate the present time, not because it is bad, but because it is Christian, and so they are not sincere in their complaints. And third: they wail about hard times because they themselves are spineless, effeminate and lazy. Two of the three fragments that were omitted by the Anglo-Saxon translator were concerned with the second thesis and one with the third.

Although Orosius rhetorically addressed pagan 'grumbling Romans' as his audience, the truth is his work was written not for them, but for faithful Christians who were dismayed by the hard times in which they lived. Consequently, his purpose was to prove that his opponents were wrong, rather than persuade them. The Anglo-Saxon translator, on the other hand, tried more clearly to demonstrate to his audience the benefits available to them, in comparison with the people of the past whose stories he told. In describing these benefits the Anglo-Saxon translator did not deviate from Orosius, but in many cases he did develop his ideas, often making them weightier, and sometimes proffering arguments which are not present in the Latin original. The main benefits in his opinion were the possibility of a peaceful resolution to conflict, whether between individuals or nations, and the absence of fear, such as the fear of despotic power, cruelty and betrayal.

> How blindly many people speak about Christianity, that it is worse now, than it was formerly – writes the Anglo-Saxon translator expanding Latin text. They will not think nor know that before Christianity no tribe of his own will ask peace of another unless it was in need; nor were any tribe obtain the peace from another by gold, by silver or by any fee without being enslaved' (Bosworth 1858, 73).

After the story of the war between the former friends of Alexander the Great, where Orosius talks about the benefits of the Christian oath on the Gospel above the oath on the holy pig, the Old English text states:

> It is very disgraceful to us that we speak about what we now called war, when strangers and foreigners come upon us and rob us of a little and soon leave us again. And we will not think what it was when no man could redeem his life from another... (Bosworth 1858, 127).

Many other quotations of such kind may be provided.

It is important to remember that the Old English Orosius was created during King Alfred's reign, a period when England was incessantly attacked by Vikings and there was a pressing need to cope with them. At the time, the tactic of buying Vikings off was used, with varying degrees of success, by the kings of England and those in continental Europe. Alfred used it himself in a rather desperate situation, paralleling that of the Romans in AD 410, so it was likely Orosius's reflections reminded the Anglo-Saxon translator of things he had experienced and felt himself. The connection of the Alfredian project with the need to communicate to an Anglo-Saxon audience explanations and ideas that could unite and inspire them in a situation of ongoing wars and fragile truces, although not explicitly expressed is not inconceivable. In the face of Viking treatment, Anglo-Saxon court scholars were not necessarily speculating on abstract matters.

This brings me back to the question I raised at the start of this paper – why Orosius? This is answered by the suggestion that Orosius's work was chosen because it contained something significant to the contemporary reality of ninth-century England. From this we can speculate that the core message that the author of the Old English Orosius wanted to communicate to his readers/listeners was bi-partite. The first idea was rooted in Orosius's polemical thesis that in Christian times even pagan invaders were less formidable than the furious enemies and brutal tyrants of pre-Christian world. The second idea was probably influenced by Anglo-Saxon perceptions of the pre-Christian past, particularly their own past, which included, amongst others, the ideals of bravery and honesty in a desperate situation. As a result, some of Orosius's conceptions of history were modified. Re-telling Orosius's stories of evils, wars and calamities, which had been the mainstream of human history from ancient times, and arguing with imaginary 'grumbling Romans' concerning the balance of good and evil in their present and past, the translator proposed a Christian reflection on the problem of Viking invasions. He demonstrated that even before Christ there were many heroes who fought bravely to defend their land, notwithstanding the prospect of inevitable defeat. He also told them that in the Christian world there was a place for mercy and hope, that calamities come and pass over and people ought to be steadfast and enduring, for now there was no reason for despair.

Reference Sources

- Bately, J. 2003. 'The Alfredian canon revised: one hundred years on'. In *Alfred the Great: Papers from the Eleventh-centenary Conferences*, T. Reuter, ed. 107-120. Aldershot: Ashgate publishing.
- Bately, J. ed. 1980. *The Old English Orosius*. London, Toronto, New York: Oxford University Press.
- Bately, J. 2000. 'The literary Prose of King Alfred's Reign: Translation or Transformation'. In *Old English Prose: basic readings*, Szarmach E. and D.A. Oosterhouse, 3-28. New York, London: Garland Publishing.
- Bosworth, J. trans. 1858. *King Alfred's Anglo-Saxon version of the Compendium History of the World by Orosius*. London: Longman, Brown, Green and Longmans.
- Deferrary, R.J., trans. 1964. *The Fathers of the Church. Paul Orosius. The Seven Books of History against the Pagans*. Washington: The Catholic University of America press.
- Godden, M. 2007. 'Did king Alfred really write anything'. *Medium Aevum* 76: 1-23.
- Bately, J. 2009. 'Did king Alfred really translate anything'. *Medium Aevum* 78: 189-215.

- Godden, M. 2011. 'Old English Orosius and its sources'. *Anglia* 129: 297-320.
- Kretzschmar, W. 1987. 'Adaptation and 'anweald' in the Old English Orosius'. *Anglo-Saxon England* 16: 127-145.
- Pratt, D. 2009. 'The Alfredian Project and its Aftermath: Rethinking the Literary History of the Ninth and Tenth Centuries'. *Proceedings of the British Academy* 162: 93–122.
- Sweet, H, ed. 1883. *King Alfred's Orosius.* London: N. Turner and Co.
- Waite, G. 2000. *Annotated bibliographies of Old and Middle English literature: VI. Old English prose translations of King Alfred's Reign*. Cambridge: Cambridge University Press.

Escaping the Island of Tyrants: Pseudo-Hugo Falcandus, Sicily, and European Historical Writing in the Twelfth Century

Philippa Byrne (University of Oxford, UK)

Introduction: a note of caution

THIS PAPER TAKES as its subject a work which the most eminent modern historian of Norman Sicily has warned 'must be used with extreme caution', a work which – even by the standards of medieval historical writing – poses seemingly insoluble riddles of authorship and provenance. This is the *Liber de Regno Sicilie*, better known in English translation as the *History of the Tyrants of Sicily*, a text usually ascribed to Hugo, or Pseudo-Hugo, Falcandus. The *History* is the major narrative source for events in the Norman kingdom of Sicily between the years 1154 and 1169, and, consequently, an indispensable text for the historian of Norman Sicily. But any historian wishing to discuss the *History* must reckon with the fact that we know so little about its composition.

It is perhaps easier to state what is securely known about the *History:* its author was present in Sicily to witness at least some of the events he narrates, and he displays considerable erudition and knowledge of the Latin classics. Almost nothing else about the work is settled, and many of the uncertainties surrounding the text stem from the uncertainty surrounding authorship. Although the oldest surviving manuscript dates from c.1230, the ascription to 'Hugo Falcandus' was first made in the *editio princeps* published in Paris in 1550, printed from a now-lost manuscript. There is no evidence for the existence of a Hugo Falcandus as an historical actor in the kingdom of Sicily, and the name may be a misreading from the Paris manuscript, its poor condition being remarked upon at the time of printing. Alternatively, 'Hugo Falcandus' may have been a pseudonym adopted to disguise the author's identity: given the slanderous tone it adopts towards almost all the power-brokers of Norman Sicily, anonymity would have been a prudent choice. As to the author's 'true' identity, various guesses have been ventured. Suggestions have included Hugues Foucaud, Abbot of Saint-Denis; Admiral Eugenius of Sicily; Robert of San Giovanni, a Sicilian royal notary; the Angevin courtier Peter of Blois; or Peter's brother, William: but there are so few clues in the text about nationality or background that no-one has put forward a singularly convincing case. Moreover, if historians do not know who wrote the text, nor can they say when it was written, or, for that matter, where – whether in Sicily or elsewhere in Europe (northern France being one likely location). All in all, this is the unfortunate type of historical enquiry which has generated far more heat than light.

The text itself narrates the history of Sicily after the death of Roger II (r.1130–54), the founder of the kingdom. The work is divided into two sections: the first covering the period 1154–66 (concluding with the death of William I); the second relates the years 1166 to 1169 in much greater detail. The *History* may have been written during the reign of William II, or composed after his death in 1189. Whether 1169 was intended to mark a deliberate conclusion to the narrative is similarly disputed. The other remarkable feature about the text is its tone, which presents Sicily as a place of entirely unparalleled iniquity in twelfth-century Europe. He considers Sicily to be unique amongst contemporary kingdoms for the depravity of its court, and makes good on his promise to relate 'a story whose frightfulness would be enough… to make it completely unbelievable… were it not that in Sicily there is nothing amazing about the performance of deeds of such extreme wickedness'. The implication is that he writes – whether for contemporaries or posterity – for an audience naively ignorant of the calamitous state of later twelfth-century Sicily.

After such an inauspicious introduction to the text, it is prudent to offer a disclaimer. I cannot offer new insight into these arguments about authorship. In the absence of new evidence being unearthed, I incline to the view that Pseudo-Hugo's 'true' identity remains undiscoverable. The reasons for very briefly rehearsing the problems with the text, however, are twofold. The first is to demonstrate how arguments over authorship can come to take precedence over a detailed examination of the contents of the *History*, and an appreciation of how the work is constructed. The second reason is to explore whether – even if we cannot name the author – it might be possible to situate the *History* in the context of broader medieval historiographical traditions. In particular, treating the text of the *History* as a carefully-crafted literary work, rather than combing it for clues to authorial identity, can provide a valuable insight into the growth of legal consciousness in twelfth-century historical writing.

Law and justice was a particularly significant – not to mention sensitive – question in this era of Norman Sicilian history. A great deal has been written about the 'justice' (or the lack thereof) of William II's grandfather, Roger II, a king often condemned for tyrannous behaviour when carving out his kingdom. But, conversely, the theme of law and justice has not been particularly high on the agenda when discussing how history was written in Norman Sicily. But scrutinising the role of law as an overarching thematic concern, rather than treating it as a narrative of episodes of immorality at the Sicilian court, offers a new way into the text, and an alternative means of 'deconstructing' the *History*. When read in this way – with a focus on what Pseudo-Hugo has to say about law and legal procedure – the *History*'s place in a common European tradition of twelfth-century historical writing becomes readily apparent.

Law in the *History*

The first half of the *History* is a tale of calamitous decline, explaining how, under William I, the Kingdom of Sicily greatly deteriorated from the heights it had reached under Roger II. This deterioration was set in motion by Maio of Bari – villain is not too strong a word to describe him – the Chancellor and amiratus amiratorum ('admiral of admirals', or supreme commander) of Sicily. Maio is described as a man of fearsome intellect, but full of sexual perversions, hungry for power, a wicked schemer and constant intriguer. He is eventually murdered by an alliance of Sicilian magnates against him. By contrast, the dominant figure in the second, more detailed section of the *History* is Stephen du Perche. Stephen's origins are obscure, but he was a relation of Margaret of Navarre, the queen-regent of Sicily during the minority of her son, William II (b.1153). At the death of her husband, William I, Margaret brought a group of Frenchmen to the court, intending to construct her own administration, rather than relying upon the factionalised Sicilian magnates. Stephen was duly appointed Chancellor of Sicily and Archbishop-Elect of Palermo. What defines Pseudo-Hugo's account of Stephen du Perche's rule is his restoration of the law in Sicily. Similarly, it is through a description of Stephen's attitude towards, and reform of, Sicilian law that Pseudo-Hugo demonstrates Stephen's virtuous character to his readers.

The catalyst for Stephen du Perche's engagement with Sicilian law arrives soon after his arrival in the kingdom, with the arrest of a court notary who had organised an attack on a group of men carrying a royal writ and royal seal. The case against him is clear cut: the notary has flouted crown authority and broken the royal peace. Stephen has the guilty man imprisoned while he considers the appropriate punishment. It is at this point, the *History* recounts, that Stephen encounters difficulties and deliberate obstruction. Pseudo-Hugo notes that the Bishop of Syracuse, complaining of the decision to punish the notary for breaking the royal peace, observed that 'perhaps it was the sort of decision that was customary in France, but such a judgment had no validity in Sicily *(sed in Sicilia nequaquam hoc iudicium obtinere)*'. The bishop adds that 'the notaries of the court had great authority, and they should not be condemned so easily'. The implication – in keeping with the criticisms voiced in the first section of the *History* – is that those who wield sufficient influence and position at court are able, with the collusion of authority, to escape the process of justice. In punishing the notary, Stephen is breaking with Sicilian custom – Sicilian justice runs according to private deals, not public punishment. Indeed, Stephen comes under such pressure from members of the court that he is persuaded to release the notary from prison, and is only able to achieve the sanction of having him banned from notarial office. It is, Pseudo-Hugo explains, Stephen's lack of success in this case which spurs him to think about how Sicilian justice might be more thoroughly reformed.

The vision of Sicily Pseudo-Hugo sketches out in this chapter is of a kingdom where the powerful are outside the processes of justice. The bishop's caustic mention of what is 'customary' in France only serves to emphasise this contrast further – Sicily is a kingdom which does not conform to the norms of twelfth-century law and jurisprudence. In the case of the royal notary, this is plainly evident: Sicilian royal authority is either unable, or unwilling, to enforce its own criminal code. That royal authority and royally-determined codes of law – not the influence of royal servants – should determine the punishment of malefactors was an increasingly widespread principle in the twelfth century. The crown's guarantee of the peace – and power over those who punish it – is common to almost all twelfth-century law codes derived from the *ius commune*. This, in theory, included the Kingdom of Sicily, where royal statements affirmed that the role of royal power was to punish the wicked in order to protect the good.

Thus, what Stephen du Perche was attempting to do – to impose appropriate punishment on a notary – was not a revolutionary proposition by common European twelfth-century legal standards. Contemporary jurists could even make the suggestion that law should recognise that when the powerful offended, they deserved to be punished more severely, because their status might make it a greater crime (C.14, q.6, c.1). In other words, there was nothing about the decision to punish an individual who had broken the king's peace that a twelfth-century European reader would have considered strange. But Pseudo-Hugo intended his educated, Latinate (and likely non-Sicilian) readers to be horrified at Sicilian backwardness. Sicily is a world turned upside-down, and a place of misrule, where law is ignored and the powerful manage to escape punishment – at least until the arrival of Stephen du Perche.

Pseudo-Hugo is, of course, not the only twelfth-century history-writer to criticise the ability of powerful members of a royal court to use their connections to escape justice and evade the punishments mandated by law codes. Laments about courtly corruption are a song common to chroniclers across Europe in this period. In this regard, Pseudo-Hugo's suggestion that Sicily is uniquely corrupt – unparalleled in any age – does not quite ring true. However, Pseudo-Hugo's narrative is founded upon the principle that the ruinous state of Sicily is, at least in part, a result of its rulers' disregard for the process of law and justice. The *History* makes implicit appeal to the idea that there are certain fixed legal requirements which are the foundations of good rule, and that there can be no basis for stable governance where certain basic legal principles are not applied in practice. Most important – and most fundamental – amongst these is a judicial system with a single centre of authority, controlled by the crown, and set beyond the influence of powerful royal subjects. Stephen du Perche's 'role' in the *History* thus becomes the task of changing this state of affairs in Sicily and enforcing royal justice. According to Pseudo-Hugo, Stephen subsequently began to reform the legal system by attempting to curtail the powers exercised by court notaries and *stratigoti* in the courts. Stephen's aim is clearly stated:

> He [Stephen] wanted to preserve the rigour of the law *(iustitie rigorem)* to such an extent that he thought that neither his friends nor even the magnates of the court should be spared. He would not allow the subject population to be oppressed by powerful persons, and would not pass over any injury to the poor by pretending to be unaware of it.

Stephen was thus demanding that justice be done according to stipulated legal procedure, and without regard for the judge's personal loyalties – a principle that might have been drawn from any twelfth-century *ordo iudicarius*. The insistence that even Stephen's 'friends' could not expect exemptions from the law also echoes the point repeatedly made by later twelfth- and early thirteenth-century jurists that proof, rather than the private sympathy of the judge, ought to be the determining factor in criminal cases.

Of course, that the 'hero' of Pseudo-Hugo's text should insist on justice being done, and particularly justice being done for the poor, is far from surprising. Justice, after all, was understood to be a cardinal virtue, essential in a ruler: 'love justice you who govern the earth', scripture instructed. Establishing Stephen's love of justice was a sure means of indicating his virtue. However, what makes this more than a straightforward demonstration of virtue – and what turns this passage into a statement about the relationship between justice as a virtue and law as a means of achieving a virtuous society – is what follows. Stephen's declaration that no-one will be immune from having their crimes considered by a court has a dramatic and immediate effect on Sicilian politics. As Pseudo-Hugo presents it, the poor clamour to utilise the law's mechanisms:

> News of this [i.e. Stephen's legal reforms] soon spread throughout the realm, and he won the favour and support of the common people and made his name so famous that everyone was saying he had been sent by God like an angel of

comfort, who would put right the state of the court so as to restore the Golden Age.

Pseudo-Hugo then relates how wronged parties flocked to the court in Palermo in order to launch legal actions against the powerful, whom they had previously feared to challenge. The influx of suitors was such, Pseudo-Hugo reports, that there were not enough judges available to examine the cases, nor enough notaries to compose the documents to begin actions. Stephen's actions begin to squeeze 'private' interests out of the kingdom's judicial system.

We cannot, of course, unquestioningly accept this narrative of Stephen du Perche single-handedly reforming the Sicilian judicial system. Even considering the relatively sparse documentary evidence available to us, it is apparent that Pseudo-Hugo embellishes, offering panegyrical praise for Stephen's re-invention of the Sicilian legal system. It is likely that Stephen's 'restoration' of justice was in fact a reorganisation of the magna curia, the body responsible for assembling the law court, determining which cases were to be heard, and assigning judges to cases. Even in this, Stephen built on older foundations: there is evidence for the administration of justice under royal auspices as early as the 1150s, with a college of royal judges established by Maio of Bari in 1156. A more difficult question to answer is whether there truly was 'popular acclaim' for Stephen's reorganisation of the judiciary, and whether any part of the motivation behind this change was to make judgment less partial, less reliant on personal connections, and more 'public'. There is probably a need for caution here, as, at the beginning of Margaret's regency, the new administration was more concerned with dealing with the practical problems stored up at the time of William I's death, than with announcing public platform of justice for the poor.

Regardless of how the historical Stephen du Perche maps onto the Stephen du Perche presented by Pseudo-Hugo, however, it is law which defines the trajectory of the *History*. The culmination of the 'reform' programme – and Stephen's career in Sicily – arrives when a powerful baron, Robert of Calatabiano, is accused of numerous offences: theft, rapine, murder, violation of women, perjury, incest and adultery. The offences listed by Pseudo-Hugo are a mixture of legal and moral accusations, and it is worth noting that general charges of 'injustice' intermingle with more specific (and well-defined) legal offences. Robert, apparently accustomed to the judicial laxity of the ancien régime, believes he can avoid the charges. He first attempts to bribe royal officials in an attempt to prevent the case coming before the courts, but under Stephen's new regime, this tactic failed. More desperate, Robert then seeks to exploit his personal links at the court: he begs Margaret and the infant William II to intercede on his behalf, falling at their feet and weeping. In what might be viewed as the twelfth-century equivalent of being 'too big to fail', Robert insists that his position as a lord is essential to the well-being of the realm, and to put him on trial would be to jeopardise the realm.

As if to underline the difference between the pre-Stephen era of 'private justice' where such charges were dealt with – and dismissed – secretly, and the new era of examination of all accusations, Pseudo-Hugo emphasises that the populace had such a desire to see Robert of Calatabiano punished that they demanded that his trial go ahead. What is more, this matter put Stephen's reputation on the line: when Robert's case did not come to court immediately, the people complained 'that the business was being handled in a negligent and lukewarm way by the chancellor, and that he seemed to be deviating from his excellent intentions'. The project of enforcing Sicilian law on an 'impartial' model is at stake. How Stephen deals with Robert will expose his true character will be exposed – revealing whether he truly loves justice, or whether simply acts out of political expediency.

Ultimately, the project of legal reform ends in compromise. Stephen brokers a deal under which Robert will not be tried for his capital offences, but will be handed over to the Church to be tried only on the charges of perjury, incest and adultery. At the trial, the testimony of many witnesses ensures that Robert is 'sentenced in accordance with the law' *(de iure)*. Flogged and imprisoned, his property is confiscated. It is an action which wins Stephen the love of the people. However, Stephen du Perche's triumph is short-lived. During the rest of his time in office, he misjudges and alienates the most powerful figures at court, who formulate a conspiracy against him, and who force him from Sicily. Stephen dies at sea as his boat makes for Syria. His French associates are driven out with him. If we subscribe to the view that the author of the *History* was one of the party of Frenchmen who had accompanied Stephen to Sicily, then this experience may partly explain the embittered tone of the narrative.

From the time of Stephen du Perche's arrival until his departure, legal scenes are prominent in the History. Pseudo-Hugo provides lengthy accounts of trials, and a wealth of detail on legal procedure. Authorial comment on these events repeatedly emphasise that the 'change' to Sicilian justice under Stephen is that legal reasoning and judicial scrutiny are now applied in every case. Thus, the master justiciars of the Royal Court preside over the trial and sentencing of a physician guilty of poisoning Robert of Bellisina, and Pseudo-Hugo comments that the physician was sentenced because 'he gave the judges every confidence that he had indeed committed the crime'. The effects of Stephen's legal reforms continue to be popularly-heralded: the people, seeing that 'no-one was being denied his rights, but that the strict rule of justice was being upheld in every judgment', bring accusations against another powerful, previously 'untouchable' figure: Richard, Stratigotus of Messina. He is indicted for robbery, murder, theft and arson, and Pseudo-Hugo describes judges listening carefully to the allegations made on both sides of the case and making careful inquiries before sentencing.

Pseudo-Hugo's decision to include the detail of criminal trials in his *History* must owe something to his classical models. A trial offered him the opportunity – as Sallust had done in his *Bellum Catilinae* – to engage in a display of learned political rhetoric, to write courtroom speeches into his work. But a desire to draw classical allusions alone cannot explain the repeated insistence that the advent of Stephen du Perche brings about justice by enforcing a change in judicial procedure. To account for this we must cast the net more broadly, and examine the connection between law and rulership in twelfth-century historical writing.

Sicilian tyranny and historians

It has long been observed that, by reason of both its classicism and its content, the *History* is quite different to the other main chronicle sources we have for Norman Sicilian history: Alexander of Telese's *Ystoria Rogerii regis* (covering the years 1127–35, probably written c.1136), and the *Chronicon* of Falco of Benevento (covering, in varying levels of detail, the years 1102–39). Both Alexander and Falco's works have been carefully examined for what they reveal about the ideological basis of Sicilian kingship in the first half of the twelfth century. Historians have long recognised that a dominant – sensitive – issue in the writing of history both in and about Sicily in this period was an argument over the reputation of Roger II. Specifically, Roger's contemporaries and near-contemporaries used chronicles and narrative histories to argue whether Roger's deeds in Sicily and southern Italy were the actions of a 'tyrant' (*tyrannus*). Alexander of Telese – a sympathetic author – excused Roger's use of violence as the only way to rule a chaotic kingdom. Other contemporaries were far less forgiving: Bernard of Clairvaux seems to have been the first – but far from the last – to refer to Roger as a tyrant. German authors (including Otto of Freising) believed Roger followed in the footsteps of the ancient tyrants of Sicily. Falco of Benevento described him as 'godless', guilty of the most unspeakable acts. Pseudo-Hugo's *History*, was of course written decades after Roger's reign and after much of this debate had taken place. Pseudo-Hugo makes only brief reference to Roger in his prologue, praising as the eminent father of the kingdom. It praises him as a man of great spirit, wise in speech and action, who used both wisdom and power (*non magis viribus quam prudentia*) to destroy his enemies and extend the kingdom. For Pseudo-Hugo, Roger's more unsavoury characteristics are far less important than his foundation of the monarchy. But Pseudo-Hugo is still, inescapably, writing in context where accusations of tyranny had long followed the reputation of Sicilian monarchs: and while he exculpates Roger II from those charges, Pseudo-Hugo does not deny the fact of tyranny in Sicily, but simply relocates it in a different period, indicting Maio and William I as wicked rulers.

Pseudo-Hugo's standards for measuring 'tyrants' and 'tyranny', however, are strikingly different to those of his predecessors. As is evident, a principle concern for Pseudo-Hugo is the operation of the law according to certain normative principles, and a ruler's adherence to that law. By contrast, in earlier discussions of Sicilian tyranny in the first half of the twelfth century, the 'legality' of a ruler's actions is a relatively minor concern. When discussing Roger II, it is Roger's reputation for cruelty and violence, and his attitude towards the church, which earns him the title 'tyrannus'. Alexander and Falco, Pseudo-Hugo's immediate and 'local' southern Italian predecessors, have strikingly little to say about the relationship between law and tyranny. When condemning Roger, they focus on his disregard for morality, and make little mention of the law. Roger is unjust because he is cruel – but those concepts are not used with any specificity. There is no sense that 'injustice' or 'tyranny' results from the breach of a particular law or laws, but rather a disregard for a more general moral code of 'Christian' behaviour – hence Falco denigrates Roger as a nominal Christian who committed atrocities worse than those done by pagans. Pseudo-Hugo, by contrast, in a history beginning with Roger's death, speaks of law and justice with assiduous attention to detail.

It is not the case that Alexander or Falco deliberately omitted law as a way of defining tyranny, or that – necessarily – they were uninterested in law. It is rather that Alexander and Falco, writing in the 1130s, inhabit quite a different conceptual world to Pseudo-Hugo.

'Law' as a measuring stick against which to assess a ruler was an obvious context for Pseudo-Hugo to consider, in a way in which it had not been for his history-writing predecessors. Breaking off from writing in the 1130s, Alexander and Falco's works do not bear witness to one of the most remarkable facets of Roger II's reign – his legal reforms. Between 1135 and 1140, jurists in Palermo worked at producing a compilation of royal legislation for Roger, a text sometimes known as the Assizes of Ariano, but better labelled as the 'Constitutions'. Roger was – with judicious borrowing from Justinian and the *Decretum* – setting out a corpus of laws for the new kingdom, and ambitious project, reflecting his own ideas about royal dignity. These reforms lie beyond the scope of Alexander and Falco's writings, but one other Sicilian narrative record for this period also hints at this change. The *Chronicon* of Romuald of Salerno offers a 'universal history' mostly derived from other chronicles. But the latter part of the chronicle – the continuation, written c.1177 – provides an account of southern Italian history between the 1120s and 1170s. This is mostly focused on the relationship between the papacy and the kings of Sicily, and provides a varying level of detail on events in Sicily. The author does, however, include one very striking detail when discussing the actions of Roger II in the 1130s: in order to maintain the peace of his new kingdom, Roger appointed chancellors and justiciars (*camerarios et iustitiaros*) across his territory. Romuald and Pseudo-Hugo were writing in a markedly different legal world to Alexander and Falco – a world in which law was a significant royal concern. Nor did royal interest in the law end with Roger: from the 1140s onwards, there is evidence for the increasing professionalisation of Sicilian judicial apparatus, with a body of judges answerable to the king alone. Little wonder then, that Pseudo-Hugo – whether a native Sicilian or an immigrant to the kingdom – should recognise that law was an increasingly important part of ruling Sicily, and a significant responsibility for the royal court, and decide to make it the centrepiece of his history.

There is one other historian who brings law to bear on a discussion of Norman Sicilian politics, but he is not a Sicilian, nor a witness to events in Sicily: John of Salisbury. Graham Loud has noted that John was the only historian who talked of Roger II as a tyrant in 'legal' terms – making an explicit connection between his disregard for law and 'tyranny'. In his *Historia Pontificalis*, John describes Roger as acting 'after the fashion of tyrants' (*more tirannorum*). Specifically, Roger was tyrannous for having 'reduced the church in his kingdom to slavery', refusing to allow free elections; treating ecclesiastical offices as his own appointments; refusing to allow papal legates into Sicily. It is in no way surprising that John, scholastically-trained, should take a keen interest in tyranny. Indeed, his rather better known work of political theory, *Policraticus*, contains a much lengthier discussion of tyrants and where they fit into schemes of government. John's verdict on Roger as a 'legal tyrant' was rendered c.1163 (the likely date of the composition of the *Historia Pontificalis*), i.e. during the reign of William I, as the events recorded in Pseudo-Hugo's History were taking place. In other words, although John of Salisbury is interested in examining the rule of Roger II, he is closer to Pseudo-Hugo than the other accounts of Sicilian tyranny offered by Alexander of Telese or Falco of Benevento.

John of Salisbury and Pseudo-Hugo are rather more alike than they may look at first glance, given the considerable difference in their reputations and the approaches of the *Historia Pontificalis* and the *History*. But both are writing on the far side of a legal 'revolution'. The legal transformation of Sicily was set in chain by Roger II, but legal reform in Sicily was only the local manifestation of a revolution in the use of law across Europe. John of Salisbury witnessed the same kind of structural reform – the redefinition of the ruler's judicial role and competencies – both in England and at the papal court. Both histories reflect this shared perspective. Both use law and adherence to correct legal procedure (as far as 'correct' procedure had been defined in the twelfth century) as a marker for just rule. Justice (*iustitia*) – and its converse – has become a more elaborately worked-out concept by the late twelfth century: it no longer means simple virtue, but adherence to a set of written rules. In that sense, I would suggest, the *Historia Pontificalis* and the *History* are almost (but not quite) mirror images of one another: John is interested in exploring how wicked men attempt to corrupt a legal system (in this case, the church courts), while Pseudo-Hugo is interested in what happens when one virtuous man attempts to remove corruption from a legal system.

More *historico*, more *legali*

The twelfth century was a century of legal revolution, imbued with a new legal consciousness, both in terms of working out legal procedure and applying that procedure in practice. It witnessed an intensity of legal study and legal discussion not seen since the time of the Roman Empire. Rulers experimented with law both in order to take control of their domains, but also to enhance their personal dignity and prestige – from Henry II in the Anglo-Norman realm, to Frederick II at the end of the 'long' twelfth century. That group of rulers included Roger II, William I, and William II. The new 'legal consciousness' undoubtedly permeated historical writing – law could not but be written into histories. Law was an essential context for history: whether it was the fact of a king who now asserted himself as the head of a legal system in a manner quite unlike any that his ancestors had done before him; or the fact, for church historians, that so much church business was now occupied with matters of lawsuits and legal arguments.

This 'legal' tendency in historical writing became increasingly pronounced across the twelfth century, and is much more observable in its latter half. It is evident across many different types of history – becoming part of the narrative in any number of ways. We may take two quite differing examples from authors active in the later twelfth century. First, Ralph Diceto, the Dean of St Paul's Cathedral in London, writing a universal chronicle running from the birth of Christ to his own times, the late 1180s, included a digest of the prologue of the canonist Ivo of Chartres in his *Abbreviationes chronicorum*. Ralph considered that work, discussing the relationship between law and morality and how law shapes human actions, to be a document worthy of study by those who would read or write histories. Secondly, the preface to Gervase of Tilbury's *Otia Imperalia* (c.1214), written for Otto IV – and a work which describes the wonders of the natural world and the history of the world, a work of recreation – begins with the authority of law, quoting from both the *Decretum* and Justinian's *Institutes*, and explaining how law and natural law shape the duties of rulership. In short, legal analysis, whether in the description of trials as important historical events, or in more careful reflection upon legal ideas and precedent, was an inescapable context for the writing of history. To ignore it would have been to ignore one of the engines of historical action. By the late twelfth century, the justice of a ruler was no longer measured as a matter of virtuous action – instead it was also about how justice was realised through adherence to legal codes and legal argument. Early twelfth century writers – particularly those critical of Roger II – understood a tyrant as a deliberately cruel ruler who prefers biblical shows of violence. Later twelfth century criticisms of tyrants are more clearly defined: tyranny now includes a failure to respect the principles of law and established legal procedure. It is unsurprising, then, that Pseudo-Hugo would use the law as a means of navigating the dynamics of Sicilian history in the 1160s; nor is it surprising that he would resort to the law to strengthen the position of the Stephen du Perche, the champion of the latter part of the *History*.

We know next to nothing about Pseudo-Hugo himself. I do not suggest that he had studied law, nor that he was as well-educated as John of Salisbury – although we may perhaps draw some inferences of from his immersion in the classics. But if Pseudo-Hugo's devotion to Sallust marks him out as a participant in a twelfth-century renaissance in historical writing, then so too does the 'legal' hue of his work indicate his place in a Europe-wide historiographical tradition. There is, however, a certain irony inherent in this observation. Pseudo-Hugo, when introducing Stephen du Perche, decries Sicilian legal standards and customs as being quite unlike those of France – that is to say, unlike those of a western European country where royal government enforced *ius commune*-derived procedure. But by lamenting the failures of Sicily to live up to common standards of European jurisprudence in his *History*, Pseudo-Hugo was writing a text which fits within the canon of twelfth-century European histories. Even while denouncing Sicilian legal standards and the uniquely-debased Sicilian level of corruption, Pseudo-Hugo aligns Sicily, in historiographical terms, with European currents of thought.

Reference Sources

- Bejczy, I. 2005. 'Law and Ethics: Twelfth-Century Jurists on the Virtue of Justice'. *Viator* 36:197–216.
- Berman, H. J. 1983. *Law and Revolution: The Formation of the Western Legal Tradition*. Cambridge, MA: Harvard University Press.
- Boreau, A. 2000. 'How Law Came to the Monks: The Use of Law in English Society at the Beginning of the Thirteenth Century'. *Past and Present* 167(1):29–74.
- Brooke, C. 1992. 'Aspects of John of Salisbury's *Historia Pontificalis*'. In *Intellectual Life in the Middle Ages: Essays presented to Margaret Gibson*, eds. Smith, L. and Ward, B., 185-195. London: Hambledon.
- Decretum Magistri Gratiani. 1959. In Corpus Iuris Canonici, volume 1, ed. E. Friedberg. Graz: Akademische Druck- u. Verlagsanstalt.
- D'Angelo, E. 2012. 'The Pseudo-Hugh Falcandus in His Own Texts'. *Anglo-Norman Studies* 35:141–162.
- Hapgood Thompson, K. 1995. 'The Counts of the Perche, c.1066–1217'. PhD dissertation, University of Sheffield.
- Hoffmann, H. 1967. 'Hugo Falcandus und Romuald von Salerno'. *Deutsches Archiv für Erforschung des Mittelalters* 23:133–8.
- Falco of Benevento. 1998. *Chronicon Beneventanum*, ed. D'Angelo, E. Firenze: Galuzzo.
- 'Falcandus'. 1998. *The History of the Tyrants of Sicily by 'Hugo Falcandus', 1154–69*, trans. G.A. Loud and T. Wiedemann. Manchester: Manchester University Press.

- Fraher, R.M. 1989. 'Conviction according to Conscience: The Medieval Jurists' Debate concerning Judicial Discretion and the Law of Proof'. *Law and History Review* 7:23–88.
- Gervase of Tilbury. 2002. *Otia Imperialia*, ed. and trans. Banks, S.E. and Binns, J.W.. Oxford: Clarendon Press.
- Hood, G. 1999. 'Falcandus and Fulcaudus, Epistola ad Petrum, Liber de Regno Sicilie: Literary Form and Author's Identity'. *Studia Medievalia* 40:1–41.
- Houben, H. 2002. *Roger II: A Ruler between East and West*, trans. G.A. Loud and D. Milburn. Cambridge: Cambridge University Press.
- Jamison, E. 1957. *Admiral Eugenius of Sicily*. London: Oxford University Press.
- ---. 1967. 'Judex Tarentinus: The career of Judex Tarentinus, magne curie justiciarius, and the emergence of the Sicilian regalis magna curia under William I and the regency of Margaret of Navarre, 1156-1172'. *Proceedings of the British Academy* 53:289–344.
- Johns, J. 2002. *Arabic Administration in Norman Sicily: The Royal Diwan*. Cambridge: Cambridge University Press.
- John of Salisbury. 1956. *Historia Pontificalis*, ed. and trans. Chibnall, M. London: Thomas Nelson and Sons.
- Kempshall, M.. 2011. *Rhetoric and the Writing of History*. Manchester: Manchester University Press.
- Liber Augustalis. 1971. Ed. and trans. Powell, J.M.. Syracuse, NY: Syracuse University Press.
- Loud, G.A. 1993. 'The Genesis and Context of the Chronicle of Falco of Benevento'. *Anglo-Norman Studies* 15:177–98.
- ---. 2007a. 'History Writing in the Twelfth-Century Kingdom of Sicily.' In *Chronicling History: Chroniclers and Historians in Medieval and Renaissance Italy*, eds. Dale, S., Lewin, A.W. and Osheim, D.J. 29-54. University Park, PA: Pennsylvania University Press.
- ---. 2007b. *The Latin Church in Norman Italy*. Cambridge: Cambridge University Press.
- ---. 2009. 'The Chancery and Charters of the Kings of Sicily (1130–1212)'. *English Historical Review* 124 (509):779–810.
- ---. 2013. 'The Image of the Tyrant in the Work of 'Hugo-Falcandus''. *Nottingham Medieval Studies* 57:1–20.
- Matthew, D. 1981. 'The Chronicle of Romuald of Salerno'. In *The Writing of History in the Middle Ages*, eds. Davis, R.H.C. and Wallace-Hadrill, J.M. 239-274. Oxford: Clarendon Press.

- ---. 1992. 'Maio of Bari's Commentary on the Lord's Prayer'. In *Intellectual Life in the Middle Ages: Essays presented to Margaret Gibson*, eds. Smith, L. and Ward, B. 118-144. London: Hambledon.
- Nederman, C.J. 1989. 'The Changing Face of Tyranny: The Reign of King Stephen in John of Salisbury's Political Thought'. *Nottingham Medieval Studies* 33:1–20.
- Pennington, K. 1994. 'Learned Law, Droit Savant, Gelehrtes Recht: The Tyranny of a Concept'. *Syracuse Journal of International Law and Commerce* 20:205–215.
- ---. 1998. 'Due Process, Community and the Prince in the Evolution of the Ordo iudicarius'. *Revista internazionale di diritto comune* 9:9-47.
- ---. 2006. 'The Birth of the Ius Commune: King Roger II's Legislation'. *Rivista internationale del diritto commune* 17:23–60.
- Ralph, D. 1876. *Abbreviationes chronicorum*. In *The Historical Works of Master Ralph de Diceto, Dean of London*, ed. Stubbs, W. London: Longmans.
- Reynolds, S. 2003. 'The Emergence of Professional Law in the Long Twelfth Century'. *Law and History Review* 21(2):347–66.
- Rogerii II Regis Diplomata Latina. 1987. Ed. C. Brühl. Köln: Böhlau.
- Romuald of Salerno. 1935. *Chronicon*, ed. Garufi, C.A.. Città di Castello: Rerum Italicarum Scriptores.
- Rouse, R.H. and M.A. Rouse, 1967. 'John of Salisbury and the Doctrine of Tyrannicide'. *Speculum* 42(4):693–709.
- Siragusa, G.B. 1897. *La Historia o Liber de Regno Sicilie e la Epistola ad Petrum Panormitane Ecclesie Thesaurarium di Ugo Falcando*. Rome: Fonti per la Storia d'Italia.
- Tounta, E. 2014. 'Terror and territorium in Alexander of Telese's Ystoria Rogerii regis: political cultures in the Norman kingdom of Sicily'. *Journal of Medieval History* 40(2):142–158.
- van Laarhoven, J. 1984. 'Thou shall not slay a tyrant! The so-called theory of John of Salisbury'. In *The World of John of Salisbury*, ed. Wilks, M., 319-341. Oxford: Blackwell.
- Walter Map. 1983. *De nugis curialium*, ed. and trans. James, M.R.. Oxford: Clarendon Press.
- Weiler, B. 2009. 'The King as Judge: Henry II and Frederick Barbarossa as seen by their contemporaries.' In *Challenging the Boundaries of Medieval History: The Legacy of Timothy Reuter*, ed. Skinner, , 115–141. Turnhout: Brepols.
- Wieruszowski, H. 1963. 'Roger II of Sicily, Rex-Tyrannus, in Twelfth-Century Political Thought'. *Speculum* 38(1):46–78.

Cultural negotiations: Eastern music in Early Modern travel writing

Claire Bardelmann (Université de Lorraine, Metz, France.)

THIS PAPER AIMS at assessing the cultural issues raised by English responses to the musical exchanges in the late 16th century and the first half of the 17th century with the Ottoman Empire, the East Indies and China. The East encompassed nearly all of Asia in the early modern cartography and geographical imagination (Hadfield 2004, 1-21).

As compared to travellers's accounts of music in the Far North or the West Indies, Eastern music is the most abundantly documented in early modern travel writing,[1] especially after 1600, when the East India Company was formed (musical exchanges mainly took place for trading or diplomatic purposes). This is illustrated by the list of early modern travel books which show an effort towards the documentation and analysis of Eastern music: William Biddulph, *The travels of certaines Englishmen into Africa, Asia [...] and to sundry other places* (London, 1608);

---

[1] As a consequence of the preoccupation of Early Modern England with the East. As Fernand Braudel remarks, England turned resolutely toward the East as a result of its relation to the larger world in which it was positioned: 'The old firm of the Mediterranean gained once more from the terrible battles of the Atlantic. Between 1583 and 1591 it was no coincidence that English agents should have made their way along the roads through Syria to the Indian Ocean, Persia, the Indies, and Sumatra. In Egypt... the English were out-manoeuvred by skillful and persistent competition from the French. The English therefore turned their attention to Syria and the roads through it'. Braudel, 1976, 627; Archer 2001, 1-22.

William Bruton, *Newes from the East-Indies, or, a Voyage to Bengalla* (London, 1638); Robert Coverte, *A true and almost incredible report* (London, 1612); Thomas Dallam, *The Diary of Master Thomas Dallam* (London, 1599-1600); Sir Francis Drake, *The world encompassed by Sir Francis Drake* (London, 1628); Richard Hakluyt, *The Principal Navigations* (London, 1599-1600); John (Jan) Linschoten, *John Huighen van Linschoten, his discourse of voyages into ye Easte & West Indies* (London, 1598); Henry Lord, *A display of two foraigne sects in the East Indies* (London, 1630); Richard Knolles, *The generall historie of the Turkes* (London, 1603); Gonzalez de Mendoza, *The historie of the great and mightie kingdom of China* (London, 1588); Peter Mundy, *Journals* (in C. Temple, *The Travels of Peter Mundy in Europe and Asia, 1608-1667*, vol. 5: *Travels in South-West England and Western India*, London, 1936); Samuel Purchas, *Purchas His Pilgrimage* (London, 1626).

The range of Eastern music accounted for in these books is considerable, but travellers had a comparatively homogeneous response to musical heterogeneity, a response answering to cultural patterns. The main forms of musical contact between English travelers and Eastern music are indeed relevant to the study of their contribution to cultural history, as are the cultural responses to this musical otherness.

Forms of musical contact: from ceremonial music to ethnographic observation

Music given and received: the musical banquet

In *English musicians in the age of exploration*, Ian Woodfield discusses the part played by music in trading exchanges with the East (but the cultural and epistemological implications of these exchanges lie largely outside the scope of his study) (Woodfield 1995, 51-74 and 87-94). Woodfield argues that the main form of musical contact came in the form of the musical banquet, given by the travellers to foreign dignitaries, most of the time on board their ships.[2] Typically, guests were escorted on board with trumpet fanfares and volleys of shot, and would then be treated to a banquet in the captain's cabin, and escorted back to land with equal ceremony.[3] The purpose of such musical entertainment was to promote good trading relations, as Sir Francis Drake's travel journal makes clear, in a passage where he describes his musical reception of the king of Tidore, in the Moluccas, in 1628.

> So was he received in the best manner we could, answerable unto his state: our ordnance thundred, which wee mixed with great store of small shot, among which sounding our trumpets, and other instruments of musick, both of still and loud noise, where with he was so much delighted, that requesting our musick to come into the boate, he ioyned his Canow to the same, and was towed at least a whole hour together, with the

---

[2] Also customary was the practice of musical gifts, which usually consisted in the gift of keyboard instruments: harpsichords, virginals, and organs, with the famous example of Thomas Dallam's organ, presented by the Levant Company to the new Sultan in Constantinople after the death of Murad III in 1595. The choice of these instruments pinpoints an important side of the English response to Eastern cultures – that they ranked high in the hierarchy implicit in their appreciation of cultural otherness. Indeed, these were valuable presents displaying the best of European artistry, not trinkets like the silver whistles which were deemed sufficient to propitiate an African chief along the trade route. There was a general agreement that cheap trinkets would be regarded as an insult in any of the great oriental courts, which reflects an awareness of the political and cultural importance of these Oriental empires. Woodfield 1995, 89-91.

[3] Such musical entertainments are regularly mentioned in the vast majority of the reports of visits made by ships of the East India Company; music was such an important asset in the diplomacy of English travelers that trading companies had musicians on their ships – the East India Company began making use of musicians as an integral part of its trading strategy after seeking advice from Hakluyt, the acknowledged authority in the field, who recommended that 'certain musicians' were very necessary for the planned voyages. Woodfield 1995, 123; Drake 1628, 89.

boate at the sterne of our ship: Besides this, our generall sent him such presents, as he thought, might both requite his curtesy already received, and worke a farther confirmation of that goodliking and friendship already begunne.[4]

Musical banquets were also the main occasions on which Eastern travellers heard foreign music, because such entertainment was usually reciprocated by foreign potentates. In his journal *Newes from the East-Indies, or a voyage to Bengalla* (1638), William Bruton gives an account of the entertainment given to the English merchants by the governor of the town of Baldakka in April 1636.

> The 28 of April in the Morning, the Governour of this Towne came and saluted our Merchant, and promised him that whatsoever was in his power to doe him any friendly courtesie, he should command it; and indeed he was every way as good as his word; for hee lent us Horses to ride on, and Cowlers (which are Porters) to carry our goods (for at this Towne the Carts did leave us, and our goods were carried on mens shoulders: then we set forwards, being accompanied with the Governour, with his Musicke, which were Shalmes, and Pipes of sundry formes, much after the formes of Waits or Hoboyes, on which they play most delicately out of Tune, Time, and Measure (Bruton 1638, 6).

---

[4] The accounts English travellers wrote of these exotic musical banquets belong to the documentation of Eastern musical otherness alongside other observations of ceremonial music, such as Richard Knolles' account of the 'magnificent pompe' attending upon the Great Sultan Selymus's chief counsellor (Schah Culi Soltan), during an embassy from the Persian king to the Great Sultan Selymus in 1603, which included 40 musicians and 'singers of the Alcoran' alongside lavish ceremonial clothing (golden turbans) and the display of fine blood horses and many camels in splendid harness. Woodfield 1995, 126.

Documenting musical otherness

Such musical exchanges were destined to facilitate trading relations, but they were not purely utilitarian. They had fundamentally cultural contents of which early modern travellers were quite aware. Indeed, accounting for the music they heard was part of the thorough observation and recording of the attributes of foreign countries, which was recommended by the *ars apodemica* treatises issued in Europe from the 1570s – the practical instructions for travel which taught the future traveler on how to travel well and which can be found, for instance, in Sir Francis Bacon's essay 'Of Travail' (1625) (McInnis 2013, 25-26; Stag 1995,47-48 and 70-80). Another well-known manual, Albrecht Meyer's *Methodus descridendi regiones* (1587), includes an exhaustive taxonomy of attributes to be observed: cosmography, astronomy, chorography, topography, husbandry, navigation, the political, the ecclesiastical, literature, histories, chronicles, and customs, including music.

The precision with which travellers recorded Eastern musical practices depended on the amount of musical knowledge they had, but even an observer with an open mind and a quick eye could provide valuable information. Such a man was Peter Mundy, a Cornish sea-captain for the East India Company in the early 1630s, whose journal is one of the most valuable travel documents of the early 17th century as regards the description of Eastern music. Mundy is, in fact, something like an early ethnomusicologist. He describes the tube zither of Madagascar, the valiha – the journal even includes a drawing.

> [B]esides their ordinary singing, they have a little Instrument about a Fote in length named Ambolo, made of a Cane. The Said Instrument and strings all of one peece, cut out off the same, being certaine thirds raised out off the grayne off the Cane which runne from Joint to Joint, which as they would have to sound higher or lower so accordingly the Force up certaine

little wedges, that are under the ends of the strings (Mundy in Temple 1936, 273).

When visiting Sumatra in 1636, Mundy also recorded his impression of the sound of the gongs.

> Another copper instrument called a gung, whereon they strike with a little wooden Clubbe, and although it bee but a small Instrument, not much more then 1. Foote over and ½ Foote deepe, yet it maketh a Deepe hollow humming sound Resembling that of a great Bell: all the aforesaid musick Discordant, Clamorous and full of Noise (Mundy in Temple 1936, 123).

And while in Agra in 1632, Mundy went so far as to attempt to understand the basis of the Indian musical system, noting how very different its harmonies were from the Western system – he noted that the musicians play 'all of one note' (in the unison) and that there are 'no thirds nor fifths in Musick as [he] could here' Temple 1936, 123).

The social uses of music

Remarkably, travellers like Mundy[5] weren't content with describing the strange instruments and sounds they saw and heard. They also usually recorded the cultural contexts in which these instruments were

---

[5] Other journals than Mundy's show genuine attempts at accounting for the strange sounds and instruments Eastern travellers came across. Scott, one of the factors who took up residence in Bantam in 1602, was the first to describe Javanese gongchimes: 'Their musique, which was ten or twelve pannes of Tombaga, carried upon a coulstaffe between two; these were tunable, and every note a note above another, and always two went by them which were skillfull in their Country musique, and played on them having things in their hands of purpose to strike them'. Purchas, 1636, 484.

customarily used, proving early ethnographers as well as ethnomusicologists. One of the best documented uses of Eastern music in this respect is the Indian practice of widow burning, the *sati*. Sati accounts were a staple of Early Modern travel narratives, from Cesare Federici's narrative of his eastern travels (published in Venice in 1587 and translated in English in 1588) to Nicholas Withington, who furnishes one of the first eyewitness English descriptions of a *sati* in 1616, and Peter Mundy, who provides a detailed account of a sati witnessed at Surat. And such accounts usually include a description of the music accompanying the ceremony. It was very solemn music involving a great many instruments, as described in Robert Coverte's account of a sati near river Tamlvo, in the Hindus region, in 1612.

> I saw a young Woman the wife of a Doctor, whose husband being dead, she made choise to be carried in a Pageant, by four men, she being clothed in lawne, and her head decked with jewels and rich ornaments, and before her went musike of all sorts that the country afforded, as Hoboies, Drums, fifes, and Trumpets, and next to her all her kindred, and so shee was brought to the place of Execution, where was a stake and a hole set to her feet in, and so being tied to the stake, all her kindred kneeling round about her, and praying to the sun and their other Idols, the fire was set to her, she having under each arme a bagge of gunpowder, and a bagge betwixt her legges, and so burnt to death, the fire being made of Beniamin, Storare, Lignomal, and other sweet woods (Coverte 1612, 35).

Similar accounts, although not so detailed, appear in Henry Lord's *A display of foraigne sects in the East Indies* (1630), in which Lord describes 'the music sounding aloud' when the fire is set to the pile; in Lindschoten's travel book (1598), with the wife's 'nearest friends singing'; and in his huge collection of travel narratives, *Purchas His Pilgrimes* (published

1625), Samuel Purchas also gives a description of a *sati* near Agra, the wife being 'pompously attended with Music'.

In all these travel narratives, music is described as part of a radical cultural otherness the reactions to which, as regards the practice of *sati*, range from absence of moral commentary (as in Mundy's description) to religious and moral horror (as in Purchas'). The feeling of cultural estrangement conveyed by musical otherness is underlined in the description of many other social practices carefully recorded by travelers, mostly weddings and funerals, but also, for instance, in William Biddulph's account of the women of Saphetta, in Turkey, lamenting the departure of their husbands for the pilgrimage of Mecca:

> Whiles we were at Saphetta, many Turkes departed from thence towards Mecha in Arabia. And the same morning they went, we saw many women playing with Tymbrels as they went along the street, and made a yelling or screeching noise as though they cried. We asked what they meant in so doing? It was answered us, that they mourned for the departure of their husbands […] It seemed strange to us, that they should mourne with music about the streets, for music is used in other places at times of mirth, and not at times of mourning (Biddulph 1606, 106).

It appears from these accounts that English travellers were not content with recording their experiences of Eastern music. They also responded to what they saw and heard, and these responses constitute a major aspect of the role of music in the cultural negotiations between East and West.

Cultural responses to musical otherness
The rhetoric of comparison and linguistic appropriation

The first pattern of response was on the linguistic level and can be described as linguistic appropriation, music being a further example of that 'renaming' which studies of the early modern pre-colonial discourse insist is part of an ideological colonization (Greenblatt 1991; Helgerson 1994; Spurr 1993). Indeed, in order to describe strange music, travellers compared it with something they knew, underlining in the process that what they saw differed from it. Scott describing Javanese gong chimes as 'their country musique', Mundy comparing their sound to that of a bell ('a Deepe hollow humming sound Resembling that of a great Bell'), or Bruton describing Indian pipes 'much after the forme of Waits or hoboys', are typical of this strategy, in which the different is translated into the code of the same through a rhetoric of comparison which still relied on the Herodotean rhetoric of analogy.[6] Similarly, early modern narratives overwhelmingly describe music instruments and musical systems by comparing them with the instruments and systems known of the travellers, as in Gonzalez de Mendoza's *The Historie of the great and mightie kingdom of China* (English translation 1588).[7] In this book, he describes the instruments associated to the celebration of the New Year in China in terms of the instruments he knew (viols, gitterns, virginals, harps, lutes), although as he underlines they 'differ something in the fashion of them':

---

[6] Herodotus, for instance, describes the hippopotamus as 'four-footed, with cloven hoofs like oxen, maned like horses', 2:71. *Herodotus* in Dewald 1998, 123.

[7] This linguistic response has political implications – it is part of the pre-colonial discourse, such as described in recent years by Stephen Greenblatt, Richard Helgerson or David Spurr, who all insist that renaming in travel writing is part of an ideological colonization, 'a mode of thinking wherein the world is radically transformed into an object of possession', Spurr 1993, 27.

This day dooth all people generally sport themselves with great singing and sounding of instruments, in the which they are very cunning. Such instruments [...] were lutes, gytternes, vuyalles, rebukes, wayghtes, virginalles, harpes and lutes, and other instruments which we doo use, although they doo differ something in the fashion of them, but yet easie to be knowen. They do tune theyr voyces unto their instruments with great admiration: they have all commonly very good voyces (Gonzalez de Mendoza 1588, 108).

Aesthetic responses to musical otherness

The second pattern of cultural response to Eastern music was esthetic. It was a reaction of surprise and wonder which certainly illustrates Stephen Greenblatt's definition of the experience of wonder in the presence of the alien as 'a fragment of a world elsewhere, a world of difference' (Greenblatt 1991, 122). Even in the not infrequent case when travellers were vague in their descriptions of Eastern music, they referred to their new musical experiences as fundamentally alien, most of the time as 'strange' (a recurrent adjective) – as in Biddulph's account of the music at Saphetta, which 'seemed strange to us'. Another case in point is Drake's account of Javanese music: the sailors of the Golden Hind were actually the first to experience the distinctive sounds of gongs and metallophones. Drake received the Javanese 'country musick' on board, and described it as 'though it were of a very strange kind; yet the sound was pleasant and delightful'.

Besides this sense of wonder, esthetic responses to Eastern musical cultures were of two kinds. The one was essentially positive, the other wholly negative. Mundy's journal and Mendoza's accounts are fine examples of the former, together with all the accounts which fail to describe the music with precision, only underlining its 'strangeness', but also emphasizing its 'pleasantness' (another recurrent adjective). Such accounts (together with the imprecision of descriptions) testify in their own way to the scale of the barriers to understanding unfamiliar musical cultures, but not so much as the attitudes of rejection such cultures often met with. 'Strange' sounds were often described as 'noise', and as such as 'harsh', 'unpleasant', 'hoarse', 'squeaking', 'disorderly'; even Mundy remarks on the 'discordant, clamorous noise' of the Javanese gongs. And William Bruton describes the musical reception of the English traders by the governor of the town of Baldakka as 'delicately out of Tune':

> then we set forwards, being accompanied with the Governour, with his Musicke, which were Shalmes, and Pipes of sundry forms, much after the forms of Waits or Hoboyes, on which they play most delicately out of tune, Time, and Measure (Bruton 1638, 6).

Purchas's account of the Javanese drums also falls into this category.

> Their drummes are huge panes, made of a mettel called Tombago, which makes a most hellish sound (Purchas 1626, 387).

Some travellers, like Purchas, relied on their knowledge of organology or of musical theory to pinpoint that the difference in perception stemmed primarily from the confrontation of radically different musical systems. Purchas says that Chinese music cannot but sound harsh to English ears, because of fundamental differences in the musical systems – the discord-concord system based on the opposition of consonant and dissonant intervals and chords being unknown in Chinese music.

> Nor doe they know the discord-concord in musicall harmonie of divers voices; so that their musike to us is harsh, in their owne opinion glorious (Purchas 1626, 387).

This response is certainly one of the most complex aspects of the part played by music in the cultural negotiations between East and West, because the backdrop to this response is not just esthetic; it implies the symbolic role of music as the expression of harmony, which pervades the Renaissance episteme. The ideas about music in the English Renaissance were encompassed by the theory of speculative music, which describes the position of music in the created universe and was transmitted from ancient Greek sources to the mainstream of Western European thought by Boethius in the 6th century. In this theory, music was a symbolic expression of harmony: the harmony of the well-ordered motions of the universe (*musica mundana*), the music of the spheres famously mentioned by Lorenzo in 5.1 of *The Merchant of Venice*; this heavenly harmony is reflected in *musica humana* – a microcosmic parallel to the macrocosmic harmony; this harmony of a human body supplied a model for the body politic.[8] In that system, music served quite literally to harmonize body, society, psyche, and gave a cosmic guarantee of meaning, an idea widely reflected in Elizabethan literature, madrigal lyrics, and in the court masque.[9]

The idea that music translated cosmic order into sensible sound was an important cultural factor in how English travellers listened to Eastern music. In this system, a musical language that was no musical language to an English ear, but mere noise, would be associated with lack of personal, moral and social harmony. Hence the moral interpretation of such dissonances as 'hellish' – it was quite attuned to

---

[8] On the role of analogy in the epistemology of the English Renaissance, see Foucault 1966, chapter 2. For a description of speculative music and of its function in Early Modern poetics, see, for instance, Heninger, 1974, esp. Section 2: 71-145 and 146-200.

[9] For instance, in Samuel Daniel's *Vision of the Twelve Goddesses* (the first full masque of James I's reign), Iris describes Britain as 'the Land of Musick and of rest': the phrase, associating music with order in society, indicates succinctly the symbolic importance of music at the time. On the politics of the court masque, see Orgel 1975; Linley 1998, 273-295.

the Early modern idea of musical ethos. Further testimony of this association between outlandish music and lack of harmony is that musical otherness appears as a ploy of satire in satirical utopias using the frame and conventions of travel writing, and prominently so in Joseph Hall's *Mundus alter et idem* (Hall 1605). In this satirical essay, the narrator takes a voyage to some great Southern continent – unless is it set in the East, for it refers to Palestine and the Holy Land, and possibly also Egypt and the Mariana Islands in the Pacific, while the English translator, John Healey, situates the narrative in the South Indies, as specified by the title, *The discovery of a new world or A description of the South Indies Hetherto Unkinown by and English Mercury*. It was a common feature of satirical prose fiction to use a remote location as a disclaimer of any direct relations between narrative and contemporary politics.[10]

---

[10]   As Davies remarks, this frame particularly challenges the idea that travel was broadening and enlightening: '*Mundus Alter et Idem* (1605) was a satiric inversion of the claims of travel literature. The ubiquitous nature of folly and immorality, their universal predominance, rendered travel futile', Davies 2008, 8. For an analysis of the structures of a model society in Hall's anti-utopian satire, see McCabe 1982, 73-109.

As David McInnis underlines in *Mind-Travelling and Voyage Drama in Early Modern England*,[11] 'one of the manifold uses of [...] prose fiction was as a vehicle to explore contemporary problems, invariably setting the individual fiction in question in a distant land or a distant time'. In Hall's tale, the remote, syncretic location aims at conjuring up different lands which answer to man's chief weaknesses or vices such as gluttony, foolishness, or thievery. Crapulia, Viraginia, Moronia, and Lavernia, populated by glutons, hags, fools and thieves respectively. Discordant music is the expression of this unvirtuous world, as shown by the description of the city of Carousi-kanikin, the capital city of Crapulia, land of the gluttons: the 'chief city of Drinke-allia, as also of the fashions and conditions of the Drink-alls'.[12]

---

[11] David McInnis underlines that the use of remote locations in these satires is within the humanist tradition of fictional text as advice book, especially considering the intrinsic pedagogical value which was attributed to travel (as enhanced in the *ars apodemica* treatises). In this tradition, fiction employs a foreign location in order to provide a disclaimer of any direct relationship between narrative and contemporary politics. McInnis gives the example of William Baldwin's elaborate anti-Catholic satire *Beware the Cat* (published 1570), and he quotes a passage in which the symbolic use of music as noise holds pride of place. In the second part of the tale, the principal narrator concocts a potion which he applies to his ears in order to enable him to understand what beasts are saying, but what he first hears is an assault to his senses: 'Barking of dogs, grunting of hogs, wawling of cats, rumbling of rats, gaggling of geese, humming of bees, rousing of bucks, gaggling of ducks, singing of swans, ringing of pans, crowing of cocks, sowing of socks, cackling of hens, scrabbling of pens... with such a sort of commixed noises as would a-deaf anybody to have heard'. McInnis 2013, 135.

[12] Foreign music and satirical dystopias: in addition to plays which incorporate travel, and have been called 'travel drama', like Wilkins' *The Travels of the Three English Brothers*, 1607), Fletcher's (*The Sea-Voyage*, 1622), Massinger's (*The Renegado*, 1624), or Daborne's *(A Christian Turn'd Turke*, 1610), a satirical response to travel can be found in a series of Early Modern plays: Jonson's *Every Man Out of his Humour*, *Volpone*, and the *Westward Ho trilogy*.

> Then steps me out one of the company and presently calling for a quart pot. An health (quoth he) unto Great Bousing-gut... he drinkes, he puffes, he belches, he talks, until within a while he had gulped downe as many quarters as his name had letters [...] This past, upstarts another, with this catch, A health for you and us, this day, and health to all Drink-allia, seasoning his song with many a goodly belche (Hall ,70-71).

This low-ethos Elizabethan music commonly associates vices with hellish music. Interestingly, despite the exotic location of his tale, Hall makes no reference to Eastern or indeed Southern instruments or foreign musical systems in general. But the projected ethos of foreign music as 'noise', such as it appears in travel writing, certainly agrees with such satirical description and contributes to conjure up an Antipodean fantasy which creates the implicit model of a good society.

Hall's satire pinpoints the complex ways in which music contributed to the cultural negotiations of the East in Early Modern England. This music did not exert any kind of direct influence – the same is true of the English madrigal, of English drama (even 'travel drama'), and the court masque. The musical settings of the few madrigals whose lyrics are concerned with the East[13] use the musical idiom of the Elizabethan madrigal. And even in 'travel drama' most closely concerned with the East, the music supposedly evoking Turkish or Indian kings follows the Elizabethan conventions of stage music –

---

[13] Numbers 7 and 8 of John Wilbye's *The First Set of English Madrigals* evoke the fabulous East: 'What needeth all this travaile and turmoiling', which mentions 'those hot climates under Phoebus broiling', and 'O fooles, can you not see a traffick neere', a blason in which the face of the poet's mistress is compared to

> 'Rubies and Diamonds daintie,
> And orient Perles such plentie,
> Corral & Ambergris, sweeter & deerer,
> Then which the South seas or Moluccas lend vs,
> Or either Indies, East or West, do send vs'. Wilbye 1598.

like the 'solemn music' which accompanies the apparition of the ghost of Mahomet in Thomas Goffe's *The Couragious Turke* (5.9, 1631). The evocation of Eastern music does not merely follow the conventions of Elizabethan stage music, but also the conventional use of musical symbolism. Thus, in John Mason's *The Turke* (1610), the Turk Mulleasses displays a surprising knowledge of speculative music. He mentions 'singing angels', the 'heavenly harmony of the spheres', and the 'dancing spheres': in other words, he refers to the music of the spheres, a well-known metaphor of harmony in Elizabethan drama.[14]

> *Mulleasses:* Oh now methinkes a chorus all of angels
> Clad with the Sun and crowned with golden starres
> Should make more heavenly music at they fall
> Then all the Spheres that dance about the ball (Mason 1619, 67-70).

Eastern characters sound very English on the Elizabethan stage,[15] where the real music of the East largely remained, to use a phrase from *Tamburlaine*, 'unconquered regions'.[16] But the musical otherness of the mysterious East fed the early modern imagination in more subterranean ways, on the epistemological, moral and esthetic levels; and that it became part of the Early Modern imagination in such a way as underlines the role of the ear in establishing knowledge of the world. Greenblatt writes that this process, since Herodotus, 'rests on witnessing, a witnessing understood as a form of significant and representative

---

[14] For a general discussion of abstract harmony, see Hollander, 1961. On the theory of speculative music in Early Modern England and its use as a metaphor of political harmony, see Daly 1979 142-179.

[15] While the English instrumentalists were increasingly foreigners from the end of the reign of Henry VIII, the foreign element remained European, as noted by Dumitrescu 2004, 113.

[16] Christopher Marlowe, 2 *Tamburlaine*, 5.3.158. Fuller 1987.

seeing' (Greenblatt 1991, 122), and we might add, 'a form of significant and representative' hearing too.

Reference Sources

- Archer, J.M. 2001. *Old World: Egypt, Southwest Asia, India, and Russia in Early Modern English writing*. Stanford: Stanford University Press.
  - Biddulph, W. 1608. *The travels of certaines Englishmen into Africa, Asia [...] and to sundry other places.*
- Braudel,. 1976. *The Mediterranean and the Mediterranean World in the Age of Philip II*, trans. Reynolds, S. New York: Harper and Row.
- Bruton, W. 1638. *Newes from the East-Indies, or, a Voyage to Bengalla.*
- Coverte, R. 1612. *A true and almost incredible report of an Englishman,*
  - *that being cast away... in Cambaya the farthest part of the East Indies... travelled by land through many unknown kingdoms, and great cities. With a particular description of all those kingdoms, cities, and people.*
- Dallam, T. 1599-1600. The *Diary of Master Thomas Dallam.*
- Davies, J.C. 2008. 'Going Nowhere: travelling to, through, and from Utopia'. *Utopian Studies* 19 (1):1-23.
- Drake, F.. 1628. *The world encompassed by Sir Francis Drake*. Daly, J. 1979. 'Cosmic Harmony and Political Thinking in Early Stuart England'. *Transactions of the American Philosophical Society* 69 (7):1-41.
- Dumitrescu, T. 2004. *The Early Tudor Court and International Musical Relations*. Aldershot: Ashgate.
- Foucault, M. 1966. *Les Mots et les choses*. Paris: Gallimard.
- Greenblatt, S. 1991. *Marvellous Possessions: The Wonder of the New World*. Chicago: University of Chicago Press.
- Hadfield, and Hammer, eds. 2005. *Shakespeare and Renaissance Europe*. Arden Critical Companions. London: The Arden Shakespeare.
- Hall, J. 1605 *Mundus alter et idem. The discovery of a new world or A description of the South Indies Hetherto Unknown by and English Mercury*. Trans. Healey J. 1609. London.
- Hakluyt, R. 1599-1600. *The Principal Navigations.*
- Helgerson, R. 1994. *Forms of Nationhood: The Elizabethan Writing of England*. Chicago: The University of Chicago Press.
- Heninger, F.K. 1974. *Touches of Sweet Harmony: Pythagorean Cosmology and Renaissance Poetics*. San Marino: Huntington Library.

- Herodotus: *The Histories* 1998. Ed. Dewald, C., Trans. Waterfield, R. Oxford World Classics, Oxford: Oxford University Press.
- Hoenselaars, A.J. 1992. *Images of Englishmen and Foreigners in the Drama of Shakespeare and his Contemporaries.* London: Associated University Presses.
- Hollander, J. 1961. *The Untuning of the Sky: Ideas of Music in English Poetry*, 1500-1700. Princeton: Princeton University Press.
- Knolles, R. 1603. *The generall historie of the Turkes*
- Linley, D. 1998. 'The politics of music in the masque'. In *The Politics of the Stuart Court Masque*, eds Bevington, D.d., Holbrook, , 273-295. Cambridge: Cambridge University Press.
- Linschoten, J. 1598. *John Huighen van Linschoten, his discours of voyages into ye Easte & West Indies.*
- Lord, H. 1630. *A display of two foraigne sects in the East Indies.*
- Christopher Marlowe, 2 *Tamburlaine*, 5.3.158. Ed. D Fuller, 1987, *The Complete Works of Christopher Marlowe: Tamburlaine the Great parts I and II*, Oxford: Clarendon Press.
- Mason, J. 1619. *The Turke A Worthie Tragedie.*
- McCabe, R.A. 1982. *Joseph Hall: A Study in Satire and Meditation*. Oxford: Clarendon Press.
- McInnis, D. 2013. *Mind-Travelling and Voyage Drama in Early Modern England*. Basingstoke: Palgrave Macmillan.
- Mendoza.1588. *The historie of the great and mightie kingdom of China*
- Mundy,1936. *Journals*. In *The Travels of Peter Mundy in Europe and Asia, 1608-1667.* C. Temple, vol. 5: 'Travels in South-West England and Western India'. London.
- Orgel, S. 1975. *The Illusion of Power: Political Theatre in the English Renaissance*. Berkeley: Berkeley University Press.
- Ortiz, J. 2011. *Broken Harmony: Shakespeare and the Politics of Music*. New York: Cornell University Press.
- Purchas, S. 1626. *Purchas His Pilgrimage.*
- Spurr, D. 1993. *The Rhetoric of Empire: Colonial Discourse in Journalism, Travel Writing, and Imperial Administration*. Durham: Duke University Press.
- Stagl, J. 1995. *A History of Curiosity: The Theory of travel 1550-1800*. London: Routledge.
- Wilbye, J. 1598, *The First Set of English Madrigals,* London: Thomas Este.
- Woodfield, I. 1995. 'English musicians in the age of exploration'. *Sociology of Music* 8, Stuyvesant, New York: Pendragon Press

Uncredited images in this book are photographs from the Othello's Island conferences held between 2013 and 2019, and from the excursions organised as part of the conference to various medieval and renaissance sites in Cyprus.

Also available from the Orage Press

Historic Cyprus
by Rupert Gunnis

Rupert Gunnis is one of the founding fathers of Cypriot historiography. Whilst working as an administrator in the British Colonial Government of Cyprus in the 1930s he visited every village, town and city on the island, recording its interesting historic buildings and sites.

In this facsimile of 1936 edition of the resulting book, not only do we gain a snapshot of a Cyprus that has now long gone, but find a text that is still surprisingly useable as a guide to the material culture of Cyprus.

ISBN: 978-0-9544523-9-1

Also available from the Orage Press

Four Essays on Art and Anarchism

by Michael Paraskos

The relationship between art and anarchism has a long but often hidden history. Artists as diverse as Courbet, Pissarro, Signac, van Gogh, Kandinsky, Tatlin, Gris, and many others, have been positively identified as being anarchists, or having sympathies with anarchist ideas. But, as Michael Paraskos suggests in the course of these essays, there is an argument to be made that anarchist ideas are at the heart of all acts of artistic creation.

Although dealing with the serious matters of art and political anarchism in the cultural sphere, Paraskos's light touch and generous writing style is filled with humour and personal anecdote, and is a pleasure to read.

ISBN: 978-0-9929247-9-9

www.ingramcontent.com/pod-product-compliance
Lightning Source LLC
Chambersburg PA
CBHW061247230426
43663CB00021B/2933